Other Books by Robert Matzen

Mission: Jimmy Stewart and the Fight for Europe

Fireball: Carole Lombard and the Mystery of Flight Three

Errol & Olivia

Errol Flynn Slept Here (with Michael Mazzone)

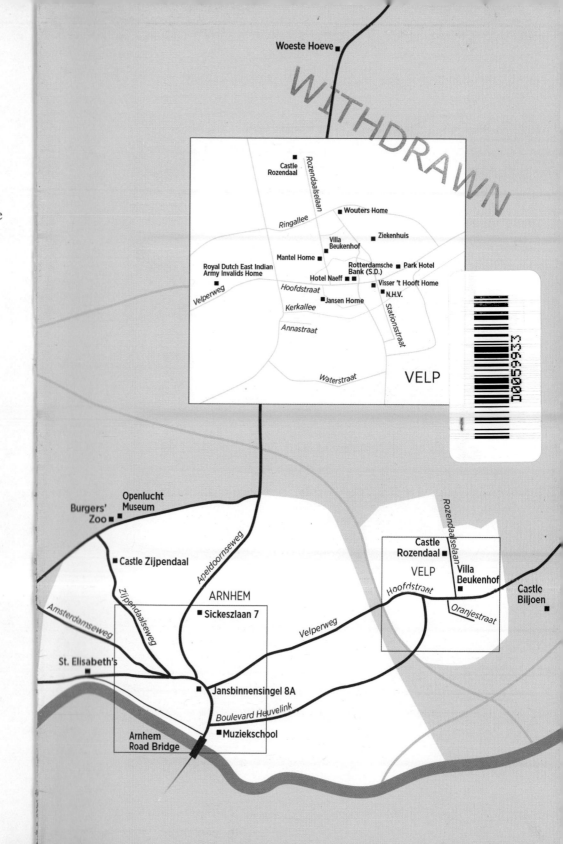

Fire

Dutch

Dutch Girl

Audrey Hepburn
and World War II

Robert Matzen

GoodKnight Books
Pittsburgh, Pennsylvania

GoodKnight Books

© 2019 by Robert Matzen

Foreword © 2019 by Luca Dotti

Published by GoodKnight Books, an imprint of Paladin Communications, Pittsburgh, Pennsylvania.

Printed in the United States of America.

ISBN 978-1-7322735-3-5
Library of Congress Control Number: 2018966886

For the people of Velp

Contents

Contents

Foreword

When I am asked about my mother, my favorite response has often been, "I don't know Audrey Hepburn."

My words always create a little stir and give me the opportunity to further explain how lucky my brother and I were growing up with a present and loving mother as opposed to a glamorous but absent movie star.

When my mother talked about herself and what life taught her, Hollywood was indeed the missing guest. Instead of naming famed Beverly Hills locations, she gave us obscure and sometimes unpronounceable Dutch ones. Red carpet recollections were replaced by Second World War episodes that she was able to transform into children's tales. We considered her lessons as tokens of wisdom, but we knew we were missing the complete story of her life in the war—until "somewhere over the rainbow" Robert Matzen wrote to me introducing himself and his book, *Dutch Girl*.

In a pure form of serendipity, Robert's message arrived just as I was trying to unite the dots between Mum's stories and my own archive and research efforts. I was understandably excited—who wouldn't be—as I knew Mum's deep self, the one that remained unchanged despite her stellar career, the one that made her the Audrey I knew, lay in these dots soon to be united by Robert's research.

Dutch Girl led me through a world of war that isn't as black and white as Hollywood's movies often suggest. Even I immediately forgot that there would be a happy ending for Audrey. As I read, I realized that bomb, that bullet, that German truck and its load of prisoners could simply be The End.

I now understand why the words Good and Evil, and Love and Mercy were so fundamental in her own narrative. Why she was open about certain facts and why she kept so many others in a secluded area of her being.

I really didn't know Audrey Hepburn, but I know more now, and I miss her more than ever.

Thank you, Robert, for your book is a true gift.

Luca Dotti
August 2018

Luca Dotti is the son of Audrey Hepburn and the New York Times *best-selling author of* Audrey at Home. *He is a former graphic designer and now chairs the Audrey Hepburn Children's Fund. Created by Audrey's family in 1994, the Fund helps children in need around the world.*

Preface

Since the death of Audrey Hepburn at the beginning of 1993, her story has been told and told again. An Amazon search of books with her name will produce 1,000+ hits. Every aspect of her life has been covered in print but one: the years of World War II when she lived in the Netherlands. There are portions of Audrey's story of the war that she wouldn't discuss and portions she felt she couldn't discuss. As a result, authors invented some situations and interpreted others incorrectly because they had no foundation in the history of the war. I can safely say that most pages about her war years in previous biographies contain errors about her life during that time.

Hepburn's definitive biographer, Barry Paris, spent a great deal of time and resources in 1993 with the backing of powerful G.P. Putnam's Sons to tell the Dutch portion of Audrey's story, and his meticulously referenced work became the starting point for my project. Paris had some advantages in his proximity to the war years—many people involved with the story were alive then who aren't now. But he also had a big disadvantage: There wasn't yet an Internet with fingertip access to prime Dutch archives. And because he based his operations in the United States (employing a Dutch researcher to do legwork in the Netherlands), Paris missed the importance of the village of Velp to Audrey's story. Velp sits just outside the city of Arnhem. That location came to mean everything to the story for reasons you will soon learn.

I love uncovering facts about Hollywood personalities in World War II, especially facts that have been lost over time because of the depth of research required to set the record straight. In the case of Audrey Hepburn, most of that research can be conducted only on the ground in the Netherlands, which is quite a deterrent for American authors. In addition, the adults that fought through and survived the war have passed on; the eyewitnesses are gone. Most vexing of all, some records stateside have vanished, which is a story in itself. These files, which should exist in the archives of the FBI and CIA (known as the OSS during World War II), concern a Dutch national named Ella, Baroness van Heemstra, who was Audrey's mother. When I began my project and sent my Washington, D.C., researcher after these files, she couldn't locate them and determined after exhaustive efforts that they no longer exist. Her professional opinion was that they had been destroyed long ago, and this conclusion begged the questions, why would these files have been removed from the record, and who would have removed them? After I spent two years investigating, the answers became evident.

Audrey Hepburn's father lived under the radar for most of his life, and her mother covered her tracks for activities from 1935 through '41, so it's no wonder that biographers shied away from chronicling those years of Audrey's life or relied on preexisting works. The trail was either cold or had been rubbed out of existence.

Was Audrey Hepburn's family rich? Was this wealth confiscated by the Nazis? Did Audrey grow up in grand Dutch castles? Did she witness her uncle and others being put up against a wall and shot? Did she perform clandestine dances to raise money for the Dutch Resistance and risk her life to perform other anti-Nazi duties at age fourteen or fifteen? My investigation took many twists and turns and provided surprising answers in the end.

Context is everything in Audrey Hepburn's war story, so I've described the times and the history that surrounded the subject. I was able to locate more than 6,000 words spoken by Audrey about World War II, and in the end I plugged them into the story of the war and the part the Netherlands played in it. And, son of a gun, her quotes made sense, including all those stories she told about the Resistance.

Combat came to Audrey's world in September 1944, and I made it my goal to recreate for the reader what she experienced over the course of eight brutal months. I wanted those who already love Audrey to know the sights, the sounds, the pain, and the terror felt by this Dutch girl during the occupation and then the battles that would forge Audrey Hepburn into a global force. I wanted the reader to get some sense of what her world was like. She saw so much blood and death before she turned sixteen, yet lived a life of such grace and never admitted what she had witnessed. The war *made* Audrey Hepburn, and so what she experienced, especially in those final months of conflict, is a story worth telling, day by day and blow by blow.

In some ways it's a miracle she made it out of the war alive; in all ways this is the tale of a remarkable young girl who would go on to become an icon for peace.

Robert Matzen
30 June 2018

Part I: Cauldron

1

Rapture

Germany
1935

Baroness Ella van Heemstra stood in the office of Adolf Hitler and offered her hand to the most famous man in the world, the man whose name was on simply everyone's lips. Hitler's deep blue eyes could have bored through her, such was their power. He was so pale, so composed as he smiled that enigmatic smile, full of humility, the one seen so often in newsreels flickering on screens around the world. He reached out his hand and accepted hers lightly. Then, with a gesture born of generations and centuries of European tradition, he bowed and touched his lips to her skin. Ella had often heard the touch of this man described as an electric shock, yet here she was, standing in the Führer's office in National Socialist German Workers Party headquarters, better known as the Braunes Haus, in Munich, Germany. She had dropped off her two sons and little daughter in the Dutch resort village of Oosterbeek so that she and her husband could come here for what promised to be a once-in-a-lifetime opportunity.

How many women would have signed away their lives for this moment, their very lives, but the baroness had earned this audience thanks to a column she had written in The Blackshirt, the weekly newspaper of the British Union of Fascists, extolling the virtues of Hitler and his British disciple in National Socialism, Sir Oswald Mosley.

It didn't hurt that Ella's dear friends in her English social class also admired the great man. British journalist Micky Burn of the Gloucester Citizen had fallen under the Führer's spell—the Führer signed a copy of his book Mein Kampf for a breathless Burn. Unity Mitford of the Swinbrook Mitfords was mad for Hitler and had become his latest pet. Unity had introduced her elegant sister Diana, and now both women were smitten. A third Mitford, Pamela, was now running in the pack, but she just seemed bemused by the whole business.

Of course, Hitler had his reasons for courting the English and sought to embrace Britain's subjects at every opportunity. Unity told of a time when the British national anthem came up, and the Führer "whistled it all the way through." So yes, he admired all things English, including women, and embracing the charming Mitfords, the so-called "scandal sisters," was no chore for the great man. What did he see in Ella van Heemstra now? A way inside the upper strata of Dutch society? Perhaps, but it didn't matter, because Ella was here and determined to enjoy this moment to the fullest. She hoped His Excellency didn't mind her lip rouge and powder—he was notorious for loathing women who wore them—but he paid no notice of the paints and powders on his foreign guests at this moment. He aimed a pleasantry at Ella, and she responded in flawless German.

Ella's husband, Joseph Ruston, and Unity Mitford were standing at her side; Ella's hand was in Hitler's. The Führer was so gallant and so pleasant, with those arresting blue eyes and such a nice face. Dear God, how heady these times were, Germany reborn and lighting the way for all of Europe after the devastation of the worldwide Great Depression. Fascism held the answer for mankind. Fascism shone the light for those wise enough to see. Fascism had brought Germany back to full employment in a matter of a few years, proving its ideals more powerful and unstoppable than economic cataclysm. Blood-red flags with the fascist crest flew everywhere in Munich; banners of fire hung from every building and crosspiece. The narrow streets of the ancient city pulsed with energy as if arteries in a stirring beast.

The enchantment of all she saw and everyone she met beckoned Ella back to Germany from her home in Belgium later that year in September; once more she parked her children in Oosterbeek so she could attend the annual Nazi Party Congress, the Reichsparteitag, in Nuremberg. She had seen images from the 1934 event shining in glorious silver thanks to Leni Riefenstahl's 1935 film Triumph des Willen, and now Ella vowed to witness it in person. Imagine a city already at a half million bulging with as many guests. Hotels filled too quickly, and all those that could not find indoor rooms or accommodations in the nine open-air tent camps were placed in commandeered factories, churches, and schools. Here the infatuated Ella became immersed in a full week of Fascist activities, from the pealing of the city's church bells to a performance of Richard Wagner's Die Meistersinger to meeting after meeting and speech after speech. She witnessed the Führer's review of his Hitler Youth at sprawling Zeppelin Field, the Nuremberg stadium, as he addressed 60,000 perfectly uniformed, precisely aligned young men. He told them, his voice booming from speakers: "You must learn to suffer privation without crumbling once. Whatever we create today, whatever we do, we will die, but Germany will live on in you. When there is nothing left of us, then you must hold in your fists the flags that we hoisted out of nothing. I know this cannot be otherwise because you are the flesh of our flesh, and the blood of our blood. In your young heads burns the same spirit that rules us."

This 1935 gathering was the Party Congress of Freedom, as in freedom from the restrictions of the horrendous Treaty of Versailles that had ended the Great War sixteen years earlier—and stripped Germany of its wealth, military might, and much of its territory. The Führer paraded his Wehrmacht, his magnificent army, before the quarter million assembled at the stadium. Overhead, German war planes flew so thick that they seemed to blot out the sun, and demonstrations of anti-aircraft fire from cannon manned by calm and able crews boomed in response.

3

The Reichstag had passed the *Law for the Protection of German Blood and German Honor,* which forbade marriages and intercourse between Germans and Jews and the employment of German females under the age of forty-five in Jewish households. The *Reich Citizenship Law* declared that only those of German or related blood were eligible to be Reich citizens; the remainder—including Jews, especially Jews—were classed as state subjects without citizenship rights. Ella had many Jewish friends in Belgium and elsewhere, but Diana Mitford summed it up beautifully quoting her dear friend Putzi Hanfstaengl: "If the Jews don't like it, they can get out. They have relations and money all over the world. Let them leave Germany to us Germans." It was the only instance Ella had for pause in an otherwise positive story, and it was easily reasoned out.

Back in the stadium, Hitler heard the affirmations of his labor force and consecrated those of the party killed in the 1923 armed Nazi uprising known as the Beer Hall Putsch, when sixteen party members were gunned down on a Munich street. It was a moving display of love, remembrance, and most of all, power. Ella felt deep in her bones that in the not-too-distant future, she would be part of a Europe united under Adolf Hitler, the man who had generated all this out of the force of his will and ended the hopelessness of Germany in the decade and a half after the Great War.

On the final day of the Reichsparteitag, Zeppelin Field bulged with more than 300,000 people, with hundreds of flags rippling in the breeze, planes flying over, tanks rolling through, drums pounding, and bands playing; the seats seemed to vibrate from the high black boots of the Führer's massed troops as they goose-stepped past. The banners, black and white swastikas inset in red, streamed past as if a river of blood. So red it hurt the eyes. The tinkling of *Schellenbaum,* the belltree staff carried in front of some army units, sent pure silver tones soaring high above the dull thuds of the drums and boots.

Finally, Hitler spoke and laid his soul bare speaking about his love for Germany and his hopes and dreams for the future. He pointed out that the world's problems centered around the Jews who had manipulated nations into the Great War, which had culminated in the defeat of Germany and then the Great Depression. The Parteitag concluded with a tattoo, a stirring, masculine presentation by the drum corps, and then Hitler climbed into a touring car and was driven all the way around the inside of the stadium to be worshiped by the throngs.

With the Party Congress concluded, Ella ventured back to Munich to bask in Hitler's presence at, among other places, his favorite restaurant, the Osteria Bavaria, and passed her time with Unity Mitford, Unity's SS boyfriend Erich Widmann, and Citizen reporter Micky Burn. Unity was so incredibly territorial over Hitler that she kept the others at bay so she could have the Führer all to herself, but Ella didn't need the great man's attention; she had already met him, and she returned home to Belgium where she took pen in hand.

Wrote Ella: "What struck me most forcibly among the million and one impressions I received there were: (a) the wonderful fitness of every man and woman one saw, on parades or in the street; and (b) the refreshing atmosphere around one, the absolute freedom from any form of mental pressure or depression."

Ella's words would boom in Sir Oswald's National Socialist newsletter, Action, as she concluded: "Well may Adolf Hitler be proud of the rebirth of this great country and of the rejuvenation of the German spirit. The Germany of today is a most present country, and the Germans, under Nazi rule, a splendid example to the white races of the world—a mighty people, upright and proud, as indeed, they have every right to be." And to these stirring words she affixed the Belgian version of her name, Baroness Ella de Heemstra, Brussels.*

---

*See the chapter notes beginning on page 321 for a description of sources consulted.

2

The Blood of Frisia

Audrey Kathleen van Heemstra Ruston, future shining Hollywood star, entered the world under a different kind of star, a dark one, on 4 May 1929. Her mother, Ella, Baroness van Heemstra, was a strong-willed, plain-speaking, high-spirited colt of a woman who at age twenty-eight still felt the need to sow wild oats, despite the fact she was now the mother of three, counting sons Alexander and Ian from her first marriage. In Ella's veins—in the veins of all the van Heemstras—raced Frisian blood. Frisia, known as Friesland to the Dutch, is a unique province in the far north of the Netherlands. Even today many Frisians bristle at being referred to as *Dutch* at all—they're too unique and independent for such a common classification.

That Audrey Hepburn should one day become an accomplished personage known around the world isn't surprising considering her bloodlines among Frisian nobility.[*] The first Frisian van Heemstra found in records came long before William of Orange, under whose reign the Netherlands coalesced. Van Heemstras were recognized as nobility from the beginning, from the Middle Ages, and the title of baron was granted officially in 1814 to Willem Hendrik van Heemstra, whose son Schelto, Baron van Heem-

---

[*]See inside the back cover for the van Heemstra family tree.

stra, represented Friesland in the Dutch House of Representatives before becoming prime minister of the Netherlands in 1861. Another son, Frans, Baron van Heemstra, also served in the House of Representatives. Frans' son W.H.J., Baron van Heemstra, had two sons, one of whom was Aarnoud Jan Anne Aleid—or A.J.A.A., Baron van Heemstra—father of Ella along with four other daughters and a son. This baron was Audrey's grandfather, or *opa*, as the position is known in Dutch.

By 1900 van Heemstra had become a family name of national honor in Holland. The path to wealth for Dutchmen cut through the East Indies, but Aarnoud went his own way and obtained a doctorate of law in 1896, the same year he married Elbrig Willemina Henriette, Baroness van Asbeck. Aarnoud set up practice as a prosecuting attorney and then became a judge in the prosperous city of Arnhem on the Rhine, capital of the province of Gelderland, forty miles west of the German border. As he pursued his practice, the Baroness van Asbeck produced babies—Wilhelmina Cornelia (1897), Geraldine Caroline (1898), Ella (1900), Marianne Jacqueline (1903), Willem Hendrik (1907), and Arnoudina Johanna (1911). By now the father of six had become *burgemeester*, or mayor, of Arnhem, a position he held for ten years until 1920. The family lived in a beautiful villa beside the Lauwersgracht, a lake that was all that remained of a moat that once encircled the ancient walled city of Arnhem. Now the lake belonged to the Park Musis Sacrum in the city center, the most picturesque spot in all of Arnhem. The van Heemstra home was one of three in the "Paadje van Bleckmann," villas owned by a wealthy local family named Bleckmann. Another of these villas, known as de Nijenburgh, was occupied by Cornelia, Countess van Limburg Stirum. The baron's daughter Wilhelmina married the countess's nephew, Otto Ernst Gelder, Count van Limburg Stirum, in 1918, meaning that the van Heemstra family presence was both strong and close in Arnhem Centraal, overlooking the Rhine. In another twenty-six years these three grand villas of the van Heemstra and van Limburg Stirum families would be soaked in blood and destroyed in the most romanticized battle of the Second World War.

Under Burgemeester van Heemstra's direction, Arnhem prospered. The land development association Nederlandsche Heidemaatschappij chose the city for its headquarters, the soon-to-be-famous Openlucht Museum and Burgers' Zoo were established, and affordable housing became prevalent.

In March 1920 Aarnoud gave his daughter Ella's hand in marriage to Hendrik Gustaaf Adolf Quarles van Ufford of Oosterbeek, the next town over. Hendrik was a former horse cavalryman and now an oil executive assigned to the Dutch East Indies. After the nuptials the couple set sail for the Far East to begin a new life together. Later that same year Burgemeester van Heemstra, who was something of a penny-pincher, suddenly relinquished his office in a squabble with the city over money. He stated that "the meager salary does not allow me to continue to do my job properly." He returned to law but not for long. The Netherlands' Queen Wilhelmina of the House of Oranje appointed Aarnoud to be governor of the Dutch territory of Suriname on the northeast coast of South America, so the baron, baroness, and three of the van Heemstra children set sail for what would become a tumultuous eight years in the far-flung Suriname capital, Paramaribo.

Aarnoud was a charismatic aristocrat. Ella described her father as "about the most handsome man I ever saw. They say he is brilliantly clever. He forms his witty remarks in a French way. On Sundays he looks subdued but bubbling over with mischief. His teeth look very white behind a small black moustache."

The new governor of Suriname had spent his life among northern Europeans and now had to deal with a South American melting pot that included native Indians and escaped slaves, called Maroons, who had formed their own independent villages in the abundant rain forests of the interior. Administering this wild area meant keeping bauxite mines producing aluminum and also ensuring the stability of rice and banana crops, and all three required lots of muscle from either free men or indentured servants. Prior governors had been figureheads, but not Governor van Heemstra, who undertook several expeditions deep into the interior—places where white Europeans rarely were seen. He took an active interest because the baron was a visionary who saw the economic potential of Suriname. He pushed hard for financial independence at the expense of a Netherlands government that he correctly labeled as disinterested in this "unimportant" piece of real estate—the *real* money was to be made in thriving Dutch East Indies enterprises that produced coffee, tea, cacao, tobacco, and rubber.

Governor van Heemstra remained a progressive who worked tirelessly on behalf of his colony. His work ethic would be seen a generation later in his young granddaughter. In 1922 van Heemstra welcomed the Aluminum Company of America, better known as Alcoa, into the Moengo forest to mine bauxite. But the honeymoon between the governor and Alcoa was short-lived: He realized almost at once that danger lurked in this U.S. company monopolizing Suriname resources.

In 1924 he traveled to Germany to negotiate with the Stinnes group, a powerful mining conglomerate. His goal was to interest the Germans in bauxite mining in the colony, figuring a second company on hand would check the aggressive Americans. But the Dutch government feared that once the equally bold and enterprising Germans got in, they might try a total takeover, and so van Heemstra was ordered to break off contact.

His worries during these years weren't just political. His wife's health was in decline, and then he learned that his third daughter on the other side of the world, Ella, had decided to divorce her husband of five years, Hendrik Quarles van Ufford, after producing two sons. Unexpectedly, Ella showed up at the governor's mansion in Paramaribo with her children after a transoceanic voyage.

Ella had become at age twenty-five a handsome and opinionated young woman with strong drives who took one look at life in primitive Suriname, said no thank you, and set sail on a return voyage back across the world to the Dutch East Indies with sons Alex and Ian in tow. Aarnoud waved good-bye while continuing to battle the mother country at every turn, holding the Americans at bay with one arm and the Germans with the other. When he tried to increase taxes on Alcoa for its bauxite exports, the Dutch government said no, while also placing Shell Oil on the shoulders of the governor as a new worry. That was it. Governor van Heemstra resigned to become Baron van Heemstra once more and returned to Arnhem's neighbor, the resort village of Oosterbeek, with wife and family.

Meanwhile, Ella had been drawn back to the Dutch East Indies by an intriguing thirty-four-year-old English ne'er-do-well named Joseph Ruston, a married man whom she had met and couldn't get out of her mind. When she showed up once more in the East Indies following the visit to Suriname, Ruston divorced his wife, and Joseph and Ella were married in September 1926.

Ruston had been born in Bohemia in 1889 of an English father and German mother. He may have casually mentioned to Baroness Ella that he was descended from the third husband of Mary, Queen of Scots. That English noble was James Hepburn, Earl of Bothwell. Ella loved the idea of being connected to British nobility and insisted that he adopt the name Joseph Hepburn-Ruston, which she would then use as well to become Ella, Baroness van Heemstra Hepburn-Ruston. He agreed to such use, but never in writing.

Ruston was Bohemian in more ways than one. He had come from money but didn't seem to have any, which might have given Ella a glimpse of their life ahead. From the Dutch East Indies the couple began a years-long global odyssey that featured Ruston's disdain for holding a steady position and then his eventual realization that the van Heemstras of Frisia were *not* weighed down by large bank accounts and treasure chests of family jewels. In fact, the only gold to be found anywhere around a van Heemstra gleamed on the impressive family coat of arms. Otherwise, they would be called upper middle class, and that didn't suit Ruston at all.

Eventually, Ruston began a position with tin merchants Maclaine, Watson and Company, working first in London and then in Brussels. It was here that their only child together, Audrey—known to her family as Adriaantje—was born in spring 1929. The first crisis faced by mother and new daughter occurred at day twenty-one, when whooping cough stopped the baby's heart. Ella's response was classically *her*: An avid Christian Scientist, she didn't bother calling a doctor. Instead, she held her daughter upside down like a newborn and began spanking her. Somehow it worked, and Adriaantje gasped for breath and began screaming. The episode would be prophetic of Ella's power over her daughter from this instant until Audrey drew her last breath sixty-three years later.

With Ruston aloof and Ella a typically forceful Frisian in the mold of her opinionated and outgoing father, Adriaantje couldn't help but grow up Dutch in key ways. Her opa, the baron, had been born near Utrecht; her mother in Velp, the village just east of Arnhem. Half brothers Alex and Ian were the sons of a Quarles van Ufford from stately Oosterbeek, just on the western side of Arnhem. The Ruston family—Joseph, Ella, Alex, Ian, and Adriaantje—were always on the move between Brussels, London (Joseph's adopted home), and Arnhem, which remained home base not only for Opa but also second cousin Schelte, Baron van Heemstra, and his wife, Mathilde Jacoba, Baroness van Heemstra van Oosterzee, known to the family as Tilly.

In fact, the Dutch province of Gelderland was crawling with titled kin—van Heemstras and Quarles van Uffords and the family that Ella's older sister Wilhelmina had married into, the van Limburg Stirums. With that marriage Wilhelmina, known to the family as "Meisje" or "Girl," had become Baroness van Heemstra,

Countess van Limburg Stirum. The titles were as impressive as the manners and sense of *noblesse oblige* of the family, but the simple fact was that while many of them had a little money or some money, none of them had a lot of money.

Lack of funds made Joseph Ruston unhappy, and he and Ella squabbled constantly. Then Joseph would hit the road to points unknown, and Ella would return home to Arnhem with the children and seek babysitting services from her father the baron and frail mother the baroness, who now resided in Villa Roestenburg, a cozy, fourteen-year-old, thatched-roof home in Oosterbeek on a tree-lined street called Pietersbergseweg.

Adriaantje's opa and oma practiced Calvinism devoutly, which meant prayers several times a day, steady Bible lessons, and more than two hours of church services on Sundays at the *Oude Kerk*, or Old Church, on the southern edge of the village, not far from the Rhine. And it really was old—built of Roman stone sometime around 1000 A.D. It fell to Adriaantje as the youngest in the house to say grace before each meal for what they were about to receive and again afterward for what they had just consumed.

But days for Ella's children also included plenty of time for play. Next door to Villa Roestenburg in a wooded setting sat an elegant hotel that bore the name Tafelberg. All around the Tafelberg Alex, Ian, and Adriaantje found trees to climb and woodlands to roam despite frequent scoldings from their mother. From the Tafelberg west to a grand resort hotel, the Hartenstein, lay woods, meadows, and a recreational facility, Sport Park Hartenstein, which were perfect haunts for marauding children.

Little Adriaantje displayed liveliness only around her brothers. Otherwise, she was shy, sensitive, and terribly quiet. She didn't like it when either parent traveled because it disrupted her comfort zone, which their home in Brussels represented. Her father seemed to her to be a lot of fun. He liked to be out of doors and taught her all about horses and how to ride. He also took her up in glider planes—gliding was a major fad of the 1930s, especially in Germany. "Audrey often spoke of the few memories she had of her father," said her son Sean, "and she remembered vividly going gliding with him, the sound of the wind, the real sense of flying."

As the girl turned five, she became aware that her father was gone a lot, and that when he returned, both parents were often cross with each other. The arguing began to affect her and brought on bouts of anxiety and asthma. Then both parents began traveling, leaving Adriaantje and her brothers in Oosterbeek with Opa and Oma.

During this period, Joseph and Ella spent increasing amounts of time in London, where both fell under the influence of Sir Oswald Mosley, former government minister and now head of the British Union of Fascists, the BUF. Hitler was all the rage in Germany for bringing back the failed German economy—Germany bolted to the economic forefront in a world gripped by depression from the crash of 1929. With Germany's rebirth came a surge in nationalism fueled by Hitler's cries of Aryan supremacy and hatred of anyone not "pure German."

English men and women heard Hitler's strident message funneled through the mouth of Mosley as depression still gripped the island nation and no upward economic swings coincided with those in the Reich. Hitler saw the potential of the fascist way of life taking hold in England; he frankly admired and respected the British for their history and global empire. With his usual cunning the Führer encouraged Mosley, his ideology resonating with many in the British upper classes whose wealth had been hacked away by the economic turmoil of the decade.

Rallies in Hyde Park drew crushing crowds in the thousands to see Mosley, clad in trademark black, deliver speeches about the potential of National Socialism to lead England out of the dark. He had long used the Great War as the dividing line that separated the overly polite "pre-war" politician from his brash "post-war" brothers. Now, Mosley railed against the use of cheap foreign labor and its crippling effect on the British economy, and he dared speak the name of the greatest threat of all: "It is the force which is served by the Conservative party, the Liberal party, and the Socialist party alike," he said, "the force that has dominated Britain ever since the war..., the force of international Jewish finance!"

Masses desperate for an answer to their economic suffering honored Mosley, the man in black, with the straight-armed Nazi salute.

Among them were the daughters of Lord Redesdale (David Freeman-Mitford) and Lady Redesdale (Sydney Bowles). Most of the six Mitford girls of Swinbrook House northwest of London became lipstick Nazis, which was quite in vogue for the social set in '34 and '35. Tagging along was their society pal known somewhat disdainfully as "Heemstra." The most glamorous Mitford sister, Diana, took the equally glamorous Nazi Mosley as a lover and then married him. The youngest Mitford, rebellious teenager Unity, headed for Munich and began stalking the Führer himself.

Joseph and Ella were in hip deep with the Mitfords and enthralled with Mosley, then with Hitler, and especially with the concept of Nazism. Ella, from her perspective as a continental baroness living in Belgium, penned a short essay on the joys of Nazism for the BUF newspaper, *The Blackshirt*. Mosley was so appreciative that he invited Ella and her husband on a BUF junket to observe the Führer and tour Germany. Accordingly, the stay of Adriaantje and her brothers at Villa Roestenburg in Oosterbeek was extended for another month.

When the touring British fascists arrived in Munich, they discovered that young Unity Mitford had earned Hitler's attention at his favorite restaurant, the Osteria Bavaria. His security people had learned that she was British and an aristocrat—a social class that Hitler coveted—and he invited her to his table. By spring, Unity had gained firm enough footing with her crush the Führer to grant access to the Mitford crowd—including Ella and Joseph—and all shook hands with the most sought-after man in the world; he would later become *TIME*'s Man of the Year for 1938.

Diana Mitford said, "It goes without saying that I saw on these occasions a very different Hitler from the man possessed by demonic energy who had changed the face of Germany." She confided in her autobiography, "The truth is that in private life he was exceptionally charming, clever and original, and that he inspired affection."

Ella was over the moon to meet Hitler and witness a Germany reborn, not only the military formations and the swastikas but the amazing autobahns and thriving factories. But as Ella would learn a little later, Joseph's trip to Germany with the BUF was more than a sightseeing tour. It was a means to an end—a stepping-stone.

Soon after Joseph and Ella had gathered up their children in Oosterbeek and returned to Brussels, Joseph walked out on his family to the horror of both mother and daughter. One story had Ella walking in on Joseph in bed with the nanny; another had the baron ordering Ruston out of the family and threatening prosecution for draining bank accounts; still a third had Queen Wilhelmina urging her friend the baron to shut up Ella because a Dutch baroness had no business being mixed up in Nazi shenanigans. Whatever happened, there seemed to have been a scene—something shocking that broke up the family for good.

Audrey would claim that the trauma of it turned Ella's hair gray overnight, which may have been a child's viewpoint as her mother lost interest in coloring her hair. Ella's emotional investment was clear, and she refused to give up on a partner who may indeed have been unreliable all along. In the autobiographical novel she wrote later in life, she alluded to Ruston when she wrote of a character who was speaking of Ella. The character wrote that Ella would "be terribly loyal to the man she loves. And if she should be disappointed in him, if she should know him to be different to what he appeared to be, if she should be warned against him by others, I would expect her to say, 'I know, but I still want to believe in him.'"

To her daughter and others, Ella was shown to be far needier than anyone would have suspected; friends feared she would kill herself. Years later, Audrey said of her mother: "She cried day in, day out. I thought that she never would stop." Seeing such heart-break in a mother whose strength she had never questioned left Adriaantje, at age six, "terrified. You say to yourself, 'What's going to happen to me?' The ground has gone out from under you." Audrey would always call it the most traumatic event of her life.

For the little girl, the abandonment would have ramifications that rippled through her time line, not just for weeks or months but for all the succeeding decades. Audrey said, "I'm not afraid to say something of that feeling has stayed with me through my own relationships."

Time and again in interviews when she was a Hollywood star and then a UNICEF ambassador, Audrey would return to that theme, when her father walked out on a six-year-old girl: "I think it is hard sometimes for children who are dumped," she said. "I don't care who they are. It tortures a child beyond measure. They don't know what the problem was. Children need two parents for their [emotional] equilibrium in life."

Ella groped to gather the shattered pieces of herself. But she retained her avid interest in Nazism, hinting that she hoped rec-onciliation with Joseph remained possible because he made her a complete person. She threw herself into planning a return to Germany with the Mitfords for the 1935 Nuremberg rally in Sep-tember. With Joseph relocated to London, he made it known that he wanted his daughter to be educated in England, and so Ella decided to take Adriaantje to a private school in Elham, a village in county Kent south of Canterbury and not far from Dover in the southeast corner of the island. It was a place the Rustons had visited on vacation.

The decision blindsided an already-fragile child. Alex and Ian, now ages fifteen and eleven, were shipped off to The Hague to live with relatives. Suddenly, the little girl was isolated with strangers in a different country hundreds of miles from home. She would never quite recover from the shock of the separation; nor would she truly overcome the actions of her mother during the ensuing weeks, months, and years.

3
Exile

As Audrey said later, "I went to a little private school in England as, at the time, we were living in Belgium and my mother thought it was right for me to speak English, being brought up as an English child." After all, she was the daughter of a British citizen and so British by birth, despite having been born in Belgium. But Audrey's explanation reinforces the theory that Ella plotted for an eventual reconciliation with her estranged husband. Later, Ella would claim that the separation from Ruston ended her interest in Nazism, but a second article written by Baroness van Heemstra for the BUF proves that the contrary was true. She seemed to consider herself an international citizen with no national allegiances. Yes, she had been born in the Netherlands, but she had traveled the world for a decade, resided in Belgium and England, and loved Germany and spoke its language fluently.

Ella rented an old brick home called Orchard Cottage on narrow Duck Street just off the village square in Elham, a countryside village dominated by the thirteenth century St. Mary the Virgin Anglican Church, which sat just across the street from the house in which Adriaantje now lived. The church dominated the view from every front window. Before long Ella was off for Nuremberg, where she would sit enthralled at Zeppelin Field and other venues for the annual Reichsparteitag, Hitler's week-long military spectacle. With emotional deafness she heard proclaimed the new laws targeting Jews, not as German but as "other." These laws, brought to reality with Ella in attendance, sealed the fate of Jews and the world and made possible all that happened afterward. And her actions here would have a crippling effect on her daughter as well.

Said Ella of the German army parade: "To watch their boundless enthusiasm as they march past in endless formations, hailing their beloved 'Führer,' Adolf Hitler, is one of the most inspiring sights on earth. Hitler has a magnetic and most charming personality, which fully reflects the spiritual aspirations of this mighty people."

From Nuremberg Ella traveled north to Munich where Unity Mitford found "Heemstra" encamped inside the Osteria Bavaria awaiting Hitler. Ella sat with her traveling companion and lover, British journalist Michael "Micky" Burn, and with Unity's boyfriend, Erich Widmann of the SS. Unity wrote in a letter to her sister Diana on 19 September 1935 that "I made them sit in the garden and I sat alone inside" so that Hitler would notice her, and only her, when he arrived. A while later the Führer showed up and invited Unity to join him.

Of this Munich leg of the trip Ella wrote, "All the time I was there I never heard an angry word, and yet, far from being sluggardly, the people are keen and alert and full of life. They are happy; they are content and fully satisfied to live today for the glory of an ever-better future."

For the girl known to Elham residents as Audrey Ruston, and more often as "Little Audrey," life was anything but colorful or inspiring or happy. Her father had been torn away, her mother was gone, and the North Sea separated her from beloved brothers, Alex and Ian. She was enrolled with thirteen other pupils at a private school in a brick row house on the village square. Four spinster governesses oversaw the curriculum: head-of-house Alice Catherine Rigden and her sisters, Norah Mabel, Maria Amelia, and Blanche Henrietta.

Music and English teacher Norah Mabel Rigden formed a special bond with the little girl in exile from mainland Europe, and both subjects, music and English, would coalesce into the foundation of a Hollywood career almost twenty years later.

The rented home on Duck Lane was owned by the Butcher family, and it was Mary Butcher who cared for Adriaantje while Ella remained on the Continent. From the front door, the schoolgirl had but to turn right, then right again at the square, and she arrived at school in thirty seconds—which came in handy given the often dreary rains and fog influenced by the English Channel just five miles south and the North Sea not much farther east. Not that Adriaantje looked forward to rushing to school. She didn't enjoy the process of education; she never would.

"I liked the children and my teachers," she said in an interview at the time of *Roman Holiday*, "but I never liked the process of learning. I was very restless and could never sit still for hours on end, learning things. I enjoyed learning the subjects I liked—I always loved history and mythology and astronomy—but I hated anything to do with arithmetic or that sort of thing. School in itself I found very dull and I was happy when I was finished."

Peggy Baker, slightly older than Audrey, lived next door on Duck Lane and said the new girl "seemed fairly lonely, especially during the long school holidays." The fear of abandonment caused by her father's departure was also on display for Baker: "Our gardens were next to each other and she was always calling out my name." During this period—late 1935 and early 1936—Audrey put on weight and soon became a sad and introverted, moon-faced girl, already tall and now heavy, with a habit of biting her nails and complaining of blinding headaches. And the asthma showed up occasionally as well; it was never life threatening, but always a concern.

Divorce proceedings commenced and through that period,

Ella remained low-key. After publication of her late September 1935 article in *The Blackshirt* entitled "At Nuremberg," she didn't communicate again publicly about National Socialism. From the perspective of the baron and the van Heemstra family, Dutch citizen Ella was behaving recklessly and making a spectacle of herself. Yes, the baron was pro-German and had courted German business while governor of Suriname. Yes, the Germans were first cousins of the Dutch, and the van Heemstra home in Oosterbeek sat near enough to the German border. But by 1937 stories abounded about German brown shirts and SS assaulting Jews on the streets of major cities. All Europe worried about Hitler's military buildup and the expansionism that could result. The beautiful, positive impression that Germany had made through August 1936, when Berlin hosted the Summer Olympic Games, was mutating into something malevolent after the Olympic torch had left the Reich.

Records don't track Ella's progress from 1936 to 1938, although she boarded the boys for a year with the Cohen Stuart family at Beverningkstaat 38 in The Hague. Despite the lack of available information about this period in Ella's life, details that are known about 1939 and 1940 indicate that she still engaged in pro-German activities and relationships.

Residents of Elham remember Baroness van Heemstra coming to visit her daughter for two or three weeks at a stretch, sometimes with one or both sons, and the more Adriaantje saw her mother and brothers, the better the growing girl handled her time in the English countryside. By now she had joined the local Brownie troop, and in 1937 at age eight participated in a production of *Humpty Dumpty*, playing one of the king's men. She was at this time still taller than the others, sporting a pageboy haircut and prone to bouts of overeating.

As she got a little older and saw her brothers more often, she loved playing with Alex, Ian, and Peggy from next door in ruins of the local brickworks. In Audrey's reminiscences about this period, she never mentions visits by her father; he must have made some or she wouldn't have been sent to England in the first place or spent so much time there over a four-year period. But her father had been and would continue to be a shady character. On the pretense of working for the European Press Agency, he traveled extensively on behalf of the Third Reich and engaged in money laundering among other activities outside the law. In practical terms Adriaantje's father had become a full-fledged German agent who caught the attention of MI5, the British intelligence service. When he became aware that MI5 was on to him, he dropped out of sight.

The eight year old must certainly have heard the name Hitler in conversations among adults. But as Audrey always said, "A child is a child." This child had had another new influence enter her life and take it over: Norah Rigden had gotten the Ruston girl interested in dance.

"I fell in love with dancing," said Audrey later. "There was a young dancer who would come up from London once a week and give ballet classes. I loved it, just loved it."

Said Joan Hawkins, a schoolmate of Adriaantje, "If anything singled her out it was the ballet lessons she used to go to in Folkestone." It was a drive of a few miles from Elham south over narrow country lanes to reach the much larger Folkestone, a harbor town on the English Channel where the Belgian girl received dance lessons from the London ballerina.

In May 1938 Adriaantje turned nine and Joan Hawkins attended the birthday party Ella threw for her daughter in the village hall. "What I chiefly remember," said Joan, "is a tape that the mother stretched along the wall, to which were pinned little gifts; and the baroness led us up, one by one and blindfolded, to grope for our present..., but I always felt she steered each child toward the gift she wanted him or her to have. She was quite manipulative that way."

That summer Ella took her three children on a two-month trip to Italy. "They visited their friends Colonna," said Luca Dotti, Audrey's son. Photos show the three youngsters at an airfield where they flew in biplanes with Don Mario Colonna, Duke of Rignano, who "would tragically crash that summer in July."

The photos show Adriaantje looking happy. At Elham she had friends and dance lessons, along with a relationship with her mother that showed signs of healing and at least sporadic visits from her mercurial father. All the while, Europe quaked every time the growing German empire flexed its muscles. Germany had announced an *Anschluss*, or union, with Austria in March 1938; in October German troops crossed the Czech border and reclaimed the Sudetenland; in November *Kristallnacht*, or "The Night of Broken Glass," began open war against Jews inside Germany. In March 1939 with German troops on the doorstep, the remainder of Czechoslovakia surrendered.

Seeing these signs of trouble for Europe, Ella applied for a Dutch immigration permit for Audrey—one less thing to worry about in the future. By now Ella had relocated from Brussels to her parents' villa in Oosterbeek and had brought Alex and Ian back as well. All stayed in the roomy villa with her youngest sister, Arnoudina. It had become urgent for Ella and her five siblings to be close to their mother, who was confined to bed and had been gravely ill for months. Elbrig, Baroness van Asbeck, Ella's mother and Adriaantje's grandmother, died at age sixty-five on 28 March 1939.

After the passing of the elder baroness, her widower husband Baron van Heemstra—Adriaantje's opa—sold the Villa Roestenburg in Oosterbeek to the Kristensen family. It had been the home and woodlands near the Tafelberg where Adriaantje and her brothers had played so lustily earlier in the decade. The baron now moved four miles east to rooms he rented in Castle Zijpendaal, a three-story, eighteenth-century brick palace in the wooded hills above Arnhem in Sonsbeek Park. The baron's daughter (and Ella's older sister) Meisje and her husband Otto, Count van Limburg

Stirum, also moved into a set of rented rooms in Zijpendaal to keep the baron company.

Zijpendaal, or "de Zijp" as all called it, offered a favorable location for the baron's business and social interests in Arnhem, along with eye appeal for a titled family. The elder van Heemstra was chairman of the board of the local hospital, Diaconessenhuis, and also involved in a number of charities. The baron believed firmly in the societal obligations of Dutch nobility to help those less fortunate and instilled in all his children similar principles. Family ties to the ruling House of Oranje also remained strong—Ella's younger sister, Marianne, Baroness van Heemstra, became a lady in waiting to Queen Wilhelmina's daughter, Princess Juliana.

An era had ended—the van Heemstras in Oosterbeek—and another had begun, with Ella now joining her father, three of her sisters, and her brother in Arnhem. By Adriaantje's tenth birthday in May, the divorce of Ella and Joseph was final, and Ella moved into a one-story, brick row house with the boys at Sickeszlaan 7 on a hill just off Sonsbeek Park above Arnhem Centraal. Ella began to entertain the idea of relocating her daughter from county Kent to Sickeszlaan as well, but Adriaantje had grown to love her ballet instruction, and so Ella resisted the move.

Then in August, Germany and the Soviet Union signed a non-aggression treaty that freed Hitler to attack Poland. He did so on the first day of September, and a few days later, Poland's ally Great Britain declared war on Germany. Bombs could be falling on England at any moment, and Adriaantje was located in Kent on the general flight path of German bombers heading for London. In a panic Ella made contact with her ex-husband, who agreed it was best to return their daughter to the Netherlands. Ella reasoned that her country had been off-limits to the Germans in the Great War a quarter century earlier. She had met Hitler and believed she knew this man—he would never send men under arms into such a peaceful, neutral place.

With Ruston's agreement, Ella petitioned the British government to allow Adriaantje to travel back to the Netherlands. By the time red tape was cleared, it was 14 December. Ella arranged by phone for Adriaantje's caretaker, Mary Butcher, to pack the girl up and take her to the train. Schoolmate Joan Hawkins was surprised to see her friend wearing traveling clothes and climbing hastily into a car to be driven away. There wasn't even a moment for a good-bye, and the next time Joan saw Audrey, it was on the silver screen.

Butcher took the girl straight to the station in Folkestone and put her on the train to London. There, father met up with daughter and he escorted her to Brighton Hove and Worthing Joint Municipal Airport, which had begun servicing KLM flights with the declaration of war with Germany.

"There were still a few Dutch planes that were allowed to fly," Audrey remembered. "Somehow my mother had contacted my father and asked him to meet me at the train in London from [Folkestone] where I was coming in. They put me on this bright-orange plane. You know, orange is the national color, and it flew very low. It really was one of the last planes out. That was the last time [before the war] I saw my father."

Tension ruled the airways—German fighter planes patrolled the skies over the English Channel and North Sea looking for warbirds taking off from British fields. On 26 September fighters had mistaken a civilian KLM DC-3 for a military plane and attacked. As a result of that incident, the entire KLM fleet of DC-3s had been painted orange to clearly identify them as noncombatant aircraft. Even Audrey noticed that the airliner, considered giant because it had two engines and twenty-five seats, "flew very low" across the North Sea as part of the pilot's effort to draw less attention from patrolling German fighters.

But she made it; the plane landed safely at Amsterdam's Schiphol Airport where Ella and the boys greeted her. Two hours later by train from Amsterdam to Arnhem, Adriaantje was walking into her new home at Sickeszlaan 7 to begin the next phase of life as a Dutch girl in a neutral Netherlands.

4

Edda

In December 1939 Adriaantje Hepburn-Ruston flew into the airport in Amsterdam as a foreigner. Yes, her blood was fifty percent Dutch, with a quarter each of English and Slovakian, but she hadn't more than visited various van Heemstra living spaces in Holland during her short life. Now, a Dutch stamp would be imprinted on the girl's soul immediately, firmly, and permanently so that, in many ways, she would always be Dutch.

Being Dutch was unlike being anything else in the world, as she would soon enough learn. The Dutch had been masters of the world at one time, particularly masters of sailing and commerce, which resulted in the booming Dutch East Indies in one direction and the equally vibrant New Amsterdam, later New York City, in the other. They excelled in the arts, producing "Dutch masters" such as Rembrandt and Vermeer, and later, van Gogh.

As Audrey put it, "Holland has been an admirable country, from the early ages to today."

The Dutch were a religious people, Protestants in the majority but with a large Catholic percentage as well and firm in their faith. They lived industrious lives, worked exceptionally hard, wore clothes neatly until they wore them out, spoke their minds, showed up early for appointments, kept homes that were tidy to a fault, ate good food meticulously and let nothing go to waste, and led the world in fitness because everyone rode bicycles everywhere over the notably flat terrain. In fact, Holland was the only country in Europe that kept growing its land without encroaching upon its neighbors—the remarkable Dutch used the power of windmills to drain seas and keep them at bay behind dikes to create rich farmlands called polders. They managed their abundant water by creating a system of canals that supplemented the many rivers and moved food and other goods easily from place to place. Above all, the Dutch didn't brag about accomplishments as individuals but knew they were the best country on the face of the earth. It was a fact; they just were.

Arnhem, the city that would become Adriaantje's new home, had once been a medieval fortress worth storming and conquering, as proved by the Burgundians, Spanish, Dutch, English, and French, all of whom possessed it or at least fought for it at one time or another. Arnhem was a most unusual Dutch city because part of it sat on significant hills that descended through the flat city center all the way to the edge of the Rhine River. Wealthy Dutch businessmen had made good lives in the East Indies and returned to Arnhem and its surrounding villages to build lavish villas for retirement, so that Arnhem showed elegance wherever one turned. Audrey's opa, the baron, hadn't quite accumulated such wealth because he had spent his life in law and government. To be a Dutch noble didn't mean wearing a crown; it meant serving as an example to others and helping those who were less fortunate. So the former burgemeester of Arnhem and governor of Suriname led a quiet and rather frugal life while managing to represent the van Heemstras as a family with an impressive history of leadership and service to the nation.

"First of all, we were not one bit wealthy," said Audrey in 1990 for the umpteenth time. She had been dealing with assumptions about the fortune associated with her mother's and grandfather's titles—baroness, baron—since new Broadway star Audrey Hepburn first made the newspapers in association with *Gigi*. She wasn't easy to anger in interviews, but this topic had a way of setting her off. "My mother didn't have a dime.... My parents divorced when I was ten, and my father disappeared and all that. But we didn't have any money at all."

They really didn't. The baron's decision to enter public service and the needs of his six children slowly chipped away at the proceeds from the sale of various family properties so that by the late 1930s, the money was gone. A dozen Audrey Hepburn biographers have alluded to Huis Zijpendaal, Baron van Heemstra's castle in Arnhem, as if he owned it. They have talked about Audrey being born with a "silver spoon in her mouth." Ella did employ a nanny in Belgium and a housekeeper in Arnhem, but that was the extent of the family silver spoon. At the time Ella arrived in Arnhem, she was working to earn a living and renting a small townhouse. Ella's father lived on a pension from government work and rented rooms at Zijpendaal after he had sold Villa Roestenburg in Oosterbeek and arrived at the status of widower with grown children.

So here came Ella's daughter from exile in county Kent, England, to a new country with a new language. The van Heemstras anticipated the return of little Adriaantje, who stepped off the orange airliner at Schiphol Airport after a tumultuous day that saw her leave Elham in a hurry and spend moments too few in number with her elusive father. Then her plane had wave-hopped the Channel and the North Sea, and after all that she had met up with her mother for a reunion during which no embrace was offered. Ella took her daughter's hand and led her to the train to Arnhem.

Audrey would always admit that Ella wasn't an affectionate person. As a result, she would say, "I spent a lot of time looking for it [affection] and I found it. She was a fabulous mother, but she came from an era. She was born in 1900—Victorian influence, still—of great discipline—of great ethics. A lot of love within her; not always able to show it. And very strict. I went searching all over

29

the place to find somebody who would cuddle me. You know? And I found it, in my aunts, in my friends. That is something that has stayed very strong [in me]." After all Adriaantje had been through that day, an embrace at the airport would have been reasonable to expect. The lack of one was typical Ella.

But Baroness van Heemstra excelled in other areas. Within three months of Audrey's arrival, Ella found a larger dwelling for her reunited family, a two-story apartment that spanned the second and third floors above a flower shop on a main thoroughfare, Jansbinnensingel, in Arnhem Centraal. It was in some respects the loveliest boulevard in the city, with the apartment overlooking green lawns and aging fountains.

Ella's son Alex began dating an Oosterbeek girl, Maria Margarethe Monné, in 1941, and they would marry two years later. The girl everyone knew as "Miepje" said of the apartment: "I was there many times.... Downstairs [on the second floor] were the sitting room and the dining room, above, the bedrooms. Ella worked for the posh home furnishings company Pander from The Hague. Her house was a showroom. It was a mixture of classic and modern. Beautiful in color. It looked good. My mother-in-law was very progressive."

Ella's job with H. Pander & Zonen of The Hague further dispelled any notion of van Heemstra wealth. She had agreed to take on a ninety-minute commute each way by train. Among its many businesses, Pander commissioned art deco furniture from the most gifted designers in the Netherlands. The job with Pander suited Ella's background and tastes given that Pander was *the* place for the upper class to shop for furniture. The fact that she arranged for her apartment to serve as an Arnhem showroom for Pander showed her practical side since it meant less commuting, and she didn't have to pay for her own furnishings.

Ella found the reunification of her family a major adjustment after spending so much of the 1930s gallivanting, chasing bad boys and excitement. But here she now was, nearing the magic age of forty and accepting the responsibility of a mother in a world facing war, single and caring for three children.

Audrey's last companion, the Dutchman Robert Wolders, knew Ella late in her life and said she was "a superior woman. Very, very humorous. Extremely well read, well educated. But critical of most everyone, including Audrey." In addition he labeled her, "Biased. Intolerant."

Audrey would spend most of the next forty-five years subjugating her will to that of her mother. Ella the benevolent dictator would see to her daughter's needs and desires on the one hand, but reinforce Audrey's feelings of inadequacy—she was worth just enough to be dumped by her father—on the other.

"I was given an outlook on life by my mother," she said, "a lady of very strict Victorian standards. It was frowned upon to bother others with your feelings. It was frowned upon not to think of others first. It was frowned upon not to be disciplined." On another occasion Audrey explained, "My mother always wanted to be useful and really impressed it upon us. 'You have to be useful.'" Ella's attitude molded her daughter into an intense loner and introvert who relied only on herself—and to a small degree her older brothers—while craving the acceptance of the adults around her. The self-discipline instilled by Ella would become legendary in Audrey, who would always be known for meticulous attention to detail as she went about every job she ever undertook.

For Adriaantje, the ten-year-old newly minted Dutch girl who had spent her first years a Belgian before becoming English, the culture shock upon arrival in Holland was profound, especially since Ella decided that her daughter must present herself as Dutch. It was that simple to Ella: Just *be* Dutch.

In theory the girl without a country could speak "Nederlands" since she had used Dutch words as a quiet young visitor to Oosterbeek years earlier. It seemed deadly logical for Ella to toss her daughter into the fifth-year class at School 21A, the Tamboersbos-je, which sat on the Sonsbeek side of the Arnhem Centraal train station. To help Adriaantje along, Ella enrolled her under a pseud-onym, Edda van Heemstra.

"I used my mother's name," said Audrey, "because it wasn't too good an idea to draw attention to the fact that I was English." This was true enough; many of Ella's Arnhem friends these days were German, some of them Nazis, and Germany was at war with England. Socially and politically, Ella needed to minimize her ties to anything English.

But the concept of "Edda" failed miserably. After three-plus years attending the Rigden's English school with a small roster of children, Adriaantje/Edda found herself alone in a large building where only Dutch was spoken, a language she didn't know. She was terrified.

"That first morning in school, I sat at my little bench, com-pletely baffled," she remembered. "I went home at the end of the day weeping. For several days I went home weeping."

On another occasion she remembered her first days "in a huge classroom not knowing a word that was being said and every time I opened my mouth, everyone roaring with laughter." Classmates made fun of her "horrible accent."

Thirteen years after "Edda" began instruction at Tamboers-bosje, at a time when the press paused to look back at the Arnhem years of *Roman Holiday* star Audrey Hepburn, her teacher H.F. van Loon would remember the agonized pupil and her troubles ad-justing. "She had a hard time speaking and writing in Dutch," the instructor recalled.

Ella now began to understand the terror Adriaantje was expe-riencing and realized that perhaps shoving her daughter into the deep end of Dutch culture might not have been the wisest choice. Ella attempted to ease the transition in an Arnhem church. A group of thirteen and fourteen year olds "were asked to continue

Sunday school at the Christian Science Church," remembered one of the teens, David Heringa, because "there would be a new young girl there and it would be helpful for her to have kids around who could speak English. It was a small Christian Science community, perhaps fifteen students and three teachers. Audrey at that time was a little quiet girl."

In the last weeks of 1939, Adriaantje kept hearing about an upcoming event that everyone in the family was going to attend. Her mother was, among her many other talents, a poet, and she would be part of the program planned at the end of the year. She also promised Adriaantje that ballet would be performed, and so anticipation built as Christmas came and went.

The evening finally arrived: Friday, 29 December 1939. The shy girl with the short bobbed hair accompanied her mother to the local auditorium, the Stadsschouwburg, or City Theater, in central Arnhem, just two blocks from the Arnhem Road Bridge. The theater overlooked a beautiful park that featured the little lake Lauwersgracht. Audrey watched crowds of well-dressed people troop inside. Here she experienced the local arts for the first time, with the evening a benefit for the Local Commission for Special Needs, which assisted victims of the recent Nazi aggression toward Poland. Baron van Heemstra, Adriaantje's opa, was chairman of the national fund for special needs, and his job was both desperate and heartbreaking: In less than four months, tens of thousands of injured and displaced Polish war victims now needed the world's help.

That evening the ten year old couldn't understand the many speeches delivered in Dutch by, among others, Arnhem Burgemeester H.P.J. Bloemers and by Ella's sixty-year-old cousin, Baron Schelte van Heemstra, and his wife, Tilly. Schelte was the queen's commissioner representing the central government in Gelderland, which meant that their entire party sat at the front of the first balcony in the Schouwburg—these seats in the Gold Circle were reserved for the queen of the Netherlands.

The Schouwburg featured an orchestra pit and 650 seats spanning stage level and two balconies. From the best seats in the house, Adriaantje watched her mother recite three poems she had written in recent years before a house that was packed up through the second balcony. Ella had written one of the poems to celebrate the birth just four months earlier of Princess Irene of the Netherlands—daughter of van Heemstra family friends Princess Juliana and Prince Bernhard. Another poem written back in 1935 looked ahead to the then-imminent departure of Adriaantje for Elham. In writing Ella could intellectualize her affection for her daughter, even if she couldn't offer embraces:

Little daughter of mine, tomorrow you will leave home—
into the world to boarding school.
Not yet permanently away—but it's a start.
From a young age on you were so much more
'free-spirited' than me.
You went (freely?), you talked (freely?),
you treated me as a friend.
That's something wonderful and also 'binding'.
You saw 'no difference' in me, no aristocratic lady.
Ah, that was wonderful and I do hope I prepared you well
for being alone.
It will be your thoughts that will shape your life.
I only gave you the foundation—a direction.
You see, first I was your friend, a good mate.
We were comrades in words and deeds.
This, daughter-mine, is over because you stand alone.
In this case friends are not enough—not one!
Even not friends like me. Completely yours.
Even not me, who loves you so much.
No child, the best comes NOW! because in your

independence no one can give you what I, as a mother,
can give you.
This you will find out.
Because: if you are away,
we will become more than good friends.
Look, if you wouldn't leave tomorrow
(you have a look on your face as if it's all so weird!),
I would say: darling, it's true—try it.
You will finally feel what's it like to be mother and her child.
Too beautiful to explain.
And as life opens up to you: don't forget that whatever
friendship you leave behind, may I call myself 'mother'.

Of the evening's festivities, the *Arnhemsche Courant* reported that Baroness van Heemstra "recited three of her own poems,
with a warm, equally moved voice. Sensitive reactions of a mother
to the farewell of her daughter who attends boarding school, of
the mothers on the departure of men and sons who were called
to arms, and on the parental happiness of the royal family. There
were flowers for the poetess...whose artful recitation set a serious
tone in the otherwise cheerful evening."

Audrey discovered at this event just how plentiful her family in
Arnhem truly was. Ella's older sister Meisje and her husband, Otto,
Count van Limburg Stirum, attended—Audrey's aunt and uncle
who lived with Opa at the castle. The count was a cheerful fellow
who laughed a lot and dressed with great style; Audrey would soon
grow to adore him. Everyone referred to him as Otto, and Audrey
learned he was a prosecuting attorney in Arnhem.

Cornelia, Countess van Limburg Stirum, Otto's seventy-one-
year-old aunt and a beloved lady by the way people reacted to her,
made a big fuss over shy Audrey. The countess was very Dutch,
with a round face and warm manner. Ella's youngest sister, Arnoudina, attended the evening's festivities, as did various other van

Heemstras from Arnhem. Ella also introduced Audrey to some Quarles van Uffords, the family of first husband Hendrik and blood relations of Alex and Ian. Oosterbeek had been their family home for generations.

Yet the crush of socializing—most of it in rapid-fire Dutch— could only confuse and frighten the shy girl who took refuge in the cultural aspects of the evening. She sat enthralled by the dance in what soon became a cataclysmic experience; she understood for the first time what dancers were able to express as human movement in response to music. This wasn't one dancer in Folkestone performing to a gramophone. It was a deep stage with many dancers moving inside spotlights and accompanied by the Arnhem Symphony Orchestra. Said Audrey, "These devices drew me into the enchanted world of music, where one didn't have to talk, just listen."

Prominent Dutch ballet master Irail Gadescov, former head of the Nederlandse Ballet, presented his troupe from the fledgling Arnhemsche Dansschool. Their spins, leaps, beating of the feet in the air, costumes—all of it mesmerized Audrey, as did the next performance by noted ballerina Winja Marova.

Also that evening, locally renowned pianist Gerald Dekker performed pieces by Chopin, Liszt, and Rachmaninoff. Then violinist Douwe Draaisma, director of the Arnhemsche Muziekschool, performed three pieces that had been composed by Austrian-born Fritz Kreisler. On this magic evening when Audrey felt the full force of her important family, when she could communicate only with those who knew English and took the time to speak it, she was simply swept away by dance and music. Soon she would be asking her mother's permission to resume her ballet lessons, this time at the Muzickschool, which had just relocated to Boulevard Heuvelink near the Schouwburg in central Arnhem. Ella, desperate to draw out her introverted daughter, accepted the idea with enthusiasm.

As a member of the Dutch aristocracy, Ella, Baroness van

Heemstra, established herself in Arnhem culture. She became patroness of the Arnhem String Quartet. She also joined the board of directors of the Muziekschool and aimed to enroll Audrey in its Dansschool at the first opportunity.

During the spring of 1940, the "Sitzkrieg," or "phony war," was in full effect. The German army stood pat, licking wounds inflicted by the Poles in a month of battles. The French braced for attack along a sturdy defensive barrier, the Maginot Line, and England prepared for an air war and invasion by the Wehrmacht. Alex Quarles van Ufford, eldest of Ella's children at nineteen, joined the Dutch army, which didn't concern Ella terribly, even with all the drilling of troops and digging of trenches around Arnhem. Ella held firm to her belief that if and when the Germans did make a move against France and England, Holland would be sidestepped, as it had been in the Great War.

By now, the full immersion of "Edda" in the Dutch language had made her passably conversant and no longer quite the laughingstock of either the Tamboersbosje school or Christian Science Sunday school. Even at age ten, she was capable of displaying a stubborn fighting spirit: "I knew I couldn't just give up," she said later. "I was forced to learn the language quickly. And I did. Considering what was to happen to me later, it was a useful basic experience."

On another occasion she painted a forlorn picture of shy Edda in a new country: "When I first got home, I cried a lot. I was whining while I ate chocolate and did my best to master Dutch. I didn't have much distraction. I learned that language because I had nothing else to do." But those who knew her in Arnhem during the war years would state her command of the Dutch language was "inadequate," and in written form "terrible." They confirmed the girl's own assessment that her accent was "horrible."

It didn't really matter to Adriaantje how well she could write anyway, because she remained as uninterested in school as she had been under the Rigdens. A classmate found her "quiet, apart," and described the girl Edda as spending a lot of time "sitting and dreaming." She would gaze out the window and sketch what she saw. All her life she would surprise friends and family with this ability to see and sketch in a natural, heartfelt way. All she needed was a pencil and paper, and magic resulted.

Meneer van Loon of the Tamboersbosje said, "She did not like normal school life, but everything that went beyond routine and spoke to her fantasies interested her." She longed for escape from this unexpected Dutch world that had ensnared her. Even with her new understanding of the language, she didn't have much to say to those around her. "I was all stilted and shy," Audrey would put it as an adult. In the sense that she minded her own business, she fit in well in a country where most people did the same.

The months ticked by in 1940 with France and England trembling at the threatened menace of Hitler's Germany. In April the Führer surprised the world again: He did not attack the Maginot Line. Instead, he ordered his armies north around mainland Europe to invade Denmark and Norway for Scandinavia's precious iron ore reserves. Hitler must steal the many natural resources he lacked. After all, his country simply wasn't that big, even with all the territory he had grabbed in the 1930s.

To listen to radio reports coming out of England, the world was slowly coming apart, but the Dutch didn't see it that way. "Dutch civilians were in denial over what was happening in Europe, even after Hitler's invasion of Scandinavia…, which was not preceded by any declaration of war," said Robert Kershaw, author of *A Street in Arnhem*. "Holland, unlike northwest Europe, had missed the devastation of 1914–18. An illusion of safe neutrality persisted."

In England, the famed Sadler's Wells Ballet of London sought to take advantage of what remained a quiet time on the mainland. As artists, they thought it their duty to spread a message of peace through dance and planned a goodwill tour to Holland, Belgium, and France that would begin in early May. The slimmed-down company featured six principal dancers, including headliners Margot Fonteyn and Robert Helpmann, and a corps de ballet of eighteen female and ten male dancers, all under the direction of forty-one-year-old ballet legend Ninette de Valois. On 6 May they performed in The Hague; on 7 May at Hengelo in the northeastern corner of the Netherlands near the German border, where they faced unexpected and hate-laced anti-English hostility. On 8 May they headed south to a much friendlier Eindhoven; and on 9 May they traveled back north and arrived at the Stadsschouwburg in Arnhem, which until recently had been considered the "backward east of the lands" in terms of the arts in general and ballet in particular. It was Ella, Baroness van Heemstra, who greeted the company on arrival.

Since the December ballet performance that had reignited Adriaantje's desire to dance, Ella had been looking for opportunities to keep her daughter interested. Ella asked for and was given responsibility for handling the appearance of the Sadler's Wells company in Arnhem in another attempt to draw out her troubled, withdrawn child.

But Ella couldn't think only of Audrey this day. Just in the past week, the fabric of "safe neutrality" that the Dutch people had relied upon had begun to unravel.

The journal of Annabel Farjeon, a member of Sadler's Wells corps de ballet, described the sights she saw from moving trains and buses as the tour wound its way into Arnhem: "Hundreds and hundreds of miles of barbed wire covered the land between these towns in deep, tangled layers. The green acres were grayed over by the filigree of wire, which was bound along fences and peered out of the pale waters of half-submerged fields." Every piece of landscape the dance company encountered foreshadowed war, including "giant, twelve-foot blocks of cement with iron spikes sticking out in all directions" that marked every roadway intersection.

Farjeon reported in her diary seeing masses of Dutch soldiers with fixed bayonets, military and civilian construction crews building fortifications, and endless checkpoints that the company's two buses had to pass. In point of fact, the Dutch had been a warrior culture for centuries, primarily fighting for their expanding Indonesian empire. But in 1940 their technology was old, laughably so, when measured against that of the Third Reich next door.

After safely arriving in Arnhem to the welcomes of a Dutch baroness, Farjeon and two others from the company wandered from the theater down toward the Arnhem Road Bridge, the magnificent steel span erected over the Rhine in 1935. As they strolled toward the bridge, they passed on their left a beautiful villa and next to it the brick van Limburg Stirum School; next to that stood another schoolhouse that had once been the villa of Burgemeester van Heemstra of Arnhem.

Then they strolled up onto the bridge deck. Farjeon said, "Along the river [to the right] stood opulent houses with gardens down to the water, where wealthy Dutchmen retired for their well-fed old age, so we decided." The spot on the bridge where they stood, surrounded by stately villas and row houses, would become the point of focus for the entire world four years later when the structure became a bridge too far.

The principal dancers of the troupe—Margot Fonteyn and Robert Helpmann—were given a more elegant private tour of Arnhem. "In the afternoon sun we stood on the bridge looking towards Germany," said Fonteyn. "'The frontier is only half an hour in that direction,' said our guide. 'Half an hour by car or ten minutes by tank!' said Helpmann."

By now, Ninette de Valois had decided that the tour must end that night and the company would head straight west toward the North Sea as quickly as possible without ever entering Belgium or France.

Late on the spring afternoon of 9 May, thoughts of war receded as the groups of English sightseers returned to the Schouwburg, but only after Farjeon and her friends spent time lost in the maze of narrow, winding streets of central Arnhem.

A few blocks away in the van Heemstra apartment, Adriaantje was dressing for a night at the ballet. "For the occasion, my mother had our little dressmaker make me a long taffeta dress," she said. "I remember it so well. I'd never had a long dress in my life.... There was a little round collar, a little bow here, and a little button in the front. All the way to the ground, and it rustled, you know. The reason she got me this, at great expense—we couldn't afford this kind of thing—was that I was to present a bouquet of flowers at the end of the performance to Ninette de Valois, the director of the company."

That evening Ella and her daughter enjoyed prime seats to watch the Sadler's Wells company dance two ballets, *Horoscope* and *Façade*, headlined by the dazzling raven-haired Margot Fonteyn, then nine days shy of her twenty-second birthday and already a star in the ballet world. The Arnhem Symphony Orchestra accompanied. At the conclusion of the performance, Ella handed Adriaantje a bouquet to present to de Valois, which the girl did with a curtsy. She would later mention with pride that she was on stage at the same time as Fonteyn.

"I remember walking onto the bright stage, with the pretty ballerinas and their costumes," she said.

Annabel Farjeon concluded her journal entry by saying, "After the performance there was supper and again those dull dull speeches that officials love to make." Chief among these speeches was that of Ella van Heemstra, who recited in English for the company and in Dutch for the locals in attendance, which accounts for Farjeon's double use of the word "dull."

Audrey reveled in what she called her "first late night," and then the company loaded costumes and equipment onto their buses and headed back to The Hague. Five days past her eleventh birthday, Adriaantje had shared a stage and a meal with three of the most famous figures in modern ballet, de Valois, Fonteyn, and Helpmann. It was a life-changing experience and in a matter of hours there would be another. The next one, however, was anything but pleasant.

5

The Unthinkable

The blackest day in the history of the Netherlands began for Adriaantje when her mother burst into her bedroom on the third floor of the apartment building on Jansbinnensingel. Ella knocked aside clouds of beautiful ballet dancers as she swept to the windows and scraped open the curtains. It was Friday morning, a school day.

"Wake up," she said. "The war's on."

Audrey would look at this moment as "the second-worse memory I have after my father's disappearance." But this was how the no-nonsense baroness settled scores in her own mind. She had been adamant that it was best to bring her daughter home to Holland because it would be safe. And it was all right for Alex to join the Dutch army, because Holland was neutral and would remain so. The how and why of Germany's conquest of France and Belgium didn't matter—Germany would simply go around Holland, because that was the gentlemanly way, and Ella knew firsthand that Adolf Hitler was every inch a gentleman.

Except that this morning planes thundered overhead heading west from Germany, and an ongoing rumble of explosions crashed in the distance. Ian was up already and agitated by the goings-on as he shuffled into the room and peered out his sister's window into the gathering dawn.

Ella now faced a hard truth: The Wehrmacht Sixth Army had

crossed the border, violating agreements that had held firm all the way back to 1914. Motorcycles, trucks, and tanks flowed in before first light, at around four o'clock. Luftwaffe planes began to overfly in ones and twos and then in large formations.

Adriaantje had slept through the thunder of distant explosions, when the Dutch army had detonated the road and railroad bridges at Nijmegen ten miles to the south, and somehow also seemed to miss the rocking detonations when the Arnhem Road Bridge and nearby railroad bridge went up with thunderous booms at about the same time just a mile away from the apartment. It was the same bridge Margot Fonteyn and Annabel Farjeon had walked upon half a day earlier.

In the ears of the van Heemstras, a siren wailed nonstop. The family radio clicked on, and after its tubes warmed up, a man was already talking in an excited voice. Usually programming didn't begin until eight o'clock, but then this wasn't a usual morning. The alarmed announcer told of paratroopers spilling out of planes near Gouda, and Delft, and north of Wijk bij Duurstede, and in the Betuwe—the broad plain south of Arnhem and the Rhine.

All across the Netherlands, people were leaning their ears near radios. West of Arnhem in Utrecht, Cornelia Fuykschot, a girl just a year older than Adriaantje, saw the fear and anger in her parents' eyes as the announcer spoke. "He never stopped!" she said of the grim reports. "It went on and on and on!" The German army was suddenly everywhere.

In eastern Netherlands Dutchmen and their families close by the German border received confirmation of what they already knew and yet couldn't believe: invasion. The overflying planes that rattled pictures on mantelpieces and plates on tables were German planes, and now it would be up to the Dutch army. Every Dutchman knew of the army because all had put in two years of compulsory service. It was a small country but a proud one, and the people were tough. Oh yes, quite tough.

In Arnhem, the siren had finally stopped and in the distance the van Heemstras heard a pop-pop-popping sound, sharp and far off. Then came a rattle of what would soon be recognized as machine-gun fire, and it went on for a quite a while. Ella knew that bullets were flying in anger and Alex was out there somewhere with the army and possibly under fire.

In the distance, the sounds of battle overlapped into a din. As the children and their mother looked down at the street below, the announcer warned, "Citizens are ordered to remain in their homes with shutters closed. Stay away from the windows because the enemy fears Dutch snipers and is shooting into windows where there is movement."

The order to stay away didn't dissuade the children; it attracted them. As Audrey would admit years later, "Naturally, we all peeped out."

Adriaantje had a view from her bedroom window onto Jansbinnensingel, the street heading one way east, and across the beautiful lawn and fountains, Jansbuitensingel, heading west, revealed a cloudless sky that was brightening by the second from gray to blue. They were the most picturesque boulevards in all Arnhem.

This particular morning, dust from the detonation of the bridges hung in the air, and pedestrians milled about on the sidewalk, most of them looking up at the sky. Above, at high altitude and low, twin-engine planes flew over in great formations. The window panes rattled with the vibrations of all those aircraft. In the distance came the chilling sound of sharp booms—they would learn soon enough that this was anti-aircraft fire from batteries of Dutch cannons aimed skyward toward the invaders.

Another ten year old, Sid Baron, lived far to the north on a Frisian farm in Opende. Baron summed up the fears of all youngsters the age of Adriaantje and Ian: "Would I survive?" he wrote. "For how long? Would we get bombed? Would my little brother get killed, too? My sisters and parents? I was afraid."

In central Arnhem the van Heemstras could now see a curious parade. People with suitcases and bundles moved along both sides of the boulevard, from right to left, east to west, with many holding white flags. They looked to be wearing layers of clothes and carrying all they could besides. Some pushed wooden carts. Some were families, with one or two or three on bicycles and others struggling to keep up on foot. All moved with nervous purpose, their heads bowed in a long, sad, silent march that went on for part of an hour. Every single person carried all he or she could— suitcases, bundles, boxes, briefcases, papers, framed paintings and photographs. There was a horse-drawn cart heavily loaded down and a little later, another.

Once more the streets grew quiet and still. Ella, Ian, and Adriaantje waited and waited as the siren came and went. Then they saw their first German soldiers: Just three, dressed in gray, came riding down the street on bicycles. They had guns strapped on their backs, gray helmets, black boots, and they scanned the city nervously as they pedaled past. The gaze of one of them swept along the line of buildings and raked the apartment windows.

The observers couldn't know that these men had a right to some nerves. They were part of the SS Der Führer Regiment that had crossed the River IJssel five miles to the east at Westervoort on rubber rafts against heavy fire from the Dutch Army—the sharp popping sounds Audrey and Ian had heard earlier. This action had been the first ground combat of the battle for the Netherlands. Now these SS scouts were scanning for snipers or any other sign of resistance. On the eastern edge of Arnhem, they had commandeered bicycles because they had a long way to go and needed to move in a hurry—they were ordered to clear the area ten miles west through Oosterbeek and beyond in preparation for the 207th Division of infantry to march in.

Adriaantje had expected fighting in the streets, but instead here came nervous men on bicycles. It took another long while for anything further to happen. In the meantime the plane traffic overhead had all but ceased. Then came the invaders en masse.

"We saw the gray uniforms of the German soldiers on foot," Audrey would remember later. "They all held machine guns and marched in looking spick-and-span and disciplined." This show of force, this first impression made by the Wehrmacht, was designed to instill fear into the Dutch population—it certainly had that effect on a girl just turned eleven and a boy of fifteen.

As the day wore on, the spectacle continued. "Then came the rumble of trucks," said Audrey, as troop carriers drove through, their bays full of German soldiers hunched forward, rifles between their knees.

"And the next thing we knew was that they had taken complete charge of the town."

6

Dancer

"I started studying ballet very soon after I arrived in Holland," said Audrey. "I had taken various lessons in England and loved dancing, and once I'd started in Holland, I decided I wanted to be a ballerina."

Before and after the Germans marched in, the desire for ballet burned within the heart of the eleven year old. Around her was a world in chaos. The Netherlands fell to the German invasion in five days. The Dutch army had been preparing for the possibility of war for years, and the troops of Gen. Henri Gerard Winkelman, fighting shoulder to shoulder with French and Belgian forces, mauled the vanguard of Hitler's Sixth Army and panzer divisions. Dutch fighter planes supported by the RAF took down scores of German aircraft, but there were simply too many and the Dutch air forces were overwhelmed. On Tuesday afternoon, 14 May, a formation of fifty German Heinkel He-111 twin-engine bombers attacked central Rotterdam with incendiary bombs. In twenty minutes a two-square-mile section of the city blazed. Water mains were hit, so there was no way to fight the fires, and up went Rotterdam in an all-consuming inferno that nearly vaporized 11,000 buildings and killed hundreds (according to the Germans) or thousands (according to the Dutch). German high command threatened to repeat the process in Amsterdam, The Hague, Arnhem, and every other major Dutch city unless the nation surrendered. With no options left, General Winkelman offered his sword that evening.

Hitler's attack plan had also included an attempt to drop paratroopers on the airfields of The Hague to capture the Dutch government—fifty-nine-year-old Queen Wilhelmina of the House of Oranje, her daughter, Princess Juliana, and Juliana's husband, Prince Bernhard, along with Prime Minister Pieter S. Gerbrandy and other authorities, and one of Juliana's staff, Ella's sister Marianne, Baroness van Heemstra. But this plan was foiled. The Germans had underestimated Dutch resourcefulness, and Queen Wilhelmina and her government escaped to London, where the House of Oranje set up camp and remained free to provide leadership from afar to a people who had been demoralized by the unexpected aggression of their neighbor.

Despite the savage bombing of Rotterdam, once Winkelman capitulated, the Germans offered Holland a firm hand in friendship. Truth was, Hitler respected the Aryan roots of the Dutch, along with their prosperity, ingenuity, and warrior traditions; he was certain they would see the value of and profit from a unified European empire. In a show of good faith, the Germans released all Dutch military prisoners taken in the five-day war on condition that the Dutch army would disband and all captured German soldiers and Dutch Nazis in the Netherlands would be freed.

Alex had survived the fighting and returned to Arnhem, but rumor was that Dutch soldiers would soon be conscripted into the German army. Alex had no intention of letting that happen, even if his mother did support the Reich. He gathered some belongings and then said good-bye to his family. Many of his mates were going into hiding, and he would join them. Adriaantje took the separation hard and Ian even harder, but at least Alex was alive and determined to remain that way.

After one day of excitement in Arnhem and a few more in other parts of the country, life settled down for the Dutch population. The sun continued to rise in the morning and set in the evening, and shops continued to operate. The trees were green, spring blooms were out, and soon people of all ages were cruising around on their bikes as if nothing had happened at all. In Arnhem proper, the only major changes to the landscape were the missing bridges, the magnificent Arnhem Road Bridge and the nearby railroad bridge, both of which lay as twisted and partially submerged piles of rubble in the middle of the Rhine. But the Germans set the Dutch right to the task of rebuilding both, and before too long the big steel road bridge and long railroad bridge were back in place. It seemed that life wouldn't be so bad under the new regime after all.

There were, however, minor changes to the scenery: All signs and placards were now printed in German; below in smaller letters were any Dutch translations needed. German eagles started to appear on documents and posters, and red flags with swastikas. Most interesting, a new color of uniform appeared on Arnhem streets: green uniforms, worn by men who seemed to be watching everything, everywhere. These were the German *Ordnungspolizei*, or order police. To the Dutch they quickly became known as the Green Police.

"The Germans tried to be civil and to win our hearts," said Audrey. "The first few months we didn't know quite what had happened.... A child is a child is a child; I just went to school." It was here that she noticed new and obvious changes to the curriculum. "It is impossible for Americans to understand the extent to which the Nazi occupation invaded our lives. In the schools, the children learned their lessons in arithmetic with problems like this: 'If 1,000 English bombers attack Berlin and 900 are shot down, how many will return to England?'"

At the beginning of June 1940, Nazi armies were working on arithmetic problems of their own, as in, how to finish off the 400,000 French and British troops they had pushed up against the English Channel at Dunkirk. It turned out they couldn't execute final maneuvers in time, and all but about 40,000 Allied soldiers escaped in a miraculous evacuation. However, France and the finest army in Europe had fallen to the Nazis, who now raised their flags all the way to the North Sea.

In Arnhem changes were subtle at first. The American movies starring Clark Gable, Ginger Rogers, and other Hollywood stars disappeared from the Rembrandt, Luxor, and Cinema Palace theaters, and only German features and short subjects were available for viewing. The *Arnhemsche Courant* stopped publishing for a short time and then restarted with some of the staff replaced by new writers chosen from the ranks of the *Nationaal-Socialistische Beweging*, or NSB, the Dutch National Socialist Movement. Official numbers showed that about 100,000 Dutch citizens joined the NSB, but more than ten percent of the population was openly supporting the German occupiers and using the raised-hand greeting to salute the Führer and his symbol, the swastika.

Terms like "Germanic brotherhood" and "people's community" were seen in print and heard on radio. A German ruling government was established in The Hague, with Austrian attorney Arthur Seyss-Inquart appointed *Reichskommissar* of the Netherlands. According to his own description of his mission: "I was responsible for the civil administration, and, within this administrative task, I had to look after the interests of the Reich. Apart from this I had a political task. I was to see to it that while Dutch independence was maintained, the Netherlands should be persuaded to change their pro-British attitude for a pro-German one and enter into a close economic collaboration." He reported directly to Hitler.

The German army of occupation was placed under Nazi Luftwaffe Gen. Friedrich Christiansen, a winner of German aviation's "Blue Max" for downing enemy planes in the Great War. This former aviator was an unlikely choice for the command of ground forces in an occupied country.

All police units in the Netherlands, including the SS and the security police, were placed under the supervision of Hanns Albin Rauter, a tall, square-shouldered man with scars on his face courtesy of student duels with the *Mensurschläger*, a heavy German saber. Rauter reported directly to Berlin and the ruthless head of the SS, Heinrich Himmler.

This was not an administration that would devote even a moment's effort to winning the hearts of Dutchmen. They didn't even try. It seemed they cared about Dutch independence only because it took a while to put the mechanisms of brutality in place. This is what some Dutch mistook as a quiet period of relative normalcy. To them, for a short time it seemed the Nazis might not be "so bad."

Seyss-Inquart made it a priority to hand-pick people for the top spots in government, the courts, the cities, the banks, and the railroads. Among his initial orders was one that set the tone for many that would follow: He decreed that German men in uniform be served first at Dutch restaurants and shops in all circumstances. This established an ominous tone, because gray-uniformed occupation troops and green-clad German police were all over the streets of Arnhem. Initially, local shopkeepers found the added foot traffic to be a boon to business; the Germans spent freely and sent Dutch goods to their families back home.

Baron van Heemstra of Huis Zijpendaal had been a proponent of German business in the 1920s, and he tried to keep an open mind now. He even shared his passion for stamp collecting with the local German officer corps, some of whom were avid supporters of the hobby.

It wouldn't take long for the viewpoint of the baron to change. The Netherlands was a bountiful nation based on its rich polderland soil and abundant water supply, and the Nazis were empire building, straining every resource to clothe, feed, arm, and equip armies that now occupied not only the Netherlands but also Belgium and France and threatened England. It would be up to the

Netherlands to help keep bellies full for the fighting men of the Reich, and just five weeks after the occupation began, the first appearance of rationing set limits on the amount of bread a family could purchase. Bread! The Dutch prided themselves as bread connoisseurs and arranged their very lives around its consumption. They loved bread, savored it, cherished it. The rationing wasn't severe at all, but when the quality of white and rye bread began to drop because white flour could no longer be imported, consumption fell correspondingly whether the product had been rationed or not. To a Dutchman, the only thing worse than no bread was bad bread. Over something so basic, discontent began to grow.

On 10 July the Battle of Britain commenced, with waves of German bombers and fighter escorts attacking England day after day and a ground invasion pending. In the Netherlands that month, butter, margarine, fats, and cream were not only rationed but disappearing from the shops. Without warning all these ingredients that had been sewn into the fabric of Dutch life were being diverted to Germany. And so it went with every commodity as bit by bit, life in Holland changed for the worse.

On 28 July Radio Oranje staged its inaugural broadcast from London over the BBC—a spine-tingling address by Queen Wilhelmina from exile. She wasn't skilled as an orator, but she was safe and feisty, and early on she refused to dignify the occupiers by calling them German. She referred to them as "moffen" or simply "moff," a very old Dutch ethnic slur meaning unwashed and backward people.

The new Dutch broadcasting network then set to the task of providing a steady stream of information from the Allies to the occupied people of the Netherlands. The Germans had anticipated the establishment of such a communication tool by the Allies and issued the "Measure for the Protection of the Dutch Population Against Untrue Information." With this act, the occupied people would be kept away from "false news" and given information they could trust from officially sanctioned pro-Nazi stations broadcasting from the Netherlands, Germany, Poland, and Czechoslovakia. Anyone caught listening to a unsanctioned station, particularly the BBC and Radio Oranje, would be severely punished.

Still, the Dutch didn't pay a whole lot of attention; they just went about their radio listening more carefully. Ella added another part-time job to her Pander arrangement by seeking work in Arnhem at the religious hospital Diaconessenhuis, located just a few blocks from Audrey's elementary school. Ella chose this hospital even though the Germans had begun placing wounded soldiers there because her father, the baron, sat at the head of the board of directors, which she figured would give her an "in." Ella tried the direct approach via the front door to speak with the facility's medical director, Willem Frederik Emaus. But Ella wasn't a medical professional and Emaus denied her request; his administrative staff was, he told Ella, full at the moment; he didn't need any help.

At the end of the war, Emaus recalled that shortly after this conversation, he was surprised to find Ella working in the hospital, supervising workers in the kitchen even though he had turned down her request for work. It was clear she had found another way in. The fact that she was speaking German to an all-German kitchen staff in a German war hospital would haunt her in the years to come.

Work was work, and Ella needed to support herself and two children, especially considering Adriaantje's burning ambition to begin ballet lessons in Arnhem. The would-be dancer finally got her wish in the autumn of 1940 when she was enrolled at the Arnhemsche Muziekschool at Boulevard Heuvelink 2, the fine two-story brick building with high-arched windows in central Arnhem across the street from the home of Cornelia, Countess van Limburg Stirum, and her girls' school. Audrey's enrollment coincided with the arrival of a new dance teacher to replace Irail Gadescov as director of the music school's Dansschool. The incoming mistress of dance was Ella's new friend, Dutch ballerina Winnie Koopman who had adopted the romantic stage name of Winja Marova with its implication that she was Russian and not a Dutch Jew. Not coincidentally, Marova was in love with virtuoso violinist Douwe Draaisma, Muziekschool director and a married man. After a quick divorce, the violinist married the new dancing teacher.

Marova found her new pupil Adriaantje to be far too "round" from poor eating habits but "very eager to learn and possessed by dance. She really had everything to do with it," said Marova. "She was also very musical: I always taught her with great pleasure. She drank in everything you said. At her first performance I already saw how good she was."

The new student was equally enthralled with her instructor: "I'd admired many dancers from afar," said Audrey, "but Winja was the first one that I really got to know and could call a friend. She was a beautiful, world-class dancer. I think that her being Dutch helped this very young girl in Arnhem to believe that she could become one too."

Adriaantje gave herself completely to the world of dance. The beginnings of an iron will forged out of Ella's unique manner of parenting served the aspiring dancer well in this initial season at the Dansschool. Whatever Marova coached or advised about routine, regimen, practice, and focus, the student adopted without question. She would do whatever was in her power to make up for getting such a late start in ballet—considering that Margot Fonteyn gave her first public performance at age four. Luckily Adriaantje was light on her feet and had the internal rhythm necessary for dance. The rest would come from sheer determination.

Ella watched with excitement as her daughter began to blossom; the baby fat she had carried with her now began to melt away under the rigors of daily instruction, and she insisted on growing out her severe Dutch-girl haircut because everyone knew ballerinas had long hair.

As the dancer danced, the baroness forged ahead in an Arnhem society just beginning to adjust to occupation. Ella saw that maintaining cordial relations with the ruling German administration in the city was the best way to get ahead in these circumstances. She could turn on great charm when she saw the need, and do it in multiple languages. She was seen with German officers at a tea house called Thee-Schenkerij in the Sonsbeek section of Arnhem, and in particular seemed fond of former AGFA businessman M.H.E. Oestreich, now *ortsgruppenführer* in Arnhem for the NSB. This Dutch Nazi official was probably the German officer that Ella's friends in the Christian Science Church, the Heringas, met when they stopped by at the apartment on Jansbinnensingel. Ella introduced the German officer as a relative, although she had no such relatives of record in the NSB. Eyewitnesses swore under oath in a post-war investigation by Dutch police that after the occupation had begun, Ella displayed a German eagle and a flag of the Reich, a red field with a black and white swastika inside it, in the van Heemstra apartment. She may have kept these items on view to impress Oestreich. Ella didn't deny later that she kept a framed photo of herself standing on the steps of Hitler's Munich headquarters, the Braunes Haus, laughing with Pamela Mitford, Micky Burn, and British aristocrat Coleridge Hills and his wife, J.C. It was a photo taken the day Ella had met Hitler in 1935, and it remained for her a happy memory.

In autumn 1940, with everything going so well, with the Germans trying to, as Audrey said, "win our hearts," Ella reciprocated. She began planning a cultural evening in Düsseldorf to benefit German war relief that would presumably involve talent from Arnhem, including perhaps Adriaantje in some capacity. Ella's beau, Ortsgruppenführer Oestreich, was involved as well, and even invited the civilian police commander of Arnhem, Cornelius den Hartog, to attend. With the near-complete destruction of Düsseldorf later in the war, records fail to indicate whether the cultural evening planned by van Heemstra and Oestreich ever took place, but the fact that they were inviting people seems to indicate that it did.

Audrey Hepburn never said a word about her mother's alliances during the war. By spring 1941 Adriaantje was enthralled with dance and making great progress under the tutelage of Winja Marova while also spending time with Ella at Castle Zijpendaal, the home of the baron, Meisje, and Otto. It was a quiet, still place where she could laze on the lawn reading books, her other passion, the one instilled by brother Alex.

She said, "Before I was thirteen I had read nearly every book by Edgar Wallace and Edward Phillips Oppenheim, who wrote a long series of romantic mysteries about secret international documents, shifty diplomats and seductive adventuresses.... To me as a girl they had far more appeal than books like *Topsy Goes to School*."

Yes, she loved the outdoors and hanging out with her brothers at every opportunity. At the same time, "I don't think I was a tomboy," said Audrey. "I'd say I was a rather moody child, quiet and reticent, and I liked to be by myself a great deal—which made me quite an easy child to raise. Nevertheless, I needed a great deal of understanding, which I always got from my mother."

Her opa enjoyed his life in the rented rooms of the castle with its little lake, broad lawns, and wooded nature trails. As a boy, Joop Onnekink lived near the castle and visited Zijpendaal with his father, a police detective in Arnhem. "My father was a stamp collector," said Joop, "and so was the baron. He was a very nice man, very friendly and outgoing." Decades later Audrey would still remember her grandfather's patience and sense of humor in the darkest times.

The castle the baron lived in was a perfect getaway for the type of person Adriaantje was becoming. As she put it, "I had a passion for the outdoors, for trees, for birds and flowers." She would retreat to watch the ducks, geese, and herds of deer. Then there were the cats, two dozen of them, belonging to the site manager, Mevrouw Mia Schulte van Zegwaart, nicknamed "Katten mei."

It was here at de Zijp in 1941, a golden time for the family despite the war, that Ian and Adriaantje grew close to Otto and Meisje, the count and countess, two warm, positive people who were fully willing to shower their niece and nephew with the affection that was so foreign to Ella. And how Adriaantje loved Opa, a grand, elegant gentleman whose family tree covered a wall in the entrance to his rooms. Both Ian and Adriaantje looked to Opa and Otto as father figures and cherished their relationships with each. Baron van Heemstra was a fixture on the lawns at de Zijp in his straw hat, cigar gripped in his teeth, as he held court with his family on picnic Sundays. Adriaantje would always love the warmth and cuddles of Tante Meisje and the warm smile and intelligent conversation of Oom Otto. Meisje and Otto were among the most renowned contract bridge players in Arnhem, and it was inevitable that Adriaantje and Ian must learn the card game with all its intricate strategy.

Travel remained a possibility in 1941, and the family went on holiday to the beach at Noordwijk, a resort town just north of Rotterdam. These were grand times, and although Alex was in hiding, he showed up frequently to see his girl, Miepje, in Oosterbeek, the next town over from Arnhem, and Adriaantje's heroic big brother would stop by at the castle. For 1941 at least, there were peace and closeness for the van Heemstras at Zijpendaal.

Part II:
Long Live Oranje!

7

Pencil Scratches

West London
30 October 1950

Like many if not most film projects, this one had taken years to come to fruition. In fact, the outbreak of war in 1940 Britain had spawned Secret People, which was to be a tale of the dangers of information falling into the hands of the enemy as a consequence of loose talk. Audrey was eleven at the time bombs first fell on London and had recently moved to the Netherlands.

A full script treatment for Secret People didn't emerge until after the war in 1946. By then it was still a dark tragedy that had mutated and now concerned a woman named Maria, who has a daughter named Nora. Their family had fled a totalitarian regime to pre-war London. There Maria meets an old comrade from her days in the Resistance, a handsome man with whom she had had an affair. He convinces her to deliver a bomb to another member of the Resistance—the bomb will be used to kill a leader of the totalitarian regime who is visiting London. The plan backfires and the bomb kills a waitress at a restaurant.

During the next four years the story treatment became a script and the plot was tweaked and tweaked again. Nora became Maria's sister and a dancer, specifically a teenage ballerina. In the same four years Audrey, now twenty-one, had become a sort of actress in front of the camera. In fact, she had just completed a bit part: one scene and a single line with Alec Guinness on the Ealing Studios production, The Lavender Hill Mob. It had been the latest role in the progression from walk-ons with no lines at all to a line here and there, and Audrey still didn't believe in this acting thing. She had been making a living as a dancer, but there was money in the moving pictures too, much easier money than dancing fifteen or twenty shows a week, and she needed all the money she could get to pay her share of the bills because London wasn't the cheapest place to reside. Her mother had been working like crazy at any jobs she could get as well—housekeeper, seamstress, florist, and whatever else came along.

Audrey took one last drag on her cigarette to calm jangled nerves and walked inside the Ealing Studios front office in West London. The building looked more like somebody's modest home than a center of British film production. Inside she met director Thorold Dickinson and his creative team. It had been Dickinson who first conceived of Secret People way back when.

Right away Audrey sensed she was wasting her time by what she could see in the faces of the people as she shook their hands. She was too tall—yet again too tall—and to make it worse, she happened to be wearing three-inch heels that must have made her look gargantuan. She completed her reading and walked back out into the daylight and did her best to put Secret People behind her.

One hundred fifteen days later, on 22 February 1951, the phone rang, Ealing calling. Could Miss Hepburn come in the following day for a second test as Nora in what was now being called The Secret People? She could? Excellent. Script pages would be delivered. After nearly four months, they wanted her back to test for the same part.

The next afternoon, a Thursday, Audrey repeated the practice, one last drag on her cigarette before walking into the cozy Ealing front office in West London. She didn't know that she had been the first choice all along; she had been correct in what she had sensed, that she was too tall when compared with the men who had already been cast. That had been the debit against her. But the "Nora" seen the previous day had been deemed unsuitable in the audition because her eyes were too expressive and showed too much worldly experience. The production team had been haunted by the young Hepburn girl and looked at her head shot again; they saw big brown eyes that seemed to reveal only pure innocence. So Audrey was back, wearing flats this time, and now noticed the crude pencil scratches on the painted plaster wall of the office where every actor and actress had been measured for height—scrawled lines and names seemingly done in anger. It was the lesson the team learned the moment she had walked out almost four months earlier: Measure everyone's height against that of the leading men.

Recently, the team had been testing potential Noras from the ranks of the London corps de ballet only to learn the dancers weren't actresses; the Nora part was big and important, requiring not only acting skill but ballet as well. Question was, could this dancer called Audrey Hepburn possibly be an actress? This girl had managed only a few lines in a few pictures and was never a classical stage actress at all.

The part of Nora had evolved since the previous October, and Dickinson, the director, ran through it with a nervous Audrey: Nora is the younger sister of the lead, Maria. She must perform two ballet sequences before the camera, and she's key to many scenes in the picture—many dramatic scenes, including one where she holds the dying Maria in her arms.

Audrey had to wonder if this was a dream—might she really be dancing ballet before cameras? Or a nightmare—she had no idea what to do as a dramatic actress and the idea of it terrified her.

She read the chosen scene with a production assistant. All she could do was feel her way through it and act and react on instinct. As a witness in the room that day noted, "After the first run-through, people start eyeing each other meaningfully; she has the quality all right. After another rehearsal it seems almost a waste of time to shoot the test."

Audrey walked out of Ealing again with no commitment from them, but three days later the official call came: Audrey had been cast as Nora. It was her first featured part in a motion picture. One week later she reported to a London church for rehearsal of a pivotal ballet sequence. For the first time in a while she was back on a ballet stage for a performance. It was beyond heaven working with the choreographer and other dancers, as around them the director of photography and technical crew assessed camera setups and lighting.

Since the end of the war she had never stopped working. Ballet lessons, dancing in chorus lines, two shows a night, night after night, modeling for the still camera, bits on television, bits in the movies. She took anything, relentlessly, never saying no. Physical activity kept the mind too busy to think about the war and all that had happened. Now she had a big important screenplay to learn, and ballets to perform on-screen. All of it made the past bearable, just so long as she didn't have too many quiet moments alone to think.

8
Unacceptable

Audrey Hepburn on the war: "I wouldn't have missed it for the world—anything that happens to you is valuable."

As years go, 1941 wasn't so bad for the van Heemstras. Ella's social calendar was full at all times with the Pander job and various cultural activities. Audrey was going to both public school and dance school and sometimes received rides from Uncle Otto, who commuted every day in his Renault from the castle on the highlands above Arnhem down to the Paleis van Justitie in Arnhem Centraal by the large Market Square, a short two blocks from the music school. There he served as a *substituut-officier*—an assistant public prosecutor working on a variety of criminal cases. In April 1939 he handled the case of a man who admitted to having six or seven drinks before getting behind the wheel and striking a woman riding a bicycle and killing her. The defendant received four months in prison. In August it was a case in which a twenty-three-year-old woman living at home had given birth to twins in secret. One was stillborn and she strangled the other, with the bodies later found floating in the Korne River. Otto's prosecution resulted in the mother with obvious mental problems sentenced to one year in prison. In September he charged three scammers for embezzling more than 25,000 gulden from an elderly woman. Otto earned convictions of one year, a year and a half, and two-and-a-half years in jail for the defendants. Usually, he showed lenience if there was genuine remorse and especially if rehabilitation was possible, but he treated these three more harshly than either the drunk driver or the killer mother.

By February 1941 the war was encroaching on his work. Adjudicating under Nazi laws, Otto was forced to prosecute a twenty-eight-year-old shopkeeper in Arnhem for listening to Radio Oranje, the "forbidden channel," in his rooms. The shopkeeper claimed that he listened to music and music only on this channel, but the Green Police heard Radio Oranje and entered the apartment above his shop to find him lying on the bed while a political broadcast played. The shopkeeper said he was asleep at the time. Otto now found himself in a tough spot. He was no longer representing true justice in the Netherlands; he was representing the occupier's twisted version of the law. The offender received a sentence of ten months in jail.

Then came the case that changed everything. In June a man was arrested for singing a forbidden song in public:

At the corner of the street
Is an NSB member
It's not a person, it's not an animal
But a Pharisee.

The attorney general of Arnhem, Wilhelmus de Rijke, insisted that Otto prosecute the offender. Otto continued to refuse, saying that no member of the NSB could possibly be offended by a rhyme that was "almost senseless." He knew his Bible—the reference to Pharisees as a sect of purists was obscure, even to him. But de Rijke found the usage "reviling and hateful."

Soon the tempest in a teapot involved J.J. Schrieke, Secretary-General of the Ministry of Safety and Justice in the Nazi Netherlands, and Otto continued to hold firm through a series of increasingly nasty letters back and forth.

As drama played out across the postal system, the Germans

were commandeering buildings for military or administrative use, nearly every large structure in town. They took over the Tamboers-bosje school and displaced all the students, including Adriaantje, and the worry was, would the Muziekschool be next, and would the new dance student see her dreams dashed after only a few months? Actually, no, because the director of the school, Douwe Draais-ma, had taken steps to join the NSB, the Dutch Nazi Party, for a number of practical reasons: He sought to maintain control over his own institution, keep his roster of students intact since his male dancers might easily have been shipped off to the German army or to labor camps, and protect his Dutch (and secretly) Jewish wife, Winja Marova. When Draaisma joined the NSB, all threats were removed, at least for the time being.

On 4 May 1941, Adriaantje turned twelve. Alex, who was still in hiding, was getting serious with Miepje Monné, the daughter of a veterinarian in Oosterbeek, and bringing her to the apartment for visits with the family. It was a time when Ella was openly friendly with the occupiers. "Ella was very English," said Miepje, "but also pro-German. That was generally known. She also dealt a lot with a German general," meaning Oestreich of the Dutch Nazis.

As spring gave way to summer and it seemed that German oc-cupation might be bearable for the Dutch after all, a military deci-sion Hitler made would begin a downward spiral for all of Europe. On 22 June the German army launched Operation Barbarossa—the invasion of the Soviet Union. Three army groups struck east in an effort to gain territory and resources and to annihilate the Slavs and any Jews they found. It was far from their policy toward the Dutch, who were Aryans with many admirable qualities. The Nazi high command believed that those in Eastern Europe de-served only to die.

All three invading German army groups made varying de-grees of progress, and mile after mile of Soviet territory became a part of the Third Reich. But the hundreds of thousands of German soldiers making the march into Soviet territory needed food, clothing, and arms, which sooner or later would mean increasing hardship for those under occupation as resources flowed out of the country for military use. In the meantime through June and July, the news of conquest reaching Arnhem was happy indeed, putting the occupiers in a marvelous mood.

Such a mood held Adriaantje captive as well, if for a completely different reason. The shy and withdrawn child who disappeared into the wallpaper in any social situation had transformed under the influence of dance and now sought only to express herself. She would do so for the first time publicly in an 18 July performance with Marova's other dance students in a program at the German-controlled *Wehrmachtheim*, the grand old concert hall just up the boulevard from the Schouwburg in Arnhem. Until recently this venue for fine music and dance had been called the Musis Sacrum and was the home of the Arnhem Symphony Orchestra. Now the German army had commandeered the concert hall to hold meetings and entertain soldiers.

Yes, Adriaantje was evolving and to such a degree that Marova now had trouble controlling her. The novice insisted she would dance "Aese's Death" from *Peer Gynt*—the dying movements of an old woman. Marova managed to redirect her pupil to a solo from Prussian composer Moritz Moszkowski's *Serenade* and also compromised by letting her choreograph some of her movements. But this wasn't the only bit of "attitude" facing Marova. "She was a curious child. With great insistence, she wanted me to call her Adriaantje," said Marova, because she thought it sounded more like the name of a ballerina. "So it was *Adriaantje* who performed in Musis, on July 18, 1941." However, in the program she would carry a different name, and *not* Edda. It seems that by this time, Ella felt so secure in her relationships with the ruling Nazi authorities, including her beau, Herr Oestreich, that she no longer felt the need to hide her daughter behind the Dutch-sounding Edda.

The young dancer was now proclaimed to be, and would remain through the war, a very English-sounding Audrey Hepburn-Ruston.

With boundless pride, Ella watched the glowing twelve year old step into the bright lights, dance to Moszkowski, and earn applause and even cheers for the first time. Something inside Adriaantje had snapped on, some inner mechanism that allowed her to project outward to the world through dance as she never had in any other way, at any other time. On a stage, for some reason, the shyness fell away, and she was temporarily released from the shackles of a wounded, awkward child. Marova admitted years later to being on the fence about Audrey—she had gotten such a late start in dance, didn't have a classic dancer's body, and was proving to be headstrong. "But when I saw her, and the reactions of the audience, then I knew: She has it; she has the spark; she has the *secret*. The people were delighted."

The next day, cultural reporter Louis Couturier of the *Arnhemsche Courant* stated, "Although many were involved in developing this evening of dance, we want to mention only the name of Audrey Hepburn-Ruston, who, although only twelve, gave a unique performance." The review shows the remarkable impression Audrey had made, considering that she had been training with Marova for a matter of months and not years. But Ella was likely working behind the scenes to assure the best possible coverage for her daughter, as when Couturier noted that the dancer had arranged "her own choreography"—something for which both Ella and Audrey were rightfully proud.

Of Audrey's situation Marova said, "Her mother was very dominant—a real ballet mother, and the other girls didn't like it. They were also jealous, because Audrey was always the one that was mentioned."

Ella had become a powerhouse in local cultural affairs. As patroness of the Arnhem String Quartet, she next organized a musical evening to commemorate the 150th anniversary of the death of Austrian composer Wolfgang Amadeus Mozart, who succumbed at just thirty-five years of age. The music of Salzburg-born Mozart was in line with the German regime's use of culture to advertise Aryan superiority, and Ella spent two full months planning the event, which was to be held at the Schouwburg on Tuesday, 11 November 1941.

But all was not well on the home front. By this time, all Dutch political parties other than the Nazi party had been abolished. Then, in November, Audrey's Uncle Otto received an official letter from Secretary-General of Justice Schrieke, who had been the first member of the Dutch Nazi party, the NSB, to enter the Department of Justice after being appointed by Seyss-Inquart for his "open-mindedness" to the occupation. In his new position, Schrieke ordered court officials in the provinces of the Nether-lands to draw up a list of Dutch who were known to oppose the Re-ich. Otto had tried to work with the new regime, but Schrieke's or-der to "name names" was unconscionable. Under-Prosecutor van Limburg Stirum refused to cooperate and now, three months later, held a letter that read: "The above-mentioned person rejected in a letter written to his superior, [Arnhem] Attorney-General Rijke, and in an inappropriate form, the drawing up of a list for the prose-cution of those called politically dissident as traitors to the country. He has also denied his superior Attorney-General Rijke the right to order him to loyal cooperation. In a summary letter addressed to him on 1 September 1941, he [van Limburg Stirum] expressly reiterated in a condensed form what he said in his previous letter. As a result, he is no longer acceptable for the post of public prose-cutor. The General Commissioner for Administration and Justice has therefore pronounced the immediate dismissal of the above from his post as Under-Prosecutor of the Arnhem District Court."

The war had created a bewildering situation for the van Heem-stras. Of course Meisje supported her husband, who had worked for the royal family, including the queen, and was one hundred percent pro-Oranje. Ella's cousin Ernestine Johanna, Baroness van Heemstra, was a notorious Resistance fighter who had already been arrested and imprisoned by the Gestapo. But Schelte van Heemstra, cousin to Ella's side of the family, remained Queen's Commissioner of Gelderland in Arnhem and was suspected of co-operating with the NSB—although in reality he was trying to do anything but. And Ella was the most pro-German of all, which caused unrest within the family.

At the beginning of November, Ella put the finishing touches on eighteenth-century period costumes for a series of scenes from Mozart's life that would be performed on stage by Ella, a group of her male and female society friends, and Ian and Audrey. The string quartet would sit beside the actors and play German-approved music. For the occasion, Alex planned to make the trip east from the town of Rhenen where he lived in hiding as what was now called an *onderduiker*. Unlike the Wehrmachtheim, which served only the German military, the Schouwburg welcomed all of Arnhem and the surrounding area to attend performances.

The evening began with Franz Joseph Haydn's Quartet in G as the actors depicted boy Mozart's visit to Prince Esterhazy. To the music of Mozart's K.V. 575 in D and K.V. 387 in G, Ella staged a scene of Mozart as guest at a foreign embassy garden party. For the final piece, Beethoven and other musicians were shown gathering a year after Mozart's death to salute their friend and inspiration.

Said Louis Couturier, "At this commemoration, one of the cleanest quartets of Mozart was played. Halfway through, the scene was darkened and with the actors hidden from view, only the four playing remained visible. The attention of the audience went to only players and their play. Then the background began to flash and only Mozart's music spoke."

Couturier went on to say, "The scenes made a very special impression. Mozart's music does not need a dramatic effect to make an impression; it has an inner power that destroys all appearance. Yet it is sometimes strange to...think back to a time when the creator of so much immortal beauty belonged to the living. All the more so if this is done in such a very artistic and indulgent way, as yesterday led by Baroness van Heemstra."

It was an evening that also featured violin solos by Maestro Draaisma and choreography by Mistress Marova in what was for Ella a crowning achievement and wonderful way to close out the cultural year. That same evening Alex and his girlfriend, Miepje, announced they were engaged to be married.

Four weeks after Ella's grand event, both German and free Dutch sources flashed bulletins that the imperial Japanese had staged a sneak air attack on the American fleet at Pearl Harbor. How the Americans had managed to stay out of the war this long was a mystery, but many Dutch grumbled that they knew exactly how the Americans felt—the Netherlands had fallen in an attack just as cowardly.

On the evening of 11 December, Arnhem heard news that the Americans had declared war on Germany, as they had three days earlier on Japan. Hitler reacted with a furious speech in the Reichstag in Berlin, aiming his venom directly at U.S. President Franklin Roosevelt. Hitler blamed a failed New Deal, the American plan to end the Great Depression, as the real reason for war with Germany. "First he incites war," railed Hitler, "then falsifies the causes, then odiously wraps himself in a cloak of Christian hypocrisy and slowly but surely leads mankind to war." Thunderous applause inside the Reichstag echoed across the German empire in a radio broadcast that electrified the air.

As Christmas arrived, there were so many reasons for Ella to be optimistic about the Germans. Their armies had all but conquered Russia and were now mere miles from Moscow. In Arnhem Ella's endlessly busy and productive social life had kept the entire family safe. Yes, the rationing was harsh, but food that couldn't be obtained with a ration coupon due to spot shortages in the shops could be secured via the black market. Yes, it had been a shock to have to register herself and her children for the trifold identification card, the *Ausweis*, which contained name, birth date, address, photo, and fingerprints. Each card was officially numbered, signed, and countersigned. It was logical that the Germans wanted to know who was in the country and why. So many things the Germans did made sense, and for that reason many people in Arnhem continued to be willing to give the occupiers a chance. It was also logical to believe that restrictions would soon be eased as the economic and political systems in the Netherlands were aligned with those of Germany and as the resources of the Soviet Union began pouring into the Reich. All the citizens of Arnhem had to do was wait a little longer.

But all was not well. By now, hunger had been gnawing at the bellies of the Dutch, both adults and children. And Otto was out at the Paleis de Justitie, which cast a pall on the holidays. This in particular became an ominous sign for a year to come, 1942, that would see unspeakable horror for the Netherlands and for all the van Heemstras.

9

Born for the Spotlight

"My mother, I think, has brought me up as well as any mother ever does," said Audrey. "I think she did a wonderful job, with three children, and I don't feel she was over-strict or that we were spoiled. She brought us up in a very natural, healthy way."

Ella grew up at the end of a time of wealth for the van Heemstras. Part of her youth was spent with her siblings at the magnificent estate Huis Doorn near Utrecht. While her older sisters, Meisje and Geraldine, reflected the ideals of their mother the baroness, Ella found herself trapped between the rigid Victorian world and a future she imagined for herself in exotic locations far from her stodgy elders. She longed for more affection, more spontaneity, even more silliness in her own family, and wrote in her unpublished novel about listening "enviously to other children who went for walks and for treats with their parents, who called them 'darling' and 'sweetiepuss.'" Unfortunately, she wrote, her own family "consider it unwise to use endearments when speaking to their children; it might be too weakening or too gratifying to a young mind. Warmth does not go well with [Dutch] austerity." For all she would surmount in life, she found herself unable to break through and offer physical affection to her own daughter—the one thing Ella herself had craved.

It was one contradiction among many. From the earliest age,

Ella had been the black sheep among the van Heemstra daughters. Three had been produced in quick succession, and from the older Meisje and Geraldine she earned the nickname "barbed wire Ella" for her frank opinions. She also possessed a rich imagination that led her to mischief, like the time at age eight she packed herself in the dumb waiter and sent herself one floor down, only to become stuck. Unsticking her required the amused wait staff—her parents, the baron and baroness, were not amused. And it was Ella and only Ella who by age ten had begun crossing herself like a Catholic because she found the Roman Catholics with their icons, relics, and traditions much more interesting than the boring old Calvinists of her own family. Her actions flabbergasted the baron.

Ella had emerged into adulthood as a Christian Scientist who saw the physical and spiritual worlds as much more connected than the Protestants allowed. But above even that she remained a stifled performer born for the spotlight, for some stage in some city, for romance and accolades, for bouquets and applause. Unfortunately, Ella had also been born into the Frisian aristocracy of 1900 and forbidden as a teenager by her father to set foot anywhere near a stage. She dreamed of becoming a ballerina or a poetess; she stated at one point that she wanted "more than anything else to be English, slim, and an actress."

"Ella was the prima donna, absolutely," said her grandson, Luca Dotti. "She was the frustrated prima donna, born a century too soon."

Her friend Alfred Heinekin III of the brewery family described her as "a born actress, very dramatic, highly emotional, with a great sense of fun."

But the baron was unrelenting. "Whatever you do," he told his daughter during her adolescence, "don't associate with actors and actresses. You'd disgrace the family."

Ella could rebel occasionally when separated from her father by countries or bodies of water. Notably, this occurred in 1935 when she wrote the public pronouncements on behalf of the British Union of Fascists. In general she had acquiesced to his wishes and by age forty was using her natural capabilities in the public spotlight only on rare, "acceptable" occasions, such as the benefit for war relief, when she read her poetry, and the dinner for the Sadler's Wells touring company, when she served as hostess and delivered a speech in two languages, and the Mozart celebration when she served as more or less a mannequin on a stage.

But Audrey—that was a different story. Ella determined that her own daughter would not be forbidden; she would be encouraged, funded, and promoted. So yes, Ella lived the life of a stage mother, unashamedly so, and yes, Ella put Audrey up on the stage at the Schouwburg in the Mozart tableau.

The family history of one of Audrey's schoolmates, Koosje Heineman, indicates that Audrey began the fall term at the Middelbare Meisjes School, the girls' college, or secondary school, in Arnhem, a building that sat above the Tamboersbosje school on the hill above the Arnhem train station. Some months later, however, the MMS building was confiscated by the Germans, and the girls had to move to other facilities. Around this time, early 1942, Ella was sending letters of introduction on her daughter's behalf along with clippings from the *Courant* to various well-placed artists around the Netherlands. Typical of these was a letter to Amsterdam cabaret artist Chiel de Boer, founder of the Cabaret De Stal. The letter read in part: "My twelve-year-old daughter is training to become a professional ballerina. She already has some very special dance compositions of her own, and she seems to have a great talent. Maybe she will perform for you...in the near future!"

A young teacher at the Dansschool, Carel Johan Wensink, said, "Haar moeder had haar op de tanden," which translates to, "Her mother had hair on the teeth," a Dutch expression meaning Ella had a sharp tongue. Wensink played piano at Audrey's dance lessons and described seeing Ella always in the wings at public performances and perpetually shoving her daughter onto some stage or other.

For the twelve year old displaced from public school, there was now dance and only dance. It wasn't just her mother's obsession, it was her own as well and her driving ambition in an increasingly harsh, colorless Arnhem. "I wanted to dance solo roles," she said. "I desperately wanted to do these roles because they would allow me to express myself. I couldn't express myself while conforming to a line of twelve girls. I didn't want to conform. I was going to hit my mark."

Many young ballerinas striving to make dance their careers developed such tunnel vision, as related by Sadler's Wells corps de ballet dancer Annabel Farjeon: "Being so highly trained in one narrow field…, dancers are seldom abashed to confess ignorance of the more elementary facts of science, politics, history, or even other forms of art. Physical demands segregate dancers more than those in most professions, for all morning and afternoon they are generally rehearsing or taking daily class…."

"I had always been sensitive to music," said Audrey. "It makes me want to move." Along with the instinct needed for dance came a drive and self-discipline uncommon in must humans. "Ballet is the most completely exhausting thing I've ever done," she said of the relentless grind of daily lessons, and yet she pushed on, stubborn and dedicated despite the war and every other obstacle.

"People don't realize that during a war of this kind, nothing basically changes inside of you," she said. "Conditions and habits change but the human doesn't. If you wanted to be a dancer before, you want to be one just as much despite the war."

Audrey shared the trait of all serious dancers—the total commitment to craft. Said Margot Fonteyn: "The necessity of going to class is not only healthy in itself—for the amount of compulsory exercise is far more than anyone would do voluntarily, just to keep fit—it is also therapeutic in times of emotional stress. No matter how often one attends a ballet class, one must still maintain a particular degree of concentration, for each class is different from all others, and the concentrating for an hour or more on the manipulation of one's limbs relieves and refreshes a mind that may be over-engrossed in emotional problems."

Every day the Dutch girl walked fifteen minutes from the apartment to the school, took her lessons, and walked home. Around her, the winter of 1942 was brutal, as indicated by journalist Steven Jansen of the nearby town of Velp. Jansen described a woman walking through town holding a basket. As she moved along the street, she would bend over, pick something up, and place it in the basket, then walk further studying the pavement and repeating the process. "She follows the trail of a coal truck," revealed Jansen. "All chips of anthracite that fall from the truck she carefully picks up because the coal assignment is not large and the winter is severe. Worse than 1941, much worse than 1940, and in fact the worst in 153 years. Almost eight weeks the IJssel has been frozen over. Sixty-five days the temperature was under zero [Celsius]."

By this point in the war, food rations were harsh, with all fats missing from Dutch diets. As a result, the cold penetrated more easily and chilled the marrow of the bones. Seyss-Inquart had pledged the previous October "that we here in Holland will get through the winter all right."

But by February the Wehrmacht had requisitioned the coal supply to keep trains running hundreds and thousands of miles to the Eastern front, where the situation was dire. Those schools in Arnhem that had managed to remain open in previous winters now closed down because they couldn't be heated. Dutch families were given enough coal to heat just one room per household.

The Germans were becoming ever more authoritarian, introducing new measures, rules, regulations, and restrictions. They no longer treated the Dutch as Aryan cousins; no longer was there an effort to win Dutch hearts. The Dutch didn't seem to be willing to walk hand in hand with the Germans, so they would be dragged along instead. In 1942 a Dutch *Kultuurkamer*, or Culture Chamber, was organized to represent musicians, writers, actors for the stage and screen, and the press. "Each profession was to have its own guild," wrote Dutch historian Louis de Jong, "but all guilds were to belong to the Chamber whose prime duty was described as the 'furtherance of Holland's culture in the light of its responsibility toward the Commonwealth of Peoples.'"

As Seyss-Inquart phrased it, "With the prohibition of the political parties, most of the organizations of the free professions became impossible, since right down to the chess players' club everything in the Netherlands was organized on a political basis."

The arts were being Nazified, including the Arnhem Symphony Orchestra and the Muziekschool, where Draaisma was already a confirmed member of the NSB, if only to keep his male students from being sent to Germany as laborers or conscripts. The move to politicize the orchestra, which included Ella's string quartet, caused internal dissension when the musicians were forced to fill out application cards to join the Chamber or be barred from further study and public performance. Draaisma and Ella didn't get along anyway—they detested each other and quarreled often. In general, Ella was experiencing disillusionment about the Nazis after her brother-in-law, Otto, had been sacked from the judicial system. It wasn't only that; the van Heemstras were suffering a second hard winter, dwindling coal and fuel supplies, and increasing regulations in all aspects of life, including now the arts. The Kultuurkamer was the last straw for Ella, who now watched as musicians she knew and respected were forced out of the orchestra because they were Jewish and couldn't obtain a registration card. Some had even become onderduikers. As a dancer, Audrey was spared from applying to join the Chamber only because of her young age at thirteen. But Marova joined, as did Draaisma.

Ella watched as the Nazi vise closed on the Jews of Arnhem.

Back in 1935 when she had run with the Mitford pack, it was easy for Diana Mitford to mouth the words of Oswald Mosley, who said that if the Jews didn't like their treatment in Europe, they could simply leave. Ella, Michael Burn, the Mitford sisters—all had been so easily seduced back then, so enamored of the promise of a revitalized Germany. Seven years later, with the streets of Arnhem stained by Jewish blood from beatings at the hands of roving Nazi gangs, reality hit Ella full force. Nazism had been twisted into something monstrous. Or had it been a lie all along?

Finally, spring arrived to break the historic winter, and with the thaw came turmoil in the family. The baron had been bickering with his landlady, Mevrouw Mia Schulte van Zegwaart, over the rent for his rooms at Zijpendaal. The quarrel erupted into open conflict, and he, Meisje, and Otto packed up their belongings at the beginning of May, with plans that by 15 May they would be vacated from de Zijp and the beautiful Sonsbeek grounds with its deer, cats, and ducks where Audrey could count many happy memories. Opa, Tante, and Oom would move three miles east to a villa the baron found that had been bequeathed to the Reformed Church by its late owner and was available for rent. The villa was located in the next town over, Velp.

Velp was a beautiful old village with money—another that had been built by business people and old soldiers with fortunes made in the Dutch East Indies. Magnificent villas dotted many streets, and the baron had managed to secure one of them, Villa Beukenhof, which was, by comparison to some others in town, more quaint than stately. It was a fine brick home just twenty-one years old, two stories tall with a high attic and tiled roof. It contained a recently expanded kitchen and living space with a half bath downstairs, plus three bedrooms and a full bath upstairs—enough room for the baron, Otto, and Meisje. A bay window stood out in the front and there was a garden behind an iron gate that wrapped around the side of the house.

The Beukenhof sat on a wide boulevard called Rozendaalse-laan, or "tree-lined road to Rozendaal." The trees were centuries old and of the beuken, or beech, variety. A stroll or bike ride up Rozendaalselaan would take the van Heemstras to the ancient Cas-tle Rozendaal with a tower dating back to the fourteenth century. Here lived Willem Frederik Torck, Baron van Pallandt, and his second wife, Aaltje, Baroness van Pallandt-Groenhof, relatives of the van Heemstras via marriage in 1837 when Baroness Henri-etta Philippina Jacoba van Pallandt—she descended from French kings—married Frans Julius Johan, Baron van Heemstra. The van Heemstras now residing in Velp knew they would always receive a warm welcome at Castle Rozendaal, and its proximity to the Beu-kenhof was the primary drawing card to this particular dwelling.

A much shorter stroll of a block and a half in the other direc-tion on Rozendaalselaan led to the downtown section of Velp and Hoofdstraat, or main street.

Ella's apartment on Jansbinnensingel was connected by a straight line and a twenty-minute ride by tram to the center of Velp, with a convenient stop at the end of Rozendaalselaan. Really, even though the baron, Meisje, and Otto had left Arnhem, the heart of the family was just a little farther away in Velp than it had been at de Zijp—Ella and Audrey could still feel connected. And it worked both ways, as the elders could still freely visit their young dancer.

On 4 May, Audrey's thirteenth birthday, she was already look-ing forward to the next public performance of the Dansschool at the Schouwburg in mid-July. She would be dancing a serenade by Haydn, while her emerging rival, Irene Grosser, would dance *An den Frühling* by Grieg. Most exciting of all was that Marova her-self would be performing a solo with Draaisma accompanying. It was the first time that the Dansschool would be filling an entire program with classical and character ballet, a clear indication that dance was beginning to make its mark in Arnhem.

It was going to be a milestone day for Adriaantje—she was now a teenager and on the verge of adulthood. She was becoming Audrey and leaving Adriaantje or "Little Audrey" behind, and with the change came a rush of insecurity and feelings that she wasn't good enough or pretty enough—a complex that would always be with her. And as if the anxieties of adolescence weren't enough to contend with, that very day, her birthday, a cruel surprise was delivered via telephone.

Meisje was on the other end of the line and told Ella the story. It had begun with a knock at the door of their rooms at Zijpendaal at eleven in the morning. When Otto answered, two members of the SD, the Dutch SS security police, presented a warrant for his arrest. He was given twenty minutes to pack a bag with necessary items and changes of clothes and accompany them at once. With Meisje looking on in horror, Otto did as instructed, somehow maintaining his usual calm. He took his wife's hands in his own and reassured her that all would be well. In moments he was loaded into the back seat of a luxury Mercedes and driven away.

Audrey had no father but she did have two father figures, Opa and Oom Otto, the cheerful, kind, and loving man and Arnhem jurist known to the world as Count van Limburg Stirum. Now he had been taken away without explanation, beginning a nightmare that, for the rest of her life, would never truly end.

10

Death Candidate

"I have a photographic memory in almost anything and there are visions of things which I will obviously never, never forget," said Audrey. "Less of Nazis on the street because that became par for the course, but certain days, certain moments, certain things that happened, I will never forget."

Otto, Count van Limburg Stirum, was a hard man to intimidate. He was an intellectual—symbolized by his wire-rimmed spectacles—and possessed a natural optimism and unwavering faith in God. The arrest didn't rattle him except for the knowledge of how his wife would take it. Now he rode in the back seat of a German automobile and was driven some distance. Then the car stopped, and he was removed from it and shoved into a poorly lit room. About twenty others had been brought to the same location to share his predicament, bewildered men—yes, all were men— and prominent men at that. For what it was worth, Otto found himself in good company; he sat among the most prominent politicians and businessmen of Gelderland. Over there den Hartog, and there, van Winter.

They remained in the room for hour upon hour until the oxygen was about used up. The space seemed increasingly damp and cold, and the heating barely worked at all. Talking among themselves, they revealed similar stories: arrest warrant, told to pack clothing, toiletries, bedclothes, jackets, and sweaters. Otto was convinced that wherever he was going, he would be away from home for some time.

Finally, after six in the evening, a German officer came into the room and called the roll of Dutchmen who had had their lives interrupted this day. In a short while, some Green Police entered and conferred with the officer. Then the prisoners were led outside and placed in a truck with their luggage, and by now the nerves of all the men had begun to fray—they didn't know where they were being taken. The truck and some Nazi staff cars set off in a procession to points unknown.

The journey took two hours. The light grew thin. Finally the stream of cars rounded some sharp turns and pulled to a stop after nightfall. The gate of the truck was opened, and Otto and the others were motioned down onto a circular driveway where the truck and cars had all parked. The group coalesced again and adjusted their eyes to look up at a magnificent building. It was tall, brick, and enormously long, extending well into the blackness of night. It seemed to be a religious institution or, perhaps, a mental hospital. They were led up a long set of stone steps and inside the main doors to an arched entryway with cornices. It became apparent at once that this was a Roman Catholic building, a seminary it turned out.

The group was herded around a corner and into a large room with an SS official's name on the door. Inside were some Wehrmacht officers and a man who looked like he was about to go riding or hunting; they were clearly German from their accents and bearing. Not one of them addressed the forlorn group standing there. Instead, a sergeant conducted another roll call. Then a little man in rumpled clothes, a Dutchman, motioned for the group to follow him out of the room.

The man had a list and assigned the prisoners to quarters. He said there were five "cell blocks" in the "villa" and that, all told, up to 600 men could be held here. "Held where?" someone asked.

"Why, Beekvliet," said the Dutchman. "You are in the village of Sint-Michielsgestel, at the seminary. The Germans have taken it over." He went on to explain that they were now in the province of Brabant, in the south of Holland.

The place was as big as a palace, but not terribly grand. It just went on and on—up stairs, down stairs, into and out of long corridors, through a series of rights and lefts. Finally they reached a dormitory on the first floor with the official name of Block IV, and there Otto entered a small room designed to hold two persons. So began his life as a prisoner. His initial impression of his new accommodations? "It looks decent," he wrote in the diary he started this night.

Otto would fill in some of the blanks the next morning. He was one of 460 Dutch men who had been rounded up for no crime other than representing the best and brightest in the country. They had been brought here to a central location in North Brabant, near its capital, 's-Hertogenbosch. Sint-Michielsgestel lay southwest of Arnhem and northwest of Eindhoven, and its best-known landmark was this complex: kleine seminarie Beekvliet, a Catholic training center for priests established in 1815 and named for the archangel St. Michael. The Catholics had been expelled so that it could be turned into a prison that would hold "death candidates" as part of a very simple plan: Since the Dutch Resistance movement seemed to be organizing at long last, then one way to head off acts of sabotage was to gather together some of the nation's irreplaceable citizens as hostages. It was an experiment born of experiences with the tiresome French Underground—maybe shooting some innocents would keep resistance movements from growing in the first place.

The SS commandant positioned all this in a speech to the assembled *gijzelaars*, or hostages. But the concept had little impact on the captives simply because this wasn't France, where the underground was organized and active and blowing up things right and left. This was Holland, where extremism had never gained much of a foothold and where acts of violence were uncommon.

In a message broadcast across the Netherlands the plan was announced—any act of violence against the Reich would call for executions of an appropriate number of death candidates who had been gathered for just this purpose. After an instance or two of capital punishment, the people would see the benefits of cooperating with the occupation forces rather than fighting them. Then maybe, finally, the Netherlands could become willing partners in the German empire. And Otto, thanks to his refusal to name names for Nazi man Schrieke, had made the list and been designated a death candidate along with another deputy prosecutor, current and former mayors, bankers, educators, business owners, journalists, and even a chef. Otto was shocked to see his younger brother, forty-two-year-old Constantijn Willem, Count van Limburg Stirum, among the catch. Constant was nothing more dangerous than a wine merchant, and yet here he was.

Otto sent a letter to Meisje immediately, then counted the days until he figured she would receive it. On 11 May, after a week of captivity, he wrote in his diary, "Have been reading in the monastery garden. Letter of M. who gave me the impression that she is a bit lonely—it's a letter, however, written on Friday night, so she must have heard from me by now and I think it will be better."

On 14 May Otto received a parcel from Meisje that contained, among other goods and clothing, snapshot photos of the Beukenhof. "It was funny but also melancholic to see all sorts of pictures of our [new] home," he wrote. He had never even had the opportunity to lay eyes on the house he was about to move into!

The next day he received a parcel containing biscuits sent by friends in Oosterbeek and the day after that another with a jar of butter, a fresh loaf of meat, and a jacket. Many of the prisoners were receiving such parcels and sharing their contents for the common good. Even more precious were two letters from Meisje announcing that she had traveled to Brabant and was now close by, staying with local friends.

Meisje was a remarkable woman; a Frisian after all and a strong Protestant. Faith alone would see her through this, he knew. In his letters he implored her not to worry, that all the captives would be held for a time and then released—this was all a big Nazi bluff. But there was also troubling news that another group of hundreds of hostages, more leading citizens, had been rounded up and placed just a few miles to the west in Haaren at the Groot Seminarie in a setup similar to Beekvliet. Among them was Rheden's mayor, W. Th. C. Zimmerman, who was married to Cecelia Emilie Louise, Baroness van Pallandt, a relative of the van Heemstras. Now, a thousand top Dutchmen were under lock and key and ready to die for the transgressions of any troublemaker with a bomb, whether a freedom fighter or a communist or just some nut.

On 18 May Otto was summoned to the commandant's office and told that he may go to the fence at the edge of the compound and there his wife would be waiting. "It was a wonderful reunion," he wrote, saying they had a half hour together. He noted that she was very brave and calm around the guard, who in turn was discreet. Otto was allowed to pass a bundle of dirty laundry to her; she gave him a picnic basket, fresh clothes, and other things. Later in the day he received a crate from the post office filled with "an incredible stock of delicious things: chicken soup, fresh strawberries, cherries in juice, all sorts of cans, and soft blankets." He ended his diary entry by saying, "It has been a wonderful day and I am so grateful to her."

May became June. In the labyrinthine building and grounds surrounded by barbed wire, with armed guards at the perimeter, the prisoners settled into a routine that was half university and half resort. Robert Peereboom, editor-in-chief of a newspaper in the city of Haarlem, joined the fraternity early in June and kept a diary that would be published in 1945.

"We lived in relative comfort," said Peereboom, "very different than the people in the concentration camps, where abuse and punishment were the order of the day. We had self-government within our hostage community. Each made his own daily schedule. There was a cheerful, clean spiritual life. We worked stubbornly. We even played: football and cricket, bridge and billiards. We sometimes heard music. Family and friends, as well as interested people unknown to us, overwhelmed us with packages. But we were locked behind barbed wire. And Death threatened us."

From the beginning, Otto believed it his duty as Dutch nobility to set a positive example for those around him. Constant was of a similar mind. They became engaged in conversation at every turn with some of the most brilliant minds in the Netherlands. Otto wrote in his diary of the relaxed mood of the prisoners and the guards; he remarked how quickly the days passed; he liked having a church so close by and went there often. The structure itself was Roman Catholic, but it would suffice for a devoted Reformed Protestant.

In general he found this a great adventure, and he determined early on he wouldn't give the Germans the satisfaction of seeing him downcast. Almost all the hostages felt that way, he learned. They gardened. They engaged in rhetorical debates about various political and religious issues. They energetically ate bad food prison-style in large dining rooms. The professors held classes in history and literature. Otto and Constant engaged in Otto's passion, contract bridge, and staged bridge tournaments. Football matches between various groups on the adjacent field—contained within barbed wire and with sentries on patrol—drew hundreds of spectators.

June became July. The countryside outside the barbed wire grew lush and the flowers reached full bloom. Otto found it wonderful to have his brother so close by; he hadn't seen so much of

Constant in years. Meisje was by now staying in the homes of various friends near Beekvliet to be near her husband. She showered him with so many parcels containing so many wonderful treats obtained from the black market that he complained about gaining weight in prison—six pounds in just ten days. Imagine, being taken away by the occupiers and eating better than at home!

Visits at the fence became a usual occurrence, but he grew frustrated, saying, "The distance and the impossibility to go to each other remains odd; but of the moment itself, the feeling of being able to see each other overrules and that's lovely."

He also exchanged letters with Ella and learned that on 11 July, Audrey performed at the Schouwburg, dancing to pieces by Mozart, Grieg, and Haydn. Otto read the clipping from the newspaper. His niece was mentioned first, as usual, leaving no doubt that she was a gifted dancer. "The performances of Audrey Hepburn-Ruston and Irene Grosser are examples of what the pupils are capable of," read the clipping. "The former, only thirteen years old, is a natural talent who is in good hands with Mevr. Winja Marova."

By mid-July Otto had gained another two pounds in confinement and decided to distribute some of the bounty from his wife to the other hostages. Meisje was delighted because she had heard such marvelous things about Otto's comrades and considered them family. "Everyone is full of admiration," he wrote, "about the way she does this [builds parcels of food] for 'her boys' and about the quantities and the variation."

More weeks passed and frustration roamed the halls with the prisoners. "It's remarkable to notice that the mood is less hopeful than some time ago," Otto wrote. "I nevertheless remain optimistic about a quick redemption. I try always to be cheerful, to cheer up others and to have a friendly word or a joke for everybody. That is, in my view, my duty here."

The air war strayed close to the compound and low-flying

planes menaced the population. At the end of July an Allied fighter attack took out the Den Bosch central train station just a few miles away—Meisje was much closer still and the detonation of three bombs startled her.

On the last day of July, control of the prison was transferred from the NSB and Green Police to the Wehrmacht, the German regular army. A few days later, Otto contracted a viral infection that landed him in the sick quarters for several days with a high fever. Then on 9 August, a Sunday, Otto saw an item in the newspaper—an act of sabotage had been committed on a railway in Rotterdam, but in good Dutch style only a railroad worker was seriously injured and a Nederlander at that. He wrote that the commandant had gathered together all in the compound and announced that "the hostages will be held liable if the culprit isn't arrested by the night of 14 August."

The next day, Otto's fever had broken, and he left sick quarters to return to his usual schedule. Hostage Robert Peereboom wrote, "Conversations remain optimistic. In our group in the dining room, van Limburg Stirum, the Arnhem substitute officer of justice, takes it very merrily and is convinced that it will end with a threat. He is a man who always tends to expect the best from his fellow men. A remarkable mentality in such a profession."

One hostage who did not exude confidence was Robert Baelde of Rotterdam, another attorney who was also secretary of the Dutch Union, a political movement that sought to improve relations between Holland and Germany to better the lives of the Dutch people. Baelde revealed to his fellow prisoners that he had "a feeling" all would not be well.

The days passed too quickly heading to 14 August, deadline day. It was rumored that seven additional hand-chosen hostages had arrived and were being kept in the front building.

On 12 August all visits by loved ones were canceled. More troubling still, each prisoner was required to turn in his Ausweis—

the identity card all carried with photo and fingerprints. In addition, twenty-five hostages were taken aside and photographed. With the exception of one, all were from Rotterdam. Robert Baelde, the man with "the feeling," was included. The one *not* from Rotterdam was Otto.

There occurred another disquieting sign: The barracks chiefs were ordered to make a strict accounting of which hostage slept in which bunk, top or bottom, in which room. Whatever was going on, it seemed that it might be more than a bluff.

On Friday, 14 August, with the midnight deadline looming, rumors spread through the seminary that the saboteurs had been caught. Spirits among the hostages lifted. Otto played several hands of bridge with his usual partner, Constant, in the afternoon, and then at dinner he sat with his new friend Peereboom, talking about his career in the justice system and offering theories about rehabilitation. Peereboom observed that Otto showed no fear at all; he was his usual friendly, upbeat self.

"After the war," said Otto, "I'll get promoted and move away from this work. It's for young men who want to gain experience. I think I can do more good in a higher position."

They remained in such deep conversation that all at once, it seemed, they were the last two in the dining hall. They hurried out to attend a football match with the rest of the hostages and then, in the long Dutch summer evening, Otto sat with his diary and wrote, "I stayed to write a letter to M. and to make notes. Lovely weather, a little wind and some sunlight now and then and soft air." Here his diary ended.

Sometime in the blackness of night, after one o'clock, Otto heard heavy boots on the plank floor outside his room. The door flew open and flashlights blinded him. He was ordered to dress and pack up all his belongings. Then two guards led him up the long corridors and stairways to a room in the front building, near the entryway.

It was the middle of the night. The sounds of shoes and boots on the floor of the seminary made an enormous and echoing noise. Every door that opened and closed had the effect of thunder.

He stood in a room that the clergy had used for consultations. He was handed a sheet of paper and a pencil and informed that he may write a final letter. He sat and wrote to Meisje as instructed. Otto still believed the actions of his captors to be a bluff, because when Constant was brought to see his brother, he found Otto to be "perfectly calm."

Otto smiled on sight of his brother. "Sit down and have a cigarette," he told Constant. "I'm busy with my letter."

With his brother's appearance, Otto must have begun to suspect that this wasn't an effort to frighten an admission out of the Rotterdam hostages. It was something more. An officer indicated it was time for Constant to go. The brothers embraced and the younger was led away.

Otto stood there in perfect stillness for a moment, with the only thing he now knew for certain: Whatever the future held, God would be with him.

After a time, he heard again the clomp of German boots approaching as another man from Beekvliet was led in to stand with Otto. Who was this unlucky soul?

Ah, but of course. It was his friend Robert Baelde, the man with "the feeling." Baelde always had such a healthy-looking face, but not now. He was pale and solemn as he stood there, hat and suitcase in hand. Outside a truck pulled up and two other civilians, obviously hostages, shuffled in the front door. Baelde recognized one of them immediately and introduced Otto to Christoffel Bennekers, superintendent of Rotterdam police. He was a bit older, perhaps fifty, his face drained of color with the weight of the moment. He seemed to be having trouble walking due to nerves. Baelde also recognized the other man to enter—Willem Ruys, director of the Dutch shipping company Rotterdamsche Lloyd.

The men took note that three of them were Rotterdam natives; only Otto wasn't. More heavy footsteps echoed in the cavernous hallways. Another gray face appeared. A young face and the last in the world that Otto expected to see.

It was young Alexander, Baron Schimmelpenninck van der Oye. No, the Germans could not do this; they could not take vengeance on two members of the van Limburg Stirum family. Constant's wife was the sister of Schimmelpenninck's wife, making it a small world of hostages who knew each other from family gatherings. But there was another connection. Alex's father had been married to Meisje and Ella's aunt—Audrey's great-aunt—Cornelia Elisabeth, Baroness van Heemstra, who had borne him three children before dying of tuberculosis in 1901 at age thirty-four. The baron had then remarried, and thus Alex and three siblings were born. Otto knew now that if the Germans did indeed carry out their threat, this night was going to be very hard on the van Heemstra family. And Schimmelpenninck was not yet thirty years old, and dear God, his twenty-year-old wife, Catharina, was with child.

Otto introduced Schimmelpenninck as a member of his wife's family, the van Heemstras. The men shook hands.

Events unfolded quickly now. The five were given a meal—if one could call bread and soup—bad soup—a meal. No one had an appetite. Then Green Police came in and pushed the men out the front door and down the long concrete stairway. If other hostages were to be included in this event, whatever the event amounted to, they must be coming from elsewhere.

The hostages were directed into the back of a truck, and Otto, lugging his effects as he was, could scarcely see to stumble his way up and inside. There was a plank bench on each long side of the truck bed, and the five found seats. More Green Police occupied the other seats and leaned on their rifles.

Doors slammed in an accompanying vehicle, presumably an officers' car. Engines started and the vehicles set out to the clatter of spraying gravel. After a couple turns, a left and then a sharp right, the truck droned on in the night, and the men held their places against the rocking, to and fro.

It was the break of dawn when the truck and car pulled to a stop in woodlands. Birds sang merry songs about the emerging morning. The air was clear with the promise of a beautiful day. The men were ordered out of the truck and jumped down on stiff legs.

The trunk of the staff car was opened and shovels and pick axes were withdrawn and tossed beside the rutted dirt path on which the vehicles had parked. The five were ordered to each take a shovel and pick axe, and they were led on at rifle point through a young forest. They saw that there was another truck full of Green Police waiting, and the total number of men with rifles was about fifty.

They picked their way through the woodland bottom over sandy ground spritzed with morning dew. The stunted height of the pine, birch, and oak trees and the abundant scrub hinted that this forest had been burned out ten or twenty years earlier.

They reached a well-secluded spot and were ordered to dig. It was a time-honored German tradition: execution victims told to open their own graves. The five stripped off their jackets and did as instructed. To resist could bring retribution down onto wives and children. Better it ended here.

It took a long while to dig the graves because even though the earth was soft and sandy, there was a great deal of it to be displaced. And the laborers had to face one more intellectual challenge: How much care does a man invest in digging his own grave? Does he want it deep? Does he want it free of rocks and roots?

Five man-sized poles were produced and set into place at intervals of ten feet near the far side of the burial pit dug by the condemned. At length, the officer in charge proclaimed that the work of the men was sufficient. He ordered them to stack their shovels and pick axes. Each was pulled or pushed to one of the five stakes and tied to it, hands behind the back. Heartbeats raced. Then blindfolds appeared, and it was almost a relief to have them fitted in place because it blotted out the sight of the hateful faces of green soldiers staring at them in the morning sun. The five could hear the Green Police being arranged into firing-squad sections, ten rifles pointed at each target. Above, the birds of morning sang on, songs about summer and sun and bugs to be eaten.

All grew still again, with the five in darkness.

"Do you have any final words?" asked the officer in charge.

There was silence a moment and a voice said, "I hope and trust that my death may yield fruit to the cause of our homeland. This is a fair thing, and for this I am willing to die." It was Schimmelpenninck.

The officer called, "Attention! Ready!" Rifle bolts clicked. "Aim!"

"Long live the Queen!" shouted a hostage.

"Long live Oranje!" yelled another.

"Shoot!"

The fusillade sent birds to flight in the forest. The hostages hung there; none showed a sign of life. The officer moved forward and checked each man. Then he motioned for his soldiers to untie the bodies, which fell to the earth. They were kicked and nudged into the pit with minimal arrangement. The poles were uprooted and tossed onto the bodies. Men produced bags of lime and dumped the white powder on each body to hasten decomposition. Green-clad soldiers tossed the sacks in last and shoveled earth at a rapid pace to get this morning over with. The officer ordered the soldiers to tramp down the earth and kick leaves and vegetation onto it. In a little while, no evidence remained of the execution; the last thing the Germans wanted was to create a place here for Dutch martyrs.

The officer complimented his men on a job well done. As they hopped in the truck to depart, one man began to sing and then all joined in, and as they drove away from the spot, the sounds of their voices became ever more distant. By now the birds had come back and it was their sweet summer lament, not the guttural tune of the murderers, that restored peace to a blood-spattered little corner of Dutch forest in Goirle.

11
Paranoid

Otto's diary, scribbled in Dutch, recorded daily life at Sint-Michielsgestel. Below the last entry, in which he had described a beautiful sunset, the last he would experience, was written in English by one of his fellow gijzelaars quoting Shelley on the death of Keats:

Peace, peace! he is not dead, he doth not sleep,
He hath awaken'd from the dream of life.

The private person who became movie star Audrey Hepburn would never think of discussing the death of Uncle Otto in a publicity piece related to a play or movie. In a 1992 interview for UNICEF, she would allow that Otto "had been shot by the Germans because he was a judge [sic]. They had taken him as a hostage and he was shot as an example."

During the war and even after it, the van Heemstras couldn't make sense of such an unspeakable horror that had taken away dear Otto and sought to bend the will of the family and nation—the losses of Count van Limburg Stirum, Alexander, Baron Schimmelpenninck van der Oye, and their three brave companions—which makes the back story important, not only to van Heemstra descendants but to the history of the Netherlands.

For Seyss-Inquart, Nazi ruler of the Netherlands, the last week of Otto's life had been a long, hard one. The failed bomb attack against German assets on Rotterdam's railroad had infuriated the ruling German administration. Soon after the railroad bombing, the SS and the Dutch Nazi secret police, the SD, had won out in arguments to take a harder line and execute fifty Rotterdam natives among the hostages being held since May. The SD ordered that even more death candidates—all prominent men—be gathered from Rotterdam and shipped south to the seminaries. The SD had made their choices for the fifty condemned and forwarded files to Hanns Albin Rauter, head of the SS in the Netherlands. At the same time, Seyss-Inquart became aware that Queen Wilhelmina was visiting the United States and had addressed the Congress in Washington. In that speech she had spoken horrible slanders about the Third Reich.

Seyss-Inquart's inner circle wondered if any of the death candidates at Sint-Michielsgestel or Haaren might be "special" to the queen. A review of the hostage lists turned up the name Otto Ernst Gelder, Count van Limburg Stirum, who had defied NSB's Schrieke the previous year. Limburg Stirum had done work for the Dutch royal court and was married to a member of the Frisian noble family van Heemstra—another that was connected to the Oranje court, as Marianne, Baroness van Heemstra, Otto's sister-in-law, was now attending Princess Juliana in Ottawa, Canada.

More importantly, Seyss-Inquart knew his history and realized the importance to the Dutch royal family of the name Limburg Stirum. Leopold van Limburg Stirum had been one-third of the "Driemanschap of 1813" along with Frans Adam van der Duyn van Maasdam and Gijsbert Karel van Hogendorp—these three men were the founding fathers of the modern nation of the Netherlands. They had formed a triumvirate in November 1813 to hold the country together when Napoleon's occupying forces withdrew following the battle of Leipzig. To keep order, the Driemanschap had invited Willem Frederick, Prince of Oranje-Nassau, to come to power, creating a Dutch monarchy that would endure. The Oranje royal line that began with King Willem I in 1813 was unbroken to Queen Wilhelmina, and so yes, thought Seyss-Inquart with glee: The death of Count van Limburg Stirum would teach the irritating old woman that perhaps it was wiser to keep her mouth shut.

Meanwhile, Protestant churches in Rotterdam tried to stop the execution of any hostages by releasing a statement that multiple congregations "strongly condemn the act of sabotage on Friday, 7 August, which puts the lives of both German and Dutch nationals at the utmost danger." They were admitting to the Germans that the resistance action committed by their countrymen was wrong.

Next, the churches sent an urgent telegram to Seyss-Inquart, which he read in his office to Rauter and Schrieke for their amusement. A representative of the church was summoned to a conference with the three leaders.

The churchman said that such an action "will lead to an uprising of the Dutch people." Several rounds of negotiations followed until the number to be executed had been reduced to five.

"There are still five too many," said the church official. "I ask for the release of all." He was sent away.

On Friday, 14 August, it seemed likely that a spy had infiltrated the Dutch Resistance in Rotterdam and might soon identify the saboteurs, which could mean the passing of the deadline without the need to carry out any executions. At nine that evening an officer telephoned Rauter and said, "Gruppenführer, I call you because...the shooting of hostages is no longer necessary." He explained the situation about the infiltrator, and Rauter asked how soon the guilty parties might be arrested. The officer said it might take a few days. Rauter conveyed the message to Seyss-Inquart, but by this time the final list of names had been decided upon: Limburg Stirum, and four from Rotterdam—Ruys, Bennekers, Baelde, and one other.

But reaching back into Dutch history to spite the queen had uncovered a more significant name at the last instant. That name was Schimmelpenninck, another tied not only to Holland but to Germany's blood enemies, the French. Rutger Jan Schimmel-penninck was a Dutch businessman and politician who became a favorite of Napoleon and was made a baron of the French empire in 1807. After the defeat of Bonaparte's armies, Rutger Jan Schimmelpenninck became part of the founding government of the Netherlands, and this name too would be important to the queen. So Rauter's SD set out to find and arrest Alexander, Baron Schimmelpenninck van der Oye. They succeeded on the third try on the afternoon of Friday, 14 August, wresting him away from his pregnant wife and driving him to Sint-Michielsgestel.

The fourth Rotterdammer was spared and Schimmelpenninck was added to the list. Only three of those to be executed had come from Rotterdam when the original intent was to make death candidates of a particular place pay for attacks by the Resistance. The other two hostages marked for death were victims of power politics. Their fates were sealed.

After a phone call confirming that the executions had taken place, Rauter ordered SS officers to call the citizenry together in Dutch cities at noon on 15 August so a proclamation could be read: "In view of the fact that despite the extremely urgent invitation by Wehrmacht General der Flieger Friedrich Christiansen, the perpetrators of the dynamiting in Rotterdam have been too cowardly to give themselves up. As a result, the following five were executed this morning: Willem Ruys, Director General of Rotterdam; the Count van Limburg Stirum of Arnhem; Robert Baelde of Rotterdam; Christophel Bennekers, former police inspector of Rotterdam; and Alexander, Baron Schimmelpenninck van der Oye of Schouwen."

Back in Velp at Villa Beukenhof, the baron, Ella, and Audrey reacted in utter shock to the news. And it wasn't only Otto but Alex Schimmelpenninck as well! With Meisje still in the south near the seminary and Alex's wife in Schouwen, there was nothing to do but sit and wait.

Audrey had missed her Tante Meisje, who had lived in Brabant for the better part of two months, and now the new widow rushed back to the Beukenhof to be with her family. It was clear that the love between Otto and Meisje was real and deep, and Audrey had so felt the loss of her wonderful uncle since he had been taken on her birthday. Now he wasn't coming back at all, and for what? He had done nothing! He was in captivity when the bomb had exploded in Rotterdam! He didn't know the saboteurs; he didn't take part in their decisions.

Meisje's first act after her return to Velp was to call the *Arnhemsche Courant* and purchase ad space. She ordered a black-boxed ad with the words: "Today died, to my unspeakable sadness, my dearly beloved husband, Mr. Otto Ernst Gelder, Count van Limburg Stirum, Substitute Officer of Justice at the District Court of Arnhem. W.C. Countess van Limburg Stirum, Baroness van Heemstra, Beukenhof, Velp. 15 August 1942."

It was a risky move to publicly acknowledge her reaction to Otto's death and to list as current his former title, considering that he had been dismissed by the Germans. But Meisje simply didn't care. As a van Heemstra and a titled person, she knew it was her duty to be seen as a leader in spite of her grief. The actions of the family were so important now; now especially. They must do honor to Otto and to Friesland. The people must have an example of grace under these impossible circumstances as she endured profound grief. Later she occupied her mind by writing a letter to the hostages left behind at the seminary:

"I am gladly sending you all a message. The last two months I have been in Gestel and have lived more closely than any other Dutch woman with the hostages from day to day. My husband has fallen with Gestel's first hostages. Some of you have known him, but most of you have not.

I sincerely hope that you will all return home safely again, but if this is not the case, and if God also summons you in the way He has done with my husband, then in your last hours He will give you the same power of dying with courage that my husband was allowed, so that he went his last way with his head raised, knowing that the Father's house awaited him. God bless you all."

The letter was read before the many hundreds of death candidates now crowding the facility. All were in shock that the Germans had actually carried out such a murderous act, and all wondered about their own fates now that the man who had given them strength, van Limburg Stirum, was dead. Meisje's letter was tacked up to a fence and read over and over by nearly everyone, and they copied down portions of it and noted her address.

A flood of letters from hostages and wives of hostages came back to the Beukenhof, including one from Robert Peereboom in which he detailed Otto's final days and his remarkable dignity and courage.

Meisje said in a letter to the wife of another hostage: "Just because you, as a hostage wife yourself, wrote to me in my great grief, did me so much good. I feel so closely connected to the Dutch hostage wives and still consider myself as one of them. Wholehearted in their love and sorrow, in their mercy and in their hope for the early return of their husbands." Of Otto she wrote:

"God has given me a very heavy cross to bear where I always try as much as possible [to honor] the life of my husband, whom I loved above all else. To see and think of his steps, his peace, his glory, for him all is well and he is in the safe haven. He has gone quietly and courageously—perhaps some anxiety or fear of death; he was allowed to give his life for his queen and his country, and I must try to follow his example and courageously bear this great suffering. Once we see each other [again], there will be no more worry and tears."

Radio Oranje announced the murders of Otto and his comrades and Queen Wilhelmina expressed her shock and sorrow. But she also ordered her people to take no action now, but to wait. Prior to the executions, Radio Oranje had warned the Germans that anyone participating in the murder of hostages would pay for their crimes at the conclusion of the war.

The executions failed to bring the Dutch people into line. On the contrary, as one German officer noted, "The last possibilities of understanding between the occupying power and the Dutch have been lost." Even the fence-sitters among the Dutch, those wishing to find peace with the Germans, expressed outrage at the killing of these wonderful, innocent men.

Among the Germans, particularly Rauter and the men who had carried out the executions, a strange paranoia set in. The select group that knew the whereabouts of the site, those who had fired the shots and their officers, returned to the fatal place two and three times a day to make sure no one had managed to find it and recover the bodies. They stumbled upon no people in that desolate location and saw no signs of disturbances. But they kept going back, and back, and back. For months. What they didn't know was that the head gamekeeper of the family-held parcel of land in question, Marinus van Heerebeek, had heard voices the morning of 15 August. After a stealthy approach he saw in the distance many Green Police scattered through the forest. Van Heerebeek's one thought was that they were searching for petrol that he kept buried in cans in these woods in case of an emergency need. But the moffen were nowhere near the petrol, so he departed not knowing what was going on. Later he heard the sharp crack of a single volley—the sound carried for miles.

When van Heerebeek heard of the execution of the five and remembered what he had seen and heard in his forest, he put two and two together. He went on an early morning excursion to the area where he had seen the soldiers. As an expert woodsman, he identified terrain that looked like it had been disturbed and made mental notes of the exact location.

The action to execute hostages had been a grand miscalculation by Seyss-Inquart, Rauter, and Christiansen. They had committed a war crime that would haunt them down the road, and it was now clear that no one among the oppressed would forget the five who were buried in the forests of Goirle. Their hearts would continue to beat inside every loyal Dutch man and woman. Long Live Oranje!

12

The Secret

"There's a curious thing about pain," said Audrey. "In the beginning, it's an enemy, it's something that you don't want to face or think about or deal with. Yet with time it becomes almost a friend. If you've lost someone you love very much, in the beginning you can't bear it, but as the years go by, the pain of losing them is what reminds you so vividly of them—that they were alive. My experiences and the people I lost in the war remain so vivid for me because of the pain."

With news of Otto's death, with word that his remains had been buried where he had fallen and that there was no way to learn where that was, the van Heemstras felt it was time to band together. Ella packed up the belongings of her children and the three of them moved from Jansbinnensingel 8A in Arnhem Centraal three miles to the northeast, up the road to neighboring Velp and the house that the Baron had just rented, the Villa Beukenhof at Rozendaalselaan 32.

Moving to Velp wasn't an easy decision for Ella because Audrey's walk from their apartment in Arnhem to the Muziekschool was a pleasant fifteen minutes. Now she would face a tram ride down the road connecting Velp and Arnhem to reach the Muziekschool, but in terms of daily living for the family, Ella thought it better to be close to the baron and Meisje now, under the circumstances, and Velp, while described by locals as a village, was a fine place to live. It included a two-story hospital called Ziekenhuis Velp as well as the sturdy Rotterdamsche Bank building with its gingerbread tower, a fine post office, and many shops. There were also two hotels—the Park Hotel and the elegant Hotel Naeff with its garden restaurant. In walking distance of the Beukenhof was everything Ella, Ian, and Audrey would need. Even dance was possible because the Johnny van Rosmalen Dansschool was located just a minute by foot down the street from the Beukenhof at Rozendaalselaan 18.

Personal factors besides the shocking death of Otto had forced Ella's move. With the Germans tightening their grip on the Netherlands, with rationing becoming more severe, with more people arrested, with the Jews being ever more cruelly oppressed, and now with the executions of innocent civilians, the population was rising up against everything that represented the Reich and the moffen. Any citizen, even a baroness, who had been seen with Germans since the occupation began was now treated by the majority with suspicion. Even though her relationship with Herr Oestreich had ended, and she was through supporting the Nazis as of the past winter, to Ella's shock she learned that a list of "people not to be trusted" had been published in the local Resistance newspaper, *Oranjekrant*. Right there in black and white was the name **Baroness van Heemstra, Arnhem**. Ella's inclination was to go to Velp to be with Meisje anyway, but the increasing wariness of the neighbors on Jansbinnensingel nudged her in the direction of the baron and relative safety. In short, Baroness van Heemstra needed a fresh start.

Ella also had her daughter to consider. She was moving into adolescence; she was quieter and more irritable; her features were maturing; she was no longer Adriaantje in any sense. She was Audrey now, and the death of Otto had wrenched from this emotionally wounded girl yet another man whom she looked up to. Thanks to the Nazis, Audrey was traumatized.

In a decision long overdue, Ella resigned as patron of the Arnhem String Quartet. The Kultuurkamer was wielding ever more power and influence as 1942 wore on. Not only Jewish musicians in the Arnhem Symphony had been dismissed—anyone who made anti-German feelings known was shoved out. Ella also stopped working in the kitchen of the Diaconessenhuis with its staff of German-born workers in a hospital that tended many wounded German soldiers. She resigned from her position at Pander & Zonen since one of the founders, Henk Pander, was a member of the NSB and now was making not only furniture but also aircraft to support the German war effort. Such things about Pander & Zonen had been common knowledge for the duration of the occupation, but now they became important to Ella's personal situation and her decision that she was finished with the Germans.

Despite the tumult of the times, Ella remained single-minded in giving Audrey everything necessary so that she could continue to immerse herself in dance. With Audrey and Ian, another introvert, now living in the villa with their grandfather, mother, and aunt, Ella could see that both children were more isolated from friends than ever. A favorite pastime for the van Heemstras became evenings at Castle Rozendaal where the Baron and Baroness van Pallandt greeted them with warm affection. This castle was like a big and worldly brother to what the van Heemstras had known at Zijpendaal. Besides a fourteenth century turret with walls fifteen feet thick, there was a hunting lodge, an orangery, a grotto, a gazebo, and a man-made cascade with rococo walls of seashells.

The titled van Heemstras could be comfortable with the titled van Pallandts. Ella said, "They [her class] differentiate very much between *people* and people. They belong to an entirely different world to the ones *they do not know*." So within the fortress Rozendaal and its grounds, the van Heemstras felt they could relax.

Audrey the nature lover was back in heaven during visits to

Castle Rozendaal, and yet inner loneliness remained. "I was growing up with people much older than myself," she said. "I was going to dancing school every day with my little satchel. In it were my sandwiches and my music. I was studying and dreaming of Pavlova and Diaghilev. To all intents and purposes I had been cut off from the world of youngsters my age because the war had made me a prisoner not just physically but mentally, never allowing me to peep out to see what was really outside."

Around her, the life was slowly being sapped from the Dutch people. In January 1942 their silver coinage had been replaced with coins made of zinc. In March coins made of nickel were taken away, and those of bronze in April. By the time the possession of all such metal coins had been outlawed, wise Dutch households were hiding their old coinage for better days.

In May Jews had been ordered to wear a yellow star outlined in black and bearing the word "Jood" on the left breast of their clothing—even the children. Restrictions on the Jews grew harsher by the day.

Rationing for all civilians kept growing stricter in concert with the Russian campaign, which had entered its second year. As progress remained slow for the German army over a massive eastern front, moods of the occupiers in Arnhem had turned dark and then darker still.

All too early for German soldiers in the east, the Russian winter set in, again, and then an unexpected Soviet military maneuver caused the entire German Sixth Army—the same army that had overrun the Netherlands two-and-a-half years earlier—to become cut off at Stalingrad. Dutch families listened to updates regarding the battle for Stalingrad on Radio Oranje, and there was ardent support for the Russians in most quarters, even though the far-flung battles and endless need for resources for those beleaguered armies would mean deepening hardships at home.

As 1942 became 1943, another unusually cold Dutch winter

set in. Meisje was there; Otto wasn't. He would have been the re-sourceful one once the coal reserves were exhausted—and it went so quickly this year. All houses in Velp were permitted to heat only one room, and with no coal for furnaces, firewood meant survival. Picket fences and trees all over town disappeared.

As the holidays approached—holidays that made Otto's absence all the more painful—a new experience brought the war even closer. Audrey was used to planes roaring over because Flieg-erhorst Deelen, the German fighter base, was located just a few miles due northwest of Velp. But most mornings now she began to hear a new sound, a deep, echoing drone of many motors high overhead. On some mornings, condensation trails could be seen in a broad unbroken ribbon of white in the blue sky, always appearing in some variation of west to east. On the clearest of days, dots were visible high above, big clusters of them arranged in intricate pat-terns, although more often than not clouds or fog hung over Velp, and only the ghostly noise signaled all those big planes flying over. Radio Oranje confirmed that the planes four miles high in the sky were American bombers, B-17s and B-24s, taking off from bases in England and on their way to bomb cities in Germany.

For Ella, the appearance of the American "bomber stream" merely confirmed the inevitability of the outcome of this war. American planes flew over nearly every morning in January and February 1943. At first dozens, then a hundred at a time to pound German cities into rubble. The RAF had been bombing at night, and the Dutch had grown used to hearing their planes fly over af-ter dusk. The Americans had been fighting for a year in the Pacific against the Japanese and in North Africa against the Germans, but now they had entered the war in northern Europe. These were the same Americans that Hitler had felt confident in disparaging back before the invasion of the Soviet Union had become a stale-mate and then a disaster. To think that the charming man with the bright blue eyes she met in 1935 had led the world to this. Back in the days of the Parteitag in Nuremberg, Ella would never have believed that Hitler's army, so proudly on display at Zeppelin Field, could ever be beaten. Now the impossible had been rendered possible: The encircled German Sixth Army surrendered at the end of January. Hundreds of thousands of German soldiers were captured in the freezing cold.

In so many ways the situation for Ella in Gelderland was impossible: under occupation, slowly being bled dry of resources, the climate brutal and no way to heat the home, with three children to worry about—one of whom was an onderduiker—and a widowed sister, and an elderly father. Alex was off playing a shell game, living here and there, finding work where he could but lying low so the Germans wouldn't conscript him or ship him off as forced labor. The last word Ella had was that he had relocated to Oirsbeek, a town in the middle of Dutch nowhere, down near Belgium. This year Ian turned eighteen, and now she would be worrying about the Germans snatching him too. Audrey was still dancing with the professional class; she had passed two years of steady progress with Marova, and, oh, what a beautiful dancer she was becoming.

On 6 February 1943, Audrey performed in a lavish program at the Schouwburg featuring the musicians, chorus, and dancers of the Muziekschool. The performance drew raves from patrons and the press. Said the *Arnhemsche Courant*, "Dance was the main course.... Only four pupils performed, but because of the talent and diversity in what they offered, it did not feel like a shortcoming. From this youthful and already well-trained dance group shone a charm that remained fascinating without interruption. The majority was solo, which made it easier to see where certain strengths lie with each of the pupils. Above all else, Audrey Hepburn-Ruston, with her graceful posture and movements, again gave the finest performance of the evening; she seems to be averse to a classicist, which more clearly gives her dance something very special." By now, it wasn't only Audrey with her original choreography earning call-out attention. She shared the press with Irene Grosser, Elisabeth Evers, and Hannie Perk because, said Louis Couturier of the *Courant*, "The Arnhemsche Musiekschool has come into a phase by steady development that has all the signs of a heyday."

Two weeks later the troupe performed again at the Schouwburg in an evening of dance honoring another school in Arnhem. "In the first part of the evening the professional class of the Arnhem Dansschool under the direction of Winja Marova came into the limelight, about which class we have already been writing extensively these days," reported Couturier. "The co-stars—the dames Audrey Hepburn-Ruston, Hannie Perk, Irene Grosser, and Elisabeth Evers—assuredly confirmed the good impression that this class has made in its recent appearances."

Audrey was simply having the time of her life developing dance routines that, with Marova's encouragement, ranged from classical ballet to the realm of interpretive dance.

Even at the age of thirteen she took herself terribly seriously as a dancer. One winter morning after a decent snowfall, Dick Mantel, a neighbor boy from across the street on Rozendaalselaan headed toward a local hill dragging his sled. He spied Audrey, who was a year older, outside and asked her if she wanted to go sled-riding with him and his friend.

Audrey gasped. "Oh, no! I can't risk having something happen to my legs!"

She was still all about dance. Dance allowed her to look past Uncle Otto, Germans, and the lack of food in her stomach. "I wanted to be Margot Fonteyn," she said, "and a choreographer as well, but life happened differently." She continued to shoot up in height now, and her feet were growing. She said, "I was an Amazon. I was taller than most of the boys in my class." As she approached her fourteenth birthday, she had already grown past the ideal height for female European ballet, a hard and fast 165 centimeters or roughly five feet, three inches. At the rate she was growing, she would surpass all limits for serious consideration as a ballerina.

"I never was a raindrop, though I was dying to be," said Audrey. "I was a 'boy.' I had to lift up the little girls because I was so tall." She would always feel this way about herself, conscious of her great height, big hands and feet, flat chest, and awkward facial features. Later in life she would say in frustration, "I didn't just make up my complex!" It had very real roots in her mind.

The dancer had entered into an ugly duckling period, and away from the dance studio and stage of the Schouwburg, she withdrew into an isolation more profound than ever. "I've had a complex all my life about being definitely ugly," she had no trouble admitting to reporters later in life. "I always was improving myself by making the most of myself, experimenting with different makeup and so forth. That was when I was between thirteen and sixteen, an age when you mind so terribly what you look like. I never thought I would succeed." She said she hated her nose and her teeth and, of course, her big hands and feet. She even hated her square, athletic shoulders. "I've always wanted really feminine shoulders that sort of slope down," she lamented.

On another occasion she said, "I didn't think much of my looks. In fact, I thought I was such an ugly thing that no one would ever want me for a wife."

Such ideas had already begun to occupy her thoughts when brother Alex married his girl, Miepje, on 11 June 1943 in a quiet and private civil ceremony. The Dutch were remarkable at carving out time away from the war for events like this one. But in the end they knew that the war must drag them back. A little earlier in the year, General Christiansen, military authority in Holland, had ordered all former members of the Dutch Army to be taken to Germany for factory work—the Green Police were already rounding up young men right and left in Arnhem and sending them away. Alex knew this would happen; he was right to remain in hiding for two years and counting.

In reaction to this order from Christiansen for the men to serve the Reich in German plants, Dutch factory workers decided not to report for work at all; some shops didn't open, and a general strike challenged German authority. In Velp alone the AKU, Thomassen, and Hermes plants located in the south by the River IJssel remained closed. In response Christiansen threatened to have everyone executed who refused to work. When workers dragged their heels, two factory representatives from Velp, Jan Tjalkens and Bartus Pessink, were taken out and shot—among hundreds who were liquidated in the ultimate strike-breaking action.

Great numbers of men in their prime were sent away—all those born in 1921, then 1922 and 1923. As many as possible "dived under" and joined the ranks of the onderduikers who were being sheltered secretly in homes, hospitals, and other buildings across the Netherlands. And every day the actions of the Dutch citizenry were directed by Radio Oranje in London.

Seyss-Inquart saw the possibility that the country he had been ordered to control by Hitler himself might be close to open revolt. "No better acknowledgment could have been desired of the immense influence emanating from London," wrote Dutch historian Louis de Jong, "than the subsequent panicky decree of May 13, 1943, in which Seyss-Inquart confiscated all radio receivers, amplifiers, and other accessories, an estimated total of about one million sets." Only members of the NSB got to keep their radios.

It was likely in this sweep that the baron was betrayed and his radio set confiscated, because soon he was visiting neighbor Jan Mantel—Jan was a radio salesman before the war and had since become a member of the Resistance—to listen to Radio Oranje at eight o'clock every evening. Sometimes Audrey would go with him to the Mantel home, but stay discreetly near the front door watching for the Green Police. Every visit to the Mantels came with a cover story about why any of the van Heemstras would be outside the Beukenhof past curfew. The best excuse of all was the time young Dick Mantel suffered from scarlet fever and a concerned Baron van Heemstra visited him faithfully.

Like a curtain descending, the situation was becoming night-marish. Protestant and Catholic Dutch saw mass deportations of Jews from Arnhem, Velp, and other areas of Gelderland to the Westerbork Transit Camp in the northeast of Holland. It was said that from there, the next stop was the Auschwitz concentration camp. The Protestant and Catholic Dutch citizenry now became horrified observers as their Jewish countrymen and women and their children were rounded up at gunpoint and sent away.

Then there were the barest of glimmers, as when Allied forces invaded Europe in Sicily and then Italy. It was very far away, but still there were now American and British boots on the ground in Europe led by two leaders the Germans seemed to fear: American General Patton and British Field Marshal Montgomery.

Overhead, the American bombers flew on every decent-weath-er day and the British every night. At the end of July, the Tommies hit the northern German city of Hamburg with incendiary bombs in a nighttime raid, and the Americans followed up the next day with general purpose bombs. After repeating the process the next night and day, a firestorm consumed central Hamburg. More than 40,000 Germans died, including 5,000 children.

The Germans had firebombed the Dutch in Rotterdam in May 1940, and now the favor had been returned by the Allies. Dutch-men were now rounded up wholesale and shipped at gunpoint to Germany to act as replacement workers for those killed in Allied bombing raids. Among the masses of Dutchmen rounded up was Audrey's big brother, Ian Quarles van Ufford. "I saw my old-er brother dragged away to a Nazi camp," said Audrey. Ian, now nineteen, eventually ended up in a Berlin munitions factory.

Ella found the toll exacted by the Germans to be much too high. First Otto and the van Heemstra cousin Schimmelpenninck, and now Ian had been removed from the family.

Ella began to look into ways she could contribute to the Dutch Resistance movement, which helped downed Allied fliers to evade capture, conducted acts of sabotage, and sheltered Jews and other onderduikers. But the Resistance members took a wait-and-see position and wondered if Ella's conversion to pro-Oranje was genuine.

Audrey kept her own feelings about her mother's past locked away. Audrey had never been pro-German—their sensibilities had always been foreign to her. She was a little girl when they marched in; she hadn't witnessed her mother's days as a lipstick Nazi. She had seen Herr Oestreich at the apartment many times, but he had never been a friend. All Audrey knew about the Germans was that they caused hunger and grief. They killed people for no reason and left empty spots at the table that would never be filled again. That was the Germany Audrey Hepburn-Ruston knew. She respected and loved her mother, and for as long as Audrey lived she would never be able to come to grips with her mother's political beliefs of before the war and during its early phase. It's possible, even likely, that Audrey and her mother never discussed the issue. It was a part of Audrey's wounded self that she kept hidden during her years as a Hollywood star, not because she feared what such information would do to her career, but because it was family business, her mother's business, and not anyone else's. It was a secret she guarded all her adult life and took with her to the grave.

Through the years, writers covering her noted her private nature. Martin Abramson writing for *Cosmopolitan* in 1955 mentioned "her aloofness toward people she doesn't know." One of her publicists said in 1959, "Interviewers are enchanted with Audrey, as long as the talk is about acting. But when the questions get personal, she changes the subject. Her private life is her own. Period."

One reporter in 1954 during the Broadway run of *Ondine* even brought up with Audrey the subject of "pryers and probers" and how she dealt with them. "It's hard work really," she responded. "Harder than preparing for a play. You keep giving performances all the time." And in 1991 a newspaper reporter called her "fiercely private and shy."

She had good reason to keep her distance from people; she would never change.

Part III: Resistance

13

Soul Sister

New York, New York
2 June 1952

"I didn't know what I was going to read," said Audrey. "I've never been the same again." She had first run into Anne Frank quite by accident in 1946. No, it wasn't an accident, not the way it turned out. It was fate—there was no other explanation—that she and Ella had left Velp and were living in Amsterdam below the apartment of a publishing house employee who was working on this soon-to-be released, strange wartime dagboek of a young Jewish girl. It carried the title Het Achterhuis, translated literally as "the house behind," with an official translation of The Secret Annex. The editor knew of Audrey's wartime experiences and saw some similarities between the manuscript she worked with day by day and what she had heard from the van Heemstras. She said of the manuscript that Audrey "might find it interesting." Oh, that didn't begin to capture the reaction of seventeen-year-old Audrey Hepburn-Ruston to the power of the entries of her contemporary, Anne Frank. They were written in Dutch by Anne to a fictional friend named Kitty.

The Frank family, including Anne's father Otto, mother Edith, and sister Margo, had fled their Frankfurt, Germany, home in 1933 after Hitler's ascension to power. Anne was four years old when the Franks began a new life in Amsterdam. Her father ran a successful business until after the German occupation, and when Margo Frank received a summons to appear before the Nazis in July 1942, the family went into hiding. Anne's diary described their experiences as onderduikers living in a secret part of her father's building from 1942 to '44.

"There were floods of tears," Audrey said of that first encounter with the writing of Anne Frank. "I became hysterical." As a resident of Amsterdam, she had been so moved that she became one of the first pilgrims to Prinsengracht 263 to experience the secret annex. Now here it was, six crazy years later. Audrey no longer lived in a one-room flat in Amsterdam; she had just completed the run of Gigi on Broadway, U.S.A., and now ran around her New York apartment packing for a trip to Rome where she would begin production of William Wyler's Roman Holiday.

This Dutch girl, the one who was a dancer and couldn't act, the one who didn't like her looks, had taken Broadway by storm. Everywhere she went in America, people fell in love with her unusual looks and quiet, humble manner. With the performances, social engagements, interviews, photo shoots, and appearances associated with a successful Broadway show, there would be times her mind shook free of memories of the war. But all that changed in a heartbeat today.

Today she learned that the American edition of Het Achterhuis was about to be released. For U.S. audiences it had been retitled Anne Frank: The Diary of a Young Girl, and former First Lady Eleanor Roosevelt had been so impressed with it that she had agreed to write an introduction that would prepare readers for the impact of what they were about to experience.

Hearing about the release of Anne Frank's diary knocked Audrey for a loop all over again, bringing back all the connections that one teenager's words had made for the other. Audrey and Anne were two dark-haired Dutch girls who had been born in countries other than the Netherlands. They were less than six weeks apart in age—Audrey born 4 May 1929 and Anne 12 June 1929. Ella's birthday was also 12

June. Separated by a distance of just sixty miles, Audrey and Anne had experienced the same war with all its milestones, from German occupation to the battles for Britain and Russia to the bombing of Berlin to D-Day—as followed by both girls with their families on Radio Oranje. They experienced the same Nazis in all their brutality. And Anne had even known of and commented upon the executions in Goirle when she wrote from the Franks' hidden rooms: "Prominent citizens—innocent people—are thrown into prison to await their fate. If the saboteur can't be traced, the Gestapo simply put about five hostages against the wall. Announcements of their deaths appear in the papers frequently. These outrages are described as 'fatal accidents.' Nice people, the Germans! To think that I was once one of them too!"

All any of the van Heemstras could manage in the years after Otto van Limburg Stirum's death was to look straight ahead and never back and to go on living. But here came a thirteen year old forcing Audrey to feel it all again. "If you read the diary," she would say to a reporter later in life, "I've marked one place where she says, 'Five hostages shot today.' That was the day my uncle was shot. And in this child's words I was reading about what was inside me and is still there. It was a catharsis for me. This child who was locked up in four walls had written a full report of everything I'd experienced and felt."

In retrospect Audrey contemplated the fact that she and Anne had entered adolescence as one and experienced the dawn of womanhood. They struggled through changing relationships with parents and felt the sting of strict parental rules. They both loved ballet and there were likely times when they practiced dance at the same moment— Anne quietly to pass time in hiding, Audrey at the Muziekschool. They imagined adulthood together, longed for love, and feared that they would never get the chance to enjoy either as they existed day to endless day in the shadow of the swastika.

Here the parallels stopped. Anne recorded her last entry on 1 August 1944, and three days later the Gestapo and Green Police discovered the Franks and four companions who had lived with them for twenty-five months. All eight were sent to Westerbork and then to Auschwitz, where seven would die. Only Otto Frank, Anne's father, lived to the end of the war.

From the heights of Broadway fame in a New York City apartment, packing fine clothes, pausing to eat any food she desired, Audrey could retrace her steps back to the beginning of August 1944 and what she was doing on those summer days. She had given up dancing by then because the food shortage had become acute, but in general, life was still life. The tram still ran from Velp to Arnhem and the Muziekschool still stood. August was just before the Airborne came and brought the September awfulness, but somehow, while Anne hadn't made it through, Audrey had.

The haunting of Audrey Hepburn by Anne Frank wouldn't end with publication of the diary in America. This slim book would become a best-seller, then a hit Broadway play. The world had become fascinated by the doomed girl; so had Hollywood. In 1958 filmmaker George Stevens would offer Audrey the role of Anne Frank in the film version of her story to be made by Twentieth Century Fox. Audrey was, by this time, one of the most sought-after actresses in Hollywood, and she paused for another read of the diary from cover to cover.

"I was so destroyed by it again that I said I couldn't deal with it," she explained, struggling to put her feelings into words. "It's a little bit as if this had happened to my sister. I couldn't play my sister's life. It's too close, and in a way, she was a soul sister...."

There were too many reasons she couldn't make the film. Audrey always looked younger than her age, yes, but by then she was almost thirty—how could she be asked to play a girl of fifteen? And as tough as she was, she simply couldn't go through the ordeal of the Nazis again—and this time not live to the end. Nor could she dream of taking a salary to portray Anne Frank or participate in a Hollywood production of this of all stories, however well intentioned it would be. There were devastating ironies, like the fact that Anne idolized movie stars from the far-flung dreamland of Hollywood. She pasted their photos clipped from fan magazines on the walls of her room in the secret annex to make life more livable. Anne had remarked that those in hiding with her "never fail to be surprised at how accurately I can list the actors in any given movie, even after a year." And that's just what the other Dutch girl had become—an international movie star. Then for Audrey there was one last unthinkable possibility: What if all this delving into wartime Amsterdam led the press to her mother's story? Or the fact that Audrey had danced for German audiences? Nothing good could come from any of that.

As a courtesy, Audrey agreed to meet Otto Frank and his second wife, Elfriede, in Switzerland—it was Otto who had taken possession of the diary after it was discovered, and it was Otto who worked through his own pain to arrive at a place where he could see his daughter's work as a miracle that could be important to the world. This beautiful, intense man whom Audrey described as having been "purged by fire" looked into her eyes and asked—begged really—for her to agree to portray his daughter in a film. After what she described as "the most wonderful day" and a visit that lasted through lunch and dinner, she had to tell him a sincere and heartfelt "I can't."

Audrey would go on to experience a full life—career, marriages, children, and a fame she never really accepted or understood. Anne had had none of that. Anne's ambition was to survive the war and turn her volumes of diary entries into a book that she herself named Het Achterhuis. She imagined that the book would make her famous, and it did, selling thirty million copies in seventy languages.

Late in her life Audrey would ultimately accept her strange relationship with soul sister Anne Frank and use Anne's words to raise funds for the cause held so close to her heart, UNICEF. In 1990 she took Anne on the road for a series of readings from the diary in four U.S. cities. The needs of the world's children had necessitated that she find the strength to face Anne. "Now, I'm very happy to read her words," said then sixty-year-old Audrey of her lost sister and her immortal writings. "I'm thrilled to do it because I think it's something very important.

They're very deep and they're pure because she was a child and she wrote them from her heart. I think it's a lovely opportunity to relay her thoughts again. Her spirit."

So there Audrey was, swathed in Givenchy and serving as UNICEF's Goodwill Ambassador for these readings that were accompanied by firebrand forty-five-year-old composer Michael Tilson Thomas, who had written music for the passages to be played by his Florida-based New World Symphony Orchestra.

"I was never cut out for public speaking," Audrey said of this tour with Anne Frank. "My mouth gets dry and my hands get clammy. It's exhausting." But she did it, reading among others her very favorite passage, one not about imprisonment or gloom or Nazis, but about life and hope: "I wonder if it's because I haven't been able to poke my nose outside for so long that I've become so crazy for everything to do with nature. Nearly every morning I go to the attic and from my favorite spot on the floor, I look up at the blue sky and the bare chestnut tree on whose branches little raindrops glisten, like silver, and at the seagulls as they glide on the wind. As long as this exists, and I may live to see it—this sunshine, these cloudless skies—as long as this exists, I cannot be unhappy."

Of the magic of these performances Tilson Thomas would say that only Audrey Hepburn could have been his partner on such a journey with Anne because both Dutch girls knew that war, and that Netherlands, and that sisterhood. He said, "To hear the fine delicate phrasing she gives...with the music providing the fabric, it's as if you were listening in to Anne Frank herself." Both Audrey and Michael knew in their hearts that Anne was with them in spirit.

From first reading and through the end of her life, Audrey went day to day with Anne her delicate secret shadow. The knowledge of Anne's life and death took its toll on a woman who had never gotten over the ordeal of the Nazis, the executions, and the Jews, not only in Arnhem and Velp, but across the length and breadth of the Netherlands where all but a fraction of the 105,000 who were sent away had perished. She had been there among them and seen too much with her own eyes, including friends who suddenly, mysteriously disappeared never to be seen again. "I tell you," she said, "all the nightmares I've ever had are mingled with that."

Thinking about the Frank family or any of the Jews in the Netherlands could always produce a shudder and suddenly the years would peel away and there it would unfold, all over again.

14

Just Dutchmen

"I have memories," said Audrey. "More than once I was at the [Arnhem Centraal] station seeing trainloads of Jews being transported, seeing all these faces over the top of the wagon."

It's no coincidence that visits to cemeteries in Arnhem and across Holland reveal many dates of death on tombstones that read 10 May 1940. The day the Germans invaded, distraught Dutch Jews committed suicide because they sensed doom but didn't have the energy or the money or the opportunity to flee their homeland. They saw no way out and for them a future under Nazi occupation meant slow death, so why not spare the torture and end it now?

A report commissioned in 1950 by the Netherlands State Institute for War Documentation noted thirty suicides in The Hague alone, with similar numbers in other cities, towns, and villages across the country. A report in 1946 looking at "the various methods of suicide (or, in the case of young children, of murder) most commonly employed concluded that 'most of these Jews took an overdose of veronal, though gassing, hanging, shooting, wrist slashing, and injections of morphine were also used.'" The report alluded to an "epidemic of suicides."

Jews had been part of the fabric of Dutch society for centuries. Since the reign of Queen Wilhelmina began before the turn of the twentieth century, all faiths were welcome in her realm. Yes, by the mid-1930s she had grown wary of accepting Jews like the Otto Frank family who were fleeing Nazi Germany because she wanted to avoid Hitler's attention. Above all, the neutrality of the Netherlands in the Great War had lulled most Dutchmen into a sense of security that was shattered when the German Sixth Army marched in on 10 May. Those Jews that Audrey had seen trudging along the twin boulevards Jansbinnensingel and Jansbuitensingel that dark day of invasion were heading to port cities where they begged and pleaded to find passage on ships headed to England. Some got out safely; most were turned away and ended up back in their homes because there was nowhere else to go. All attempting to leave the Netherlands had to contend with the fact that they were hemmed in to the north and west by water and to the east by Germany. Escape south into Belgium or southwest into France was impractical because the Nazis were there too. It then became a matter of waiting at home for the inevitable.

To the Nazi occupation government, a Dutch citizen was considered a Jew based on having at least one grandparent who was "known to have been a member or temporary member of the 'Jewish community.'" At first the administration of Seyss-Inquart seemed to be treating the Dutch Jewish population with far more lenience than their counterparts in Germany. Seyss-Inquart was making no reference to Jews, and for a number of months they were considered "just Dutchmen." Yes, as early as July 1940, Jews were forbidden in the Dutch Air Raid Precaution, or ARP, Service. But then life went on as before until October, when Jews were forbidden from all civil service positions. When university professors and their students protested, they too fell under the administration's scrutiny. Soon all businesses had to register whether they had a Jewish owner or partner. The answer to the question "Who is a Jew?" grew much more granular, and all people in this category were recorded. From there, the situation grew increasingly grim. Soon Jews were being openly discriminated against and barred from theaters and other public places.

In February 1941 for the first time, Jews were confronted and beaten on the streets of Amsterdam as they had been for years in Germany. The attacks were organized and carried out by the Dutch SS, known as the WA, and by the NSB, the Dutch Nazis. The reaction by the Dutch mainstream was instant: Citizens on the street defended their Jewish brethren, fighting back and bloodying the attackers. More than bloodying them; the defenders frightened and humiliated the WA and NSB thugs. Hanns Albin Rauter, head of the SS in the Netherlands, responded with furor and unleashed terror raids in Amsterdam that arrested hundreds of Jewish Dutch citizens between the ages of twenty and thirty-five. The Dutch countered with a general strike in support of the city's Jewish population on 25 and 26 February 1941. The ruling authority then dissolved all municipal councils to short-circuit future plans to disrupt public services.

So it escalated through 1941, as the ruthless Rauter worked in concert with Himmler toward the systematic annihilation of the Jews in Holland. In May 1942 it was required that Jews wear the yellow Star of David on clothing. They were forbidden to ride in trains and required to surrender their bicycles and automobiles to limit the ability to travel. Then the registrations of Jewish Dutch from eighteen months earlier were put to use rounding up individuals to be sent as forced labor in work camps and families to be deported at a rate of 600 people per day. It was around this time, July 1942, when the Franks went into hiding in Amsterdam. Audrey had just turned thirteen in Arnhem and the stroll from the apartment on Jansbinnensingel to the Arnhem Centraal Station was just two blocks.

"I'd go to the station with my mother to take a train and I'd see cattle trucks filled with Jews," she said, describing it to a British reporter in 1991 as "the worst kind of horror. I remember, very sharply, one little boy standing with his parents on the platform, very pale, very blond, wearing a coat that was much too big for him, and he stepped on the train. I was a child observing a child. I don't know how much longer it was before we knew what was happening—sooner than you did in Britain. Then I realized what would have happened to him."

In interviews later in life she recalled time and again the horror of what she witnessed in Arnhem: "I saw families with little children, with babies, herded into meat wagons—trains of big wooden vans with just a little slat open at the top and all those faces peering out at you. And on the platform were soldiers herding more Jewish families with their poor little bundles and small children. There would be families together and they would separate them, saying, 'The men go there and the women go there.' Then they would take the babies and put them in another van."

Soon, van Heemstra neighbors and family friends disappeared. Favorite shop owners, musicians in the orchestra, dance students, were now gone. From the summer of 1942 through 1944, more than 97,000 Dutch Jews were shipped to Transit Camp Westerbork seventy miles north of Arnhem. From there 89,000 were sent on to their deaths in Auschwitz or Sobibór in Poland—including Anne Frank, her mother, and sister. From the beginning of the war to the end, almost 105,000 Dutch Jews died at the hands of the Germans.

"Don't discount anything you hear or read about the Nazis," said Audrey. "It was worse than you could ever imagine." What would Otto have thought about the injustice of it all? Of man's inhumanity to man? He had been the eternal optimist, and this was a new and terrible world.

But all was not lost for the Jewish population of the Netherlands. Somewhere around 30,000 Jews became onderduikers, taken in and hidden by the largely Protestant population who shared more than their homes and ever-tightening rations. The daring Dutch also risked machine-gunning if they were found hiding

Jews. In the village of Velp alone, about 600 Jews were onderdui-kers. A few were rooted out and shot or sent to Westerbork, but in the end, most survived thanks in large part to a band of stubborn and ultimately compassionate Dutch civilians who simply wouldn't let the Nazis win.

15

Warmest Praise

Audrey was all about dancing as 1943 wound down. "It's good discipline and sheer drill," she explained of the rigors of ballet. "When you dance you must keep fit—go to bed early, get up early, drill, drill, drill."

She certainly wasn't up on the politics of war, but when she returned home on the tram from Arnhem and the Muziekschool, she couldn't help but learn of the latest bit of intrigue in Velp. Buildings and villas were being confiscated by the Green Police seemingly at random. But there was nothing random about their actions—the SD had moved their national headquarters into the Park Hotel on Hoofdstraat, just four blocks from the Beukenhof. The Germans now expected invasion by Allied armies from England on the coast of France, and were moving their offices inland to the east, closer to Germany. Velp with its beautiful villas and other infrastructure—a sturdy bank, luxury hotels—became a safe harbor for the ruling administration. In short order, Velp, the home of Audrey Hepburn-Ruston and her family, became the most important place to the Nazi occupation government in the entirety of the Netherlands.

Arthur Seyss-Inquart commandeered a home on Parkstraat, the next street over from Rozendaalselaan. Now the number-one Nazi in Holland, the man most responsible for Otto's death, was a neighbor to the van Heemstras just yards away.

Hanns Albin Rauter, the ruthless SS man with the dueling scar, took over one of the finest red brick villas in Arnhem at Velperweg 101, just across the city line from Velp.

Eviction from a home built with loving care after a lifetime of dealings in the East Indies would always begin with a pounding at the door by the Green Police at any hour and then a demand for the departure of the citizens living there. But, oh, by the way, leave your furniture and dishes behind. It was a new sword of Damocles hanging over van Heemstra heads as around them more than a hundred villas were claimed by the occupiers. It became a situation so dire for the population that a new evacuation agency was established in Velp to find housing for those displaced from its finest homes. And every hour the baron, Meisje, Ella, and Audrey feared the dreaded knock on the door of the Beukenhof or a phone call from their landlord, the Reformed Church, to say they must vacate.

German soldiers' pounding at the front door did finally come, but it wasn't to confiscate the structure; it was to place a radio monitoring station in the attic, which meant a steady stream of Wehrmacht soldiers tramping up and down the stairs whenever the need arose.

With so many Germans commandeering seemingly anything of value in the village, Meisje decided to stash Otto's Renault sedan and found help from F.J. "Frits" Besseling, a member of the Resistance who worked at his mother's flower shop on Hoofdstraat. Besseling concealed the Renault in the barn behind his parents' home where this unusual onderduiker remained in safety, hidden under straw.

Just as relentless as the aggressions of the Green Police were the missions of the American Air Forces in the skies above, and by now Fliegerhorst Deelen, the German fighter base just up the road from Velp, scrambled fighters often to intercept American bombers at 20,000 feet. Deelen also launched fighters to go against British formations at night. By late 1943 the daylight hours often featured burning American B-17s and B-24s falling all over the Netherlands from brutal air battles that covered dozens and hundreds of miles. Surviving air crews would abandon their crippled planes by parachute and float to earth to be picked up by the moffen or sheltered by lion-hearted Dutch civilians.

Friday, 19 November, had begun like any other, quiet at first then with the roar of an American formation heard at late morning through low, dense cloud cover. The Allied planes must have been flying directly over Velp because at midday the batteries of big 88mm German anti-aircraft cannon in the entire area began to thunder skyward, aiming at the planes flying over. The Diogenes command bunker at Deelen used radar to track the planes through the clouds and feed coordinates to fire control. Boom-boom-boom went the German guns, punching up through the cloud cover, in a twenty-mile radius of Velp. To ears at the Beukenhof, it was a cacophony like nothing Velp had experienced.

Deelen's fighter aircraft scrambled next and dogfights broke out; it couldn't be seen but it could certainly be heard as high-rpm engines roared, climbed, dove, and fired machine guns above the cloud deck.

Then, the van Heemstras heard a booming explosion nearby. Black smoke wafted skyward just north of the Beukenhof from the direction of Castle Rozendaal. The family's thoughts immediately went to the local kin, the van Pallandts. The Velpsche fire brigade sped north toward the scene, followed shortly by the Arnhemsche fire brigade. The van Heemstras were shocked and saddened to learn that the ancient castle, their favorite destination for day trips, had indeed been hit by an American incendiary bomb, which had been jettisoned by a crippled B-17 heavy bomber that was trying to lighten its load. The German press reported gleefully that the 100-pound bomb fell through the roof of the castle and exploded in living quarters between the main building and coach house. In other words, the Allies were the real enemy here.

By some miracle, Baron and Baroness van Pallandt, their family, and their staff escaped with their lives, but the phosphorus in the bomb ignited centuries-old timber, and up went a large portion of the family's living space along with priceless artwork and mementos. The event reminded all inhabitants of the Beukenhof that no one was safe from the war, even on a day that had started out lazy and quiet.

For the van Heemstras, the Christmas holiday came and went. The baron and Meisje attended services at the Reformed Church in Velp South on Kerkstraat. Ella still practiced Christian Science alongside Audrey in Velp with their friends the Heringas. Said David Heringa, "Her mother the Baroness van Heemstra came to our house in Velp to practice reading the Scriptures and the Science of Health, the Christian Science Bible. She and my mother or father changed being first and second readers."

Churches had become the last refuge for the people of Velp to renew their strength when facing another brutal week, and another winter without enough heat and with a dwindling food supply. There weren't even tires for the bicycles anymore—what bicycles that hadn't been stolen by the Germans, that is. Civilian motor cars were a distant memory by now because there simply wasn't petrol to run them. There hadn't been for a long time.

But for Audrey, through it all, there was still dance, even if the war exacted a running toll. "It was almost impossible to buy tights or slippers," she said. "As long as there were any old sweaters to pull out, my mother would re-knit my tights. Sometimes we were able to buy felt to make slippers, but they never lasted more than two classes."

The slippers and costumes were still performance-grade for events at the Schouwburg. On 8 January 1944 the Dansschool performed its most lavish "dansavond," or dance evening, yet with the star pupils of its professional dance class taking the stage accompanied by the Arnhem Symphony. Winja Marova headlined, performing sections of Grieg's *Peer Gynt Suite*. Audrey soloed the *Danseuse de Delphus* by Debussy, then shared the stage for a Bavarian Rhinelander dance with Elisabeth Evers, the latter aligning with the edict to focus on German culture.

Audrey was given the concluding number of the evening as the lead soloist, dancing to *La Danza* by Rossini. Hannie Perk and Katy de Jongh also earned praise in Louis Couturier's *Courant* review. It was an evening of such popularity that encores of the entire program were held in various venues, including at the Schouwburg on 31 January and again on 14 February.

At one of the performances, the baron had a bouquet of *bloemen* handed to his granddaughter with a card that read, "I want to bestow my warmest praise on Adriaantje, who today performed so poignantly and graciously."

This grand series of encores for the winter recital proved that, despite a late start in dance and her gangly height, Audrey had arrived as a dancer of promise and become an Arnhem celebrity. And yet the war was closing in from all directions, including and now especially from above, and the winter 1944 performances would serve as her last hurrah in the footlights of the Schouwburg for the duration of the occupation.

In the third week of February 1944, the U.S. Eighth Air Force, composed of heavy bombers and the fighters to protect them, found an unusual stretch of good winter weather over Europe and launched Operation Argument, an attempt to knock out the German aviation industry. Before the Allies could invade Hitler's "Fortress Europe," they had to neutralize the Luftwaffe, and a week was devoted to the task of sending hundreds of bombers against the German aircraft-manufacturing industry. On 20 February the target was the German city of Brunswick. That morning, anti-aircraft batteries again opened up. In a country as flat as the Netherlands, with wide-open skies overhead, the anti-aircraft shells booming up from the ground and bursting high in the sky among the seemingly endless procession of bombers produced a terrifying spectacle. Debris from the exploded shells rained down on Velp and its citizens for hours.

Two days later on 22 February, Allied fighters staged attacks on the German anti-aircraft cannon in the area. Bombs and rockets deluged Arnhem, and more fell to the south in Nijmegen, where fires blazed and black smoke rose so high in the sky it was visible in Velp at a distance of ten miles. Civilians simply weren't used to bombs so close, but as Audrey had said, the war had to draw nearer before it could end.

Following the attacks on Arnhem and Nijmegen on 24 February and again the next day, Dutch skies bulged with American bombers aimed at the city of Gotha in central Germany. What went on in the skies over Velp on these two days was like nothing the citizenry had ever seen. Four miles straight up, a deadly dance played out as German fighters faced hundreds of American heavy bombers and their fighter escorts. The skies blazed fire and smoke as the big German flak guns, those that survived the attacks to destroy them, thumped over and over and their shells exploded among the bomber formations. Then, as soon as the cannon fell silent, German fighters swooped in by the dozens and aerial combat raged. Planes exploded or tumbled from the sky in flames. Parachutes brought survivors to earth, and the Germans rushed in to offer aid to their own pilots and capture the enemy as they hit the ground.

But some Allied fliers were helped to evade capture by members of the Resistance, which had a strong presence in Velp located right under the noses of the Nazis. With so many powerful representatives of the Reich gathered in the village, the local Resistance grew just as fervent, and Velp's hospital, het Ziekenhuis, became de facto Resistance headquarters. The two-story, eighty-bed facility sat on Tramstraat, just three blocks from the Beukenhof—which for the van Heemstras involved a five-minute walk directly past Seyss-Inquart's villa.

"The mafia had nothing on the doctors of Velp," kidded Ben van Griethuysen, whose father, Bernhard, served as a radiologist at the Ziekenhuis and also worked at St. Elisabeth's Hospital in Arnhem. "They all knew each other very well and kept each other's secrets." And those secrets on behalf of the Resistance were legion. Dr. Willem Portheine was hiding a small Jewish boy and shuttling other Jews to and from his home, as did Dr. Vince Haag.

Elly Röder-Op te Winkel, daughter of Dr. Wim Op te Winkel, said, "In our home [at Hoofdstraat 7A] were about thirteen Jews and other onderduikers hiding for a shorter or longer period. And our neighbors were members of the SS and SD!"

In fact, all the doctors on staff at the Ziekenhuis were aiding Velp's sizable onderduiker population. "All doctors hid Jews in their homes," said Velpsche historian Gety Hengeveld-de Jong. "The Jews—from Amsterdam, Rotterdam, etc.—were brought by the Resistance to het Ziekenhuis Velp and from there the doctors took them in their cars to their own homes and later to different families in Velp."

Dr. Adriaan van der Willigen Jr., served as chief of staff at the hospital and also a key member of the Resistance. Perhaps the most energetic of the physicians working for the Resistance in Velp was thirty-nine-year-old Dr. Hendrik Visser 't Hooft, who lived in the shadow of the hospital with his wife, Wilhelmine, and four children in a beautiful early nineteenth century villa called de Leeuwen-hoek. The doctor had been a silver-medalist field hockey player for the Netherlands at the 1928 Amsterdam Summer Olympic Games and now used his extensive network of connections reaching out through Gelderland in service of the local Resistance movement.

"He was a charming and good-looking person, a sportsman, hockey, skating, etc., and he was a reliable doctor," said one of his former patients, Rosemarie Kamphuisen. "As children we loved him and called him 'Uncle Doctor.' When we were ill, even with a high fever, we looked forward to his visits and made drawings for him."

Among his myriad duties, which spanned the length and breadth of Velp, Dr. Visser 't Hooft served as *de huisarts van de Pallandts*—visiting doctor to Baron van Pallandt, his wife, and their adult children at Castle Rozendaal. With their kin and frequent guests the van Heemstras so close by, it was natural that connections would be made between the baron, Meisje, Ella, Audrey, and Dr. Visser 't Hooft.

By this point in the war, the young doctor worked every waking moment. He practiced at an office in his home as well as at the hospital. He also made house calls and his wife, Wilhelmine, helped him keep track of appointments. But she also helped him with a variety of other tasks, some of them menial. Wilhelmine's responsibilities also included four children as well as family and patients who shuttled into and out of their home on a regular basis—every time the doctor offered shelter to someone displaced or in trouble. Both the Visser 't Hoofts needed another set of arms and legs in his practice. Given the situation, he asked one of the few people in Velp possessing the vitality to keep up with him, Audrey, for some assistance.

The offer by a key Resistance man in the village demonstrated just how much Ella's sympathies had changed during the course of the war. Dr. Visser 't Hooft likely would have used his contacts to research the van Heemstras, and the intelligence must have come back favorable. At the beginning, Audrey's role meant only handling the most menial assignments, which would free up the doctor to better serve his many patients. She had her career to think about after all, as her training continued at the Dansschool under the tutelage of Marova.

Audrey turned fifteen on 4 May 1944 and faced pressure to

register as a member of the Dans Kultuurkamer with its deep ties to the Reich. "You had to be a member of that Chamber in order to study," said Audrey. "A good Dutchman simply was not."

Ella and Audrey together faced the inevitability that, for the moment at least, she must give up dance because she must *not* obtain a Kultuurkamer card. Ella could reason with her daughter that the war couldn't last much longer, and once it ended Audrey could resume her training with Marova. Ella knew it was past time for both mother and daughter to sever their ties to the Arnhem cultural scene. Louis Lieftinck, director of the employment office in Arnhem and a member of the NSB, had been appointed as an honorary member of the board of directors of the Muziekschool. There was nothing honorary about the appointment, and with this move the Nazi grip on the arts in Arnhem became complete. Rather than sit at a table with an NSBer, the entire board resigned in protest, Ella included, and her final tie to Arnhem, which she had kept in support of Audrey's career, was severed.

It seemed, according to the BBC and Radio Oranje, that the Germans would be out of power any time now and that Allied victory was inevitable—if, said Queen Wilhelmina, every freedom-loving Dutch man and woman continued to fight. And, true enough, the bombers kept flying over, and kept on, and kept on. Almost every day, hundreds passed by at a time. At night, similar RAF bomber formations made a ghostly noise to break the silence of the late hours.

"As we heard the allied bombers roaring overhead every night bound for Berlin," said Audrey, "I could not help but think of my brother...though of course I knew the bombers were bringing the end of the war nearer." Ella and Audrey had heard nothing from Ian other than a message that he was in or near Berlin working at a munitions factory.

The question on everyone's lips remained: When will the Allies invade northern Europe? The Allied landings in Italy had come to nothing, and they were stalemated on "the boot." The occupation of the Netherlands couldn't possibly be broken without an invasion in France because, despite the bombing campaign and devastation of German civilian centers, manufacturing in the Reich had continued, and more tanks and planes than ever were rolling off the assembly lines. Allied bombing had only stiffened the resolve of the Germans, just as had happened for the population of London and, for that matter, for the Dutch after Rotterdam.

Yes, the war dragged on. Day by endless day the nutritional needs of the fighting men of the German war machine were ravaging the civilian population of the Netherlands. Too many vital nutrients had been extracted from the food supply and diverted to German forces; the store shelves had become too empty; animal proteins were nowhere to be found; and a dancer's muscles could endure it no longer.

The usual description of Audrey at this time: She was "tall and skinny, with big hands and feet." Said Marova of her star pupil, "She didn't get the right nutrition, and she fell apart. I agreed with her mother that she should stop dancing temporarily." It was just as well because she couldn't perform publicly anyway unless she agreed to join the Kultuurkamer. True enough, Audrey could keep dancing in Velp at the studio of Johnny van Rosmalen just down the street from the Beukenhof, but there was no substitute for the brilliance of Marova and the resources of the Muziekschool.

With time on her hands, Audrey began giving public dance lessons to local children in Velp at the Netherlands Hervormd Vereniging, or N.H.V., a church building on Stationsstraat that also served as the local civic auditorium. "I wanted to start dancing again," she said, "so the village carpenter put up a barre in one of the rooms. It had a marble floor. I gave classes for all ages, and I accepted what was about a dime a lesson. We worked to a gramophone wound by hand."

One of her former pupils described Audrey as "very serious for her age, and she really tried to make something out of the lessons."

Annemarth Visser 't Hooft became one of Audrey's students at age eight, and said, "There are two ways to teach ballet. One is doing all the pliés and classical movements, and the other is, when it's ballet with children, looking at their way of movement, taking that up, and making a ballet out of it. She was good in that, but she also introduced the basic steps."

Audrey would say with pride in the 1950s that, "Some of the pupils still correspond, and they always say they don't know what they would have done without the school. Everyone was made to keep his mind off things. You have to remember that there were no parties, no radios, no new books. I don't suppose it taught me much as a dancer, but it taught me a great deal about people and work."

She also booked some more expensive private lessons for the children of prominent families, including Hesje van Hall, who lived in Het Witte Huis on Biesdelselaan in Velp. Hesje's older brother Willem certainly noticed Audrey, who had just turned fifteen. "I was beginning adolescence and sometimes opened the door and took her coat," he said. "Audrey had a very interesting look back then. When she came in, the house suddenly seemed completely different. She was very slender and walked so gracefully." This way that she could cross a room as if gliding, with the gait unique to ballerinas, had drawn the attention of Edouard Scheidius, a young Arnhem attorney and friend of Marova. His nickname for Audrey was *Poezepas*, or cat-walk.

Audrey devoted part of her week to volunteer work for Dr. Visser 't Hooft and also provided dance lessons as May, a beautiful month in the Netherlands, gave way to June. Then, on the morning of 6 June, the BBC broadcast an urgent bulletin that ended a year of expectation among the oppressed and the occupiers: The Allied invasion of Fortress Europe had begun! The beaches of France had been stormed at Normandy by the largest fleet of sailing vessels ever assembled! Thousands of Allied troops from a multinational force were trying to establish a foothold and facing fierce resistance!

The day passed with agonizing slowness across the Netherlands. By nightfall it could be reported that the boots of the liberators held firm in northern Europe. Men and supplies of the liberation army began flowing into France, and the Germans rushed troops west to beat back the Allied attack in desperate combat that sprawled across the French countryside.

In the ensuing weeks, thousands of Allied soldiers died in an attempt to move inland. During the long back-and-forth series of battles for France, word came that Hitler's own generals had tried to kill him at the Wolf's Lair in East Prussia on 20 July and that he had barely survived the attempt. Supporters of the House of Oranje—ninety percent of the Dutch population—rejoiced at this new sign that the Reich was finally showing signs that it might crumble.

In August after a long stalemate, Allied armies under Patton and Montgomery punched through the German lines and began gobbling up great parcels of French territory. An entire German army was cut off and captured at the Falaise Gap south of the city of Caen.

It seemed to the people of the Netherlands that everything was going remarkably well, and Ella wasn't wrong: The war might soon be over. Little did anyone at the Beukenhof know just how incorrect she was; the people of Arnhem and Velp were about to learn the cruelest possible lessons about the art of war. Quite simply, their world was about to explode.

16

Black Evenings

"Food started getting scarcer and scarcer and scarcer," said Audrey. "We ran out of everything. Holland had no imports or exports. It was just a closed country. And, of course, the German army took the best of everything."

Expectation hung in the air of Gelderland in August 1944. Some units of the German army that had been mauled in the Soviet Union were transferred to the new western front to fight the American and British armies pouring into the heartland of France from the Normandy beaches in the north. Activities by the Dutch Resistance picked up as Oranje Dutch—those loyal to the royal family—began to entertain the idea that one of these days, their country would be liberated. Why not help the situation along where possible?

Through the summer, Audrey's work for Dr. Visser 't Hooft, including tours of duty in the Ziekenhuis working directly under the head nurse, Sister van Zwol, brought the Dutch teenager closer to the web of Resistance activities by necessity—the Velpsche doctors working inside the hospital were key to many anti-German efforts, from forging identity documents to facilitating the movement of onderduikers. The hospital became the obvious center for their activities. It was the place where they could talk in safety, and where their imaging equipment—key to document forging—was located.

"The Velp Hospital...was a very important central institution," said Velp resident Rosemarie Kamphuisen, "not only for the inhabitants [of the village], but also for the doctors who met each other after their visits practically every day."

These physicians were members of the Landelijke Organisatie Voor Hulp Aan Onderduikers, the L.O., one of four Resistance groups active in the Netherlands by the summer of 1944. At this point in the war, all the Jews in Velp had been "dealt with," all but those who had gone into hiding. The great number of onderduikers hidden across the village, about 600 Jews plus many others like Audrey's brother Alex who were hiding for different reasons, served as evidence of the sophistication of the L.O. enterprise supervised by Dr. Visser 't Hooft and his colleagues.

The doctor for whom Audrey volunteered was quite a swashbuckling character. Earlier in the war, the car he kept hidden in the village had been "betrayed"—an informant had told the Germans about it, leading to confiscation. Somehow he managed to obtain a German motorcycle for transportation, possibly from the black market—a doctor on foot in an area serving several thousand people wouldn't be effective. One day his ten-year-old daughter Clan stood in front of their house as her father returned home. "He came into the driveway, and I was standing there," she recalled. "And he put this running motorcycle in my hands and ran off. And I thought, 'What's going on?' A few seconds later, a German patrol came into the driveway to arrest him. And he was gone. And I stood there with this running motorcycle. I didn't know what to do with it."

Her enterprising father had earlier cut an escape hole in the iron fence around the family property for just such an occasion, and within minutes of his encounter with Clan, he had hopped a train out of town. He was confident that the Germans wouldn't harm a ten year old; they would have been satisfied with the confiscation of a motorcycle that a Dutchman had no business possessing. The simple fact was, the Germans walked a fine line with the physicians of Velp—every doctor in wartime was a vital resource, so gazes were averted from some basic transgressions by Visser 't Hooft, like motorcycle stealing.

Ironically, not long after this incident, the doctor was summoned to the villa on Parkstraat of none other than Seyss-Inquart, who was suffering some ailment. A key member of the Resistance in Velp now faced the moral dilemma of treating his bitter enemy, knowing that if he didn't, his family might suffer. He also had to wonder if he might be walking into a trap. What did he decide to do? "He went," said Clan with a shrug. And it wasn't a trap.

Biographers and many Dutch who lived through the war have doubted the participation of a young Audrey Hepburn in work for the Resistance, saying, "She was just a girl. What could she possibly have done?" But as she was under the influence of such an enterprising and patriotic character as Visser 't Hooft, the many stories she told about her activities in the war become highly plausible.

First and foremost, with the encouragement of the doctor for whom she volunteered, she could dance. Audrey's celebrity as a dancer for nearly four years at the Schouwburg made her talents valuable to Dr. Visser 't Hooft and the Resistance for illegal musical performances at various by-invitation-only locations. These events, called the *zwarte avonden*, or "black evenings," had first been introduced by musicians as a way to earn money after they had been forced out of the Dutch mainstream by the Kultuurkamer. Soon the zwarte avonden were helping to raise funds in support of those sheltering the tens of thousands of onderduikers hiding across the Netherlands—including those in Velp. They were known as black evenings because windows were blacked out or darkened so the Germans didn't know of the activities going on inside.

The first documented involvement of the van Heemstras with the zwarte avonden took place on 23 April 1944 when at least one van Heemstra, and likely both Ella and Audrey, attended an illegal performance, their family name listed among those present. From that point on, Audrey wanted to participate.

By this time she, like most Dutch young people, was already suffering symptoms of malnutrition, yet still she danced. "I was quite able to perform and it was some way in which I could make some kind of contribution," she said.

In another interview Audrey said: "I did indeed give various underground concerts to raise money for the Dutch Resistance movement. I danced at recitals, designing the dances myself. I had a friend who played the piano and my mother made the costumes. They were very amateurish attempts, but nevertheless at the time, when there was very little entertainment, it amused people and gave them an opportunity to get together and spend a pleasant afternoon listening to music and seeing my humble attempts. The recitals were given in houses with windows and doors closed, and no one knew they were going on. Afterwards, money was collected and given to the Dutch Underground."

Many of the events in which Audrey performed were staged in the home of homeopathic physician Dr. Jacobus T. Wouters, who lived in a large villa at the corner of Ringallee and Bosweg in Velp, not far from the home of the van Heemstras. Wouters wasn't a member of Velp's inner circle of physicians, but his willingness to host a series of black evenings proved his patriotism. Ella also hosted at least one illegal black evening at the Beukenhof, during which her daughter danced.

The Resistance events were high risk, with danger always present. "Guards were posted outside to let us know when Germans approached," said Audrey, who reported that "the best audiences I ever had made not a single sound at the end of my performance."

They had reason to be cautious because lives depended upon

it. Evil lurked in Velp. It had arrived with top Nazis like Seyss-In-quart and Rauter and the basing of national SD operations inside the Park Hotel. Audrey passed close by this evil in downtown Velp one day, and what she heard stayed with her for the remainder of her life. She was walking with her mother along Hoofdstraat past the Hotel Naeff. At the intersection with Vijverlaan, just four blocks from the Beukenhof, they waited for traffic to clear by the venerable Rotterdamsche Bank, a brick and stone building with a turret on the corner. Audrey looked up at the bank, the city's most solid structure, which the Dutch security police had comman-deered to hold political prisoners. She said she heard "the most awful sounds coming out of this building. It was then explained to me [by my mother] that it was a prison and perhaps people were being tortured. Those are things you don't forget."

By now, every life in Velp had been affected, if not outright ruined or taken away, by the German or Dutch Nazis. Village doc-tors enjoyed some degree of immunity, but not so the local reli-gious leaders. Pastor J.A. Schaars of the Catholic Church, one of the most charismatic men in Velp, had been arrested in 1942 and was now in a concentration camp. Reverand Adriaan Oskamp of the Reformed Church was also arrested and sent to a camp. Fa-ther J.H. Campman, who had worked tirelessly for the Resistance until he was captured, died in a concentration camp. These were the village leaders, and all had been forced out by the Germans—which only spurred on the activities of Dr. Visser 't Hooft and his companions in the L.O.

One of their most important efforts arose out of the air war and the Allied bombing campaign against Germany that was bringing down so many heavy bombers and their crews over Holland. The Velpsche L.O. helped many American and British fliers to evade capture as they went "on the lam," armed only with a service .45 and an escape kit that contained a silk map of Europe, a translation card of key Dutch and German phrases, and some Dutch coins.

Upon landing, if he didn't break a leg or a back, each individual airman was responsible for avoiding capture. The Dutch Resistance did what it could to keep the airmen, most of them aged nineteen or twenty, hidden from the Germans. If all went well, they would be delivered into the Dutch Resistance network and spirited south over the "Freedom Trail" through the Pyrenees Mountains and into northern Spain.

In a 1951 interview with Sidney Fields of the *New York Daily Mirror*, Audrey tossed off the fact that her role with the Resistance had included "running around with food for the pilots," referencing the Allied airmen shot down over the Netherlands during the 1944 bombing campaign and hidden by the Resistance in and around the village before being moved south. Dr. Visser 't Hooft sent her at one point during this period to take a message, and perhaps food, to one of the downed fliers. Her qualifications were simple: She spoke English fluently whereas other young people within easy reach in the village did not. Many versions of the story exist, a story that originated with Audrey herself when she told it to American writer Anita Loos. The most reasonable interpretation is that as a fifteen year old—still young enough to be deemed "safe" by the German Green Police—she sought out this flier, likely a fighter-pilot who had been shot down and now hid in the woodlands just north of Velp. He must have been quite close to the village because the Germans decreed that no civilians could trespass in the forests of the Veluwe, which lay just beyond Rozendaal. The reason: Deelen Air Base sprawled across the edge of the Veluwe north of Arnhem and Velp. For any Dutch civilian, venturing near this complex meant death, so Audrey must have been closer to Velp when she made contact with the fugitive.

By this point in the war, hundreds of Allied airmen had been shot down over the Netherlands, mostly from B-17 or B-24 heavy bombers on their way to or from Germany. Audrey, through her work for Dr. Visser 't Hooft, would have been at least vaguely aware of the activities of the local Resistance to funnel these fliers south through local towns and cities to Belgium, where they would be handed off to the underground network.* Her task here and now, completed in mere minutes, helped to keep that machinery running.

After delivering the message to the flier successfully—*Go to this place, say these words, and the people will help you*—she saw Green Police approaching. Another fifteen year old might have crumbled at this moment. Not the Dutch girl; not the dancer with the iron will and self-discipline to fight to the top of Arnhem ballet. Audrey kept her wits and began picking wildflowers in the rough countryside. When the Germans in the green uniforms reached her, she remained silent and sweetly presented her flowers to them. After the soldiers checked her Ausweis, she was allowed to pass.

Something along these lines must have taken place because Audrey described the events—British man in forest, message delivered, flowers given to soldier.

"Every loyal Dutch schoolgirl and boy did their little bit to help," said Audrey. "Many were much more courageous than I was."

But it seemed to Ella that the situation was becoming more dangerous by the day. As August 1944 wore on, she put a plan in action to take Audrey from Velp and move farther west, away from the German border. The Hague seemed like a good place to relocate. There were many van Heemstras there and perhaps they were better connected to the black market. Maybe they could help Audrey put on some weight and regain her health; maybe there was even a way for Audrey to return to dance in another part of Holland. Who could say in wartime what was the best decision? But Ella's gut continued to tell her: It's time to go.

---

*See the story of Clem Leone of the 445th Bomb Group in *Mission: Jimmy Stewart and the Fight for Europe.*

17

Het Vaderland

"I don't think you ever forget anything, totally," said Audrey in May 1990 as UNICEF's ambassador. "But life, and especially time, gives you a way to deal with it, to live with it. I have a good cry every so often, like everyone else."

The inhabitants of the Beukenhof arose on 15 August 1944 to a somber anniversary: It had been two years since the murders of Otto, Schimmelpenninck, and the others in the forests of Goirle at the hands of the oppressor. Two years! How could it be so long already since this optimistic, loving, and jovial man had been alive and enriching all around him?

Late in the morning they heard the drone of heavy bombers on their way to Germany, except this time there was something different about that sound. Nothing one could quite put into words, but, different. Hearts of all, including Audrey, must have skipped a beat when the air-raid siren began to wail in Arnhem and then the siren in Velp. Distant muffled thumps signaled anti-aircraft cannon shooting at something in the sky. Thump-thump-thump went the guns on the ground with supreme energy. The first deep booms that answered from the planes overhead rattled the floor underneath their feet, and then came a furious chorus of explosions—detonations as constant as pounding on a kettle drum. It was a few miles off and so the van Heemstras and their neighbors ventured outside to see what went on.

The group wandered to an open spot of sky away from the cover of the beech trees, and the day's action became apparent: Formations of Allied bombers were releasing their deadly loads on the Deelen Air Base just over the high ground to the northwest, up in the Veluwe. The pounding went on for a quarter hour as the orderly, dark-colored dots in the sky, American Flying Fortresses and Liberators, flew through clouds of exploding flak and released bomb loads on their target. All the while, swooping and swarming groups of Allied fighter planes glided by in formations of four over and under the bombers to engage the German fighters that had been launched from Deelen before the pounding began.

Dogfights broke out between British Spitfires and Focke-Wulf 190s, and they chased each other up and down across the blue summer sky. A puff of smoke meant a plane had been hit, and the viewers murmured or gasped and a parachute would or would not appear. Life and death came that fast up there in the topaz blue.

It was fascinating spectacle. And then came the rain—bits of metal and gunpowder fell onto the spectators from the heavenly battle, gritty remnants of the flak bursts that had been sizzling hot way up there and by now had cooled and become souvenirs for the children. All the young ones stood mesmerized at the magnificent air ballet without quite understanding that boys of eighteen and twenty and twenty-two were living and praying and dying high above.

To the adult Velpenaren, the weight of the world pressed down or was lifted, depending on one's loyalties. The NSBers—the German lovers—understood that this strike on Deelen meant the vault of safety they had lived within for four years was finally threatening to collapse. For the Oranje Dutch it meant liberation in the air, literally in the air above, dreamed of for so long and a possibility since D-Day. For those who were once pro-German and now the opposite, like Ella, standing there watching history in the sky over

Deelen meant siding with the only possible future she could enjoy with her children. The time of the Germans was ending; the time of the Allies was still to come.

On 26 and 27 August the bombers returned and hit Deelen again. The first time it had been big four-engine planes with heavy bombs to plow up the runways. These new attacks were made by nimble medium bombers and fighter planes with rockets to target the barracks and hangars that had been so cleverly disguised as Dutch farm buildings. For so long that ruse had worked but today it didn't matter. Up went everything the British pilots could see.

By the end of August 1944, it had become clear to Ella that she must implement her plan to spirit Audrey away from Velp. The war was closing in fast. It could be seen growing closer every day in the form of German soldiers meandering up Hoofdstraat from Arnhem and on toward the German border forty miles farther on. The moffen came with shoulders slumped under the burden of their equipment and the oppression of an enemy army that had come ashore in Normandy and fought like tigers every day ever since. It had been relentless. Many of these men had faced the Russians, and they never expected an enemy as ferocious in the west. The Führer had said the Americans were soft, that they couldn't fight—well, that Patton fellow was dangerous.

The Germans were trudging up over the Arnhem Road Bridge from Nijmegen and points south, their only thought to get away from the mighty, well-equipped, and growing forces that had pushed them out of France. The drivers of half-tracks and tanks coming up from Arnhem had adopted the annoying habit of turning left off Hoofdstraat and parking under the protective cover of the magnificent shade trees of Rozendaalselaan. There the Germans would rest and picnic. These drivers knew that under such cover the "hunters"—as Dutch civilians called Allied fighter planes—could not see them. Word got passed south down the line that Rozendaalselaan was the safest street between Arnhem and the German border. It also happened to be home of the van Heemstras.

Velp had become, by the end of August, a Wehrmacht hive buzzing with activity. German soldiers swarmed the Hotel Naeff and overran the garden restaurant. All the cafes and restaurants in town served only Germans these days. And it wasn't just in Velp. Of course they had overwhelmed Arnhem. In Oosterbeek Germans had long ago commandeered the Hotel Schoonoord, but now word had it that the high command had taken over the Hotel Tafelberg, and their support staff had snapped up all the rooms in the nearby Hotel Hartenstein. It was suddenly a good time not to be living in Oosterbeek as Opa once had, in that beautiful villa on Pietersbergseweg that Audrey still remembered from her time there as a six and seven year old. Now the entire area from Oosterbeek east through Arnhem to Velp had become the Wehrmacht base of operations.

There were German regular army soldiers everywhere—desperate, hungry, tired, and scared soldiers so unlike those square-shouldered lads who had marched in on 10 May 1940. They had been a sight to behold, and how could Ella not think back on the glorious Parteitag at Nuremberg in 1935? But most of the 1940 bunch that had rolled through the Netherlands had died in the Soviet Union, and the troops of August-going-on-September '44 were mere shadows of the glory days. There were older men and younger boys, and they retreated on foot, on stolen Dutch bicycles, hitching rides in horse-drawn carts and on tanks and trucks. Any way to put distance between themselves and the advancing Allies seemed to be a good way. They looked so weary, in some cases dragging their weapons, in others carrying no weapons at all.

Whatever control Ella had had over life within occupation in earlier times—back when the German officers kept control of all their subordinates and thereby kept mother and daughter safe—was now gone. At the Beukenhof, with only the baron and Meisje and Audrey living there and with Germans traipsing up to the top floor and their radio set, who and what was to stop those soldiers parked on Rozendaalselaan from pushing their way in and taking what they wanted? No one in the Reich command would know or care at this point. With her perfect ear for German, Ella heard the grim tone of the conversations of those soldiers: The western front was collapsing. The high command was a bunch of fools. There was nothing to return to at home because the bombing day and night had left Germany a wasteland. These men were fighting now only for each other and their own survival. They appeared to be a mob and anything might happen.

Ella knew that Audrey had experienced too much already, and Ella dared not imagine Audrey touched by a German soldier.

"I was awfully young," Audrey would remember later. "I was younger than most fifteen year olds mentally, if you like. I was brought up that way. I wasn't exposed the way young people are today. I had a totally different background. I was very young in my behavior."

It was a good thing now that Audrey had stopped attending Marova's classes. How could Ella have allowed her daughter to make the commute by tram under these conditions when it couldn't possibly be safe? Nothing was safe these days. No one and nothing.

Some families in Velp and Arnhem were packing up their key belongings, filling bottles with water, squirreling away a little food, getting ready for a hasty escape because of the attention British and American fighter planes would be giving to that writhing, snaking German column of beaten men that grew ever longer.

At the end of August Ella sent off wording for a newspaper advertisement that ran on Saturday, 2 September, as a boxed classified in The Hague's German-controlled newspaper, *Het Vaderland*. Under the heading "Twee Ruime ZIT SLAAPKAMERS," the ad asked for two bedrooms preferably with sitting rooms in the banking district of The Hague for a woman with daughter. The contact information read: E. Baroness van Heemstra, Rozendaalselaan 32, Velp.

Why did Ella run this ad with her father and sister settled in the quiet and out of the way village that had been spared any ground fighting? And why now? Ella had a feeling, a very strong feeling, that she should take Audrey and go. She was an intuitive woman and she believed in signs, in gut feelings, in magic, and in what even then was called the supernatural. Every instinct told her that something bad was coming and that she shouldn't waste a single moment. If they were going to escape, now was the time.

18

If, If, If

The German high command didn't really *believe* any longer. Honestly, how could they? The Führer was a wreck of a man, deafened, crippled, and scarred emotionally from the assassination attempt led by a battle-hardened nobleman, Colonel von Stauffenberg. After the 20 July bombing at the Wolf's Lair in Prussia, Hitler had become obsessed with loyalty from his generals at the expense of what was happening in his two-front war. Worse, he had long ago shown himself to be, at heart, a corporal, a battlefield message carrier, and not a military strategist. After the recent purge of "traitors" that had cost so many lives in high command, morale among the officer corps had hit bottom. It didn't benefit any German general to maintain friendships in times like these, and yet they did. Many of these men went back decades with one another, and they were human after all. Friends were friends. Many, perhaps most, of the high-ranking officers knew the end was near and came to the realization that now, they were fighting for their country, and for each other, and to the devil with Hitler.

Here it was September. France and Belgium had been lost, and Field Marshal Walter Model studied his maps on a table in his headquarters at the Hotel Tafelberg. Out his window he could see wooded, quiet, elegant Oosterbeek. He had chosen the Tafelberg over other hotels in the resort village because its tree cover would keep any snooping Allied reconnaissance planes away.

Model controlled a large portion of the men on the western front, and from his Oosterbeek headquarters he could follow the retreat of German forces that had been mauled across a broad front. He figured that here in the eastern Netherlands a good ways from the front, he could establish a rallying point. Among the units needing a rest were the 9th and 10th SS Panzer Divisions under the command of Gen. Wilhelm Bittrich. These battle groups had fought valiantly at several key points in Normandy and helped to stem the tide of the invading 2nd Army. There wasn't much left of either unit now, with both divisions seeing 16,000 men whittled down to about 6,000 in the past couple months. His once mighty tank column was now down to about thirty of the big tanks in all, many of them the biggest of all, the Tiger. After the tanks rolled into the Arnhem area from the front lines, the idea was to send some tanks back to Germany for refitting and keep some near Arnhem so they could head south to tangle again with the Allied 2nd Army along the border with Belgium.

Arnhem was the perfect spot for the German army to lick its wounds. Arnhem sat far from the front and yet only forty miles from the German border, with solid rail lines and excellent security under Arnhem's city commander, Generalmajor Friedrich Kussin, and his efficient security force. The citizens were docile and their Resistance units amateurish, meaning that sabotage of his tanks or the murder of his men simply didn't concern Bittrich. Here they could get some sleep, take a bath, and live off the fat of the land courtesy of the many farms in the area.

By the second week in September, Bittrich had placed his tanks and personnel, including the grenadiers, outside Arnhem in the pretty little village of Velp and beyond, keeping them out of sight from the damned British fighter planes constantly snooping around and shooting at anything that moved. Bittrich figured if Velp was good enough for Reichskomissar Seyss-Inquart and SS man Rauter, it would do for weary Panzer troops.

The situation really did look bleak to Model and Bittrich, and the conclusion inevitable except for the intervention of some sort of miracle. Perhaps Hitler's secret weapons could snatch victory from defeat. The jet fighter-bomber held such promise, as did the V2 rocket. If only both could be produced in sufficient quantities and deployed at once, the strategic advantages of the enemy might be checked.

If, if, if: Playing that game only led to frustration because the key ingredient remained a man at the top with skill and cunning, and that simply wasn't the Führer. Maybe at one time, six or eight years ago, but not anymore.

Ah well, the end wasn't coming today or tomorrow. There was time yet, and the job remained the job, to do the best with what was on hand and pull the occasional rabbit out of the odd hat. Both Model and Bittrich were very good at these things, and what better place to sit back and do a little relaxing than Arnhem, with its rolling hills so uncharacteristic of flat, waterlogged Holland. Arnhem had a zoo, an open-air museum, cinemas, restaurants, a city theater, and the Wehrmachtheim, a grand old concert hall. Maybe they could treat the staff to a ballet—just the tonic for men who had seen too much suffering and too much death, men who had earned a respite. Just a little one. A few weeks of peace and quiet; was that so much to ask?

19

The Hun on the Run

The world had just seen the passing of the fifth anniversary of war—five long years since Hitler had ordered blitzkrieg on Poland. The German Reich was being squeezed by the Russians from the east and the Brits and Americans from the west. Dutch Resistance reports said the dispirited German soldiers that were trudging north over the Arnhem Road Bridge and up Hoofdstraat—the men Audrey and Ella saw pass by every day—no longer wished to fight. But Eisenhower, the Supreme Allied Commander, knew the Germans hadn't quit. In fact, they had dug in across the southern border of the Netherlands with Belgium, along the east-west Meuse-Escaut Canal.

It was the Netherlands that would become the next battleground, and that was a problem because this was a watery country with many rivers to cross. Eisenhower's army couldn't move through it if the Germans were to destroy the bridges across the Maas, Waal, and Rhine rivers. They might also blow up key dikes and flood major sections of roadway, which would trap his forces for months. But British Field Marshal Montgomery had an idea to change the game in the west, an idea that, if successful, could bring the war to a close by Christmas and get the Yanks and Brits to Berlin before the Russians. Why not load crack American and British paratroopers onto transport planes and drop them behind enemy lines at all the key bridges in the Netherlands? Use surprise to capture and hold all these bridges while the Allied Army under the command of Monty himself marched up through the Netherlands to the last and most important bridge of all, the span over the Rhine at Arnhem—right by the Muziekschool and the villa and girls school of Cornelia, Countess van Limburg Stirum.

The British paratroopers dropped on Arnhem would face nothing more than some Green Police and barracks troops that had grown fat and lazy in the restaurants of the city center. They would simply capture and hold the bridge and wait for Monty and the British 2nd Army to come rolling in from the south. Montgomery assured Eisenhower the armored column could make seventy miles in two days, but Lt. Gen. Frederick Browning, who was also in command of the British 1st Airborne, the paratroopers that would take Arnhem, offered the opinion that he thought his men might hold the Arnhem Road Bridge for a few days if necessary, then paused and added, "But I think we might be going a bridge too far." To Browning it seemed especially ambitious to try to capture four major bridges spanning the Netherlands in forty-eight hours, as if there were no Germans along the way at all.

There were so many risks with the plan, which was designated as Operation Market Garden, that any one of them could have merited second thoughts. By their nature, paratroopers traveled light and wouldn't have the support of tanks or heavy cannon. But Montgomery said their invasion would be so "rapid and violent" that they wouldn't need heavy equipment.

Other risks involved getting 35,000 American and British jumpers into planes and over their drop zones. There simply weren't enough planes in England for that number, so the planes would have to make drops spread out over three days to get all the men in. And at Arnhem, there was no good spot near the bridge for the parachutists and gliders to land. They'd have to come down nine miles from the bridge and make their way on foot.

But it would be all right. Arnhem was such a lovely, quiet city that had been spared during the war to a remarkable degree. The Germans didn't pay it particular mind and except for the Deelen Air Base, which had been neutralized, Arnhem didn't have a significant military presence. Montgomery saw his plan as a cakewalk, a nearly bloodless operation, and a dagger through the heart of the Reich.

Part IV:
The Liberators

20

The Netherlands in Five Days

Oosterbeek, the Netherlands
5 November 1954

International movie star Audrey Hepburn and her new husband, American actor Mel Ferrer, neared the end of a whirlwind Dutch tour. They had wed six weeks earlier in Switzerland, and after the crush of the Dutch press these past few days and the unending adoration aimed squarely at Audrey—with reporters and photographers all but pushing the tall Ferrer out of the way to get to his wife—the honeymoon was just as over as the tour.

Audrey had returned to the Netherlands to raise money for the Dutch Association of Military War Victims and had been run to exhaustion. She suspected she was pregnant, which she longed to be, and she and Mel had ripped through public appearances in major Dutch cities in which she urged her countrymen and women to donate for war relief. Along the way she had for the first time seen evidence of the heights she had achieved, as in the Amsterdam department store where thousands of fans of the Roman Holiday princess, mostly teen-aged girls, had stormed security lines and instilled fear for her safety that Audrey hadn't known since the war. In The Hague she managed to carve out a forty-minute visit with her opa, the baron, and his second wife, Mevrouw Anna Roosenburg. It was a crime to spend so little time with Opa after spending so very much—and depending on his calm maturity—through the last and most horrible year of the war.

This Friday morning she had visited a rehabilitation center in Doorn and offered each of the 225 young war victims a warm smile and simple, heartfelt words. She also had taken a one-hour tour of the facility to learn about the latest rehabilitation methods being employed and had made it a point to speak to every doctor, nurse, and administrator at the facility, telling them that she had come "to convey the gratitude of the Dutch people, who have a great respect for you." In total she had shaken 250 hands.

After a drive east and a quick lunch, they reached the outskirts of quaint old Oosterbeek. In a moment their limousine glided to a stop opposite the Hotel Hartenstein, a gleaming ivory building behind expansive lawns that represented the best that this resort village had to offer. Across the street from the Hartenstein stood a tall obelisk in a landscaped circle: the Airborne Memorial. A group of silent, well-dressed people awaited Audrey and Mel there. The couple carried a black wreath down a long path of cut stones, the only sound the clicking of their heels along the way. They set the wreath at the base of the monument. Each said a prayer, shook the hands of the dignitaries, and walked back.

The limousine drove them down into the center of Oosterbeek, which still showed some pockmarked villas, vacant lots, and broken trees to serve as reminders of the nightmare of September '44. Their car swooped to a stop in front of Villa Maria, the Monné home at Utrechtseweg 136. Audrey and Mel rushed in past an iron fence still riddled with bullet holes for a quick hug and kiss for Dr. and Mevrouw Monné, for Miepje, Alex's wife, and her two children. Alex was conducting business in Indonesia, but Audrey insisted that they stop and see her sister-in-law, the last of her relatives still in the area. Then the celebrities rushed back to their limo so it could zoom through a moment of countryside before reaching dear old battered Arnhem. They passed St. Elisabeth's Hospital in a blur and shot down the hill past the train station and through the streets she knew so well in a lightning tour of ten minutes. There, the Schouwburg, unchanged from her last performance in February of '44, now appeared small and sad after all she had seen of the world. There, the red brick apartment building on Jansbinnensingel and the third-story window that had been her perch to watch the Germans march in almost fifteen years earlier. Over there, the Musis Sacrum where she had first danced in public—long ago its name had been changed back from the Wehrmachtheim.

Arnhem was no longer a dead city, thank God. It had been cleaned up if not rebuilt, and she noted that the debris and the wrecked buildings had all been removed. She used to know every street and interesting building; now she looked upon a weed-covered expanse of flat nothingness in what had been Arnhem Centraal with only the odd building standing alone. They were all that remained of grand old Arnhem. In the pit of her stomach at times like these was the horrible old awfulness—memories of a blood-red sky.

In a flash they were off on a mad dash to reach Schiphol Airport in Amsterdam in time to catch a plane for Rome. During the walk to their gate, one of a group of reporters asked Audrey for a few minutes' chat to get her impressions after five days in the country that had once been hers.

"Naturally," said Audrey with a smile.

Ferrer had her at the elbow. "No you don't," he snarled, patience shot. "They've gotten enough." As he pulled her away from the press she gave a gesture of "I wish I could help," and a resigned smile. Then, one last obstacle stood before the six-foot-three actor and his five-seven wife: a three-foot nothing Dutch girl, age four, in traditional Volendam costume. She held tightly to an Edam cheese that covered her entire chest; it was all she could handle.

Audrey began to bend down to greet the child, and Mel stepped between them to disrupt the cameramen poised to capture the sweet moment. Audrey reached around her husband to lightly take the cheese from the Dutch girl and thank her with a smile, just as Mel *pulled his bride up the steps of the plane. "Bye!" she called back, waving to the small crowd gathered to gawk one last moment at an international movie star. "Bye!" She was practically Dorothy, ready to be yanked by balloon out of Oz.*

Every moment Audrey carried with her the understanding that her mother didn't like Mel. In fact, she loathed him for stealing Audrey away and taking over her life. Ella didn't hold back about it either; she told Audrey exactly how she felt and exactly what she didn't like about the man, which was everything. There Audrey was, caught in the middle. She knew Mel worshiped her and, oh, how she had longed for a man to make her the center of his universe. He was eleven years older, and she found that dreadfully important because it meant he was mature and worldly, but mother didn't like the fact that he had been three times divorced. She thought him a cad, like Ruston. The truth was that Audrey adored Mel for so many reasons, even though he could be intense and impatient, like now at the airport.

As she stepped into the cabin of the airliner, her feet were once again off Dutch soil. In her wake she had raised enough money to buy a seventeen-hectare parcel of land in Doorn that would see construction of twelve bungalows for handicapped war victims.

The wealthy, award-winning, married, and probably pregnant twenty-five year old settled into her seat and in a half hour watched the flat and green countryside recede beneath her. These days she could flit so easily from Switzerland to the Netherlands to Italy and then the United States. But the pregnancies of the coming several years, beginning with this one, would each end in miscarriage and cause deep depression and what seemed a bottomless well of grief.

Then there was that other sadness, the one that went wherever she did, always and forever. The war was her constant companion; she said so herself in many ways. And chief among the memories for Audrey and anyone else who had lived through it was that bright blue September day, a Sunday, when it all began, and the days that followed.

21

Ultimatum

"It was the war, and the war diet, and the anxiety and the terror," said Audrey of the ever-worsening situation under the Nazis in Velp.

As August turned to September 1944, the people of Velp heard Radio Oranje report that the shooting war was out there. Among the Dutch, illegal radios had been treasured and kept safe, and daily the baron, sometimes with Audrey, would hurry across the street to the home of the Mantels for the 8:00 P.M. fifteen-minute Radio Oranje update of the Allied dash across France into Belgium. Now, the reports said the British and American armies had set up camp just across the Dutch border to the south, a mere seventy-five miles away. And when the Brits and the Yanks marched north and ran headlong into all the Germans in Oosterbeek, Arnhem, and Velp, life would not be pleasant.

Ella had had her gut feeling long before she had done the arithmetic—all those Allied troops out there plus all these Germans around here equaled trouble. Ella knew she must think about life after the war and away from those who knew her here in the early days of occupation. It might have seemed logical to take Audrey to Amsterdam, center of cultural activities in the country; then after the war, probably London. She would go wherever Audrey's dance career dictated. She would live for Audrey.

But instead of Amsterdam, she had chosen The Hague. Said Dutch historical researcher Maddie van Leenders: "Ella and her family had some connections to The Hague that might have made her desire to move there more explainable. For example, Ella lived in The Hague for a while after she married her first husband, Hendrik Quarles van Ufford, and before they set off for the Dutch Indies. They lived on the Koningin Sophiestraat 4. Besides, The Hague has always been a city that was ruled by old, noble families, as in the Golden Age. When you enter the name 'van Heemstra' in the digital pedigree system of the [municipal] archive, about 157 results pop up. I don't know how they are exactly related to the baron or Ella, but it shows that there have always been some connections between the city and this noble family. In addition, The Hague was a more thriving city than Arnhem, and the Dutch government has always been established there."

The same day that Ella's classified ad appeared, 2 September, Seyss-Inquart read reports of the Allied army poised to strike north from Belgium into the Netherlands and saw the need to order all German Nazi civilians living and working in Holland to return to the sanctuary of Germany. The order terrified the NSB Dutch living in Arnhem and Velp and all across the country; these Nazi loyalists knew they would be arrested by the Oranje Dutch or worse if the Allies seized control of Gelderland. Those with the means packed up and headed east in case the Allies were to suddenly appear and unleash Dutch nationalism that had been heating up like a covered kettle in the past couple of years.

Three evenings after the "rooms wanted" ad ran in *Het Vaderland* came something that would be known in the Netherlands as *Dolle Dinsdag*, "Mad Tuesday," when rumors shot along the countryside and waterways that the Allies had blown through the German front line at the Belgian border and were rushing northward into the Netherlands. The baron brought this incredible news home to the Beukenhof, and it seemed to be true since the flow of

Germans through town had become a sudden flood, with weary, beaten soldiers stopping only long enough to loot some homes and steal what they could before they moved on. At times, gridlock occurred as thoroughfares crowded by Germans and every manner of escaping vehicle exceeded capacity.

But the euphoria of Dolle Dinsdag faded in succeeding days as no liberators appeared, and then the radio confirmed that the Allied ground forces remained stuck way down at the border of Holland and Belgium. Liberation remained a long way away.

Hoofdstraat in the center of Velp resembled a major European city, so crowded were the streets and sidewalks. Mother and daughter listened to a new sound, the Hawker Typhoon, a speedy British fighter plane that had been boasted of on the BBC. By this time every Dutch man, woman, and child knew the sound of each type of aircraft engine. They knew instantly what the Allied fighter planes sounded like, what was a Spitfire, Thunderbolt, or Lightning, and what was a German Focke-Wulf 190, Messerschmitt Bf-109, or Junkers 88. The Typhoon had a high and deadly buzz-saw growl about it. And Audrey didn't find it a comforting sound, as it was the Allied planes that dealt death in Velp, the Tommies mostly, attacking moving trains or trucks or tanks riding along Dutch streets, and God help any Velpenaren who happened to get in the way. The Germans even put up propaganda posters about it around Velp. The poster showed bombs raining down from the skies with the words in red, *van je vrienden*—from your "friends" the Allies.

On 9 September, a Saturday, British planes strafed a train and ammunition dump in Wolfheze, nine miles to the west just past Oosterbeek. Both the train and munitions went up in explosions that boomed for an hour within easy earshot of Velp.

But even though the air attacks were increasing by the day and the Americans and Brits ruled the skies with no German fighter planes seen anywhere, the German retreat seemed to have stopped. German troops were gathering around Velp. Ella knew who they were because she remembered them well: They were Waffen SS from the Panzer Corps. Lots of them suddenly appeared in the village. Gaunt, stone-faced, battle-scorched men lazed about on Rozendaalselaan. They sat and talked, smoked cigarettes, ate food that the Dutch could only dream about, and enjoyed the renowned shade trees, their tanks, cannon, and half-tracks dented and bullet-riddled from combat in Normandy. The worst thing about them—they weren't passing through. They were said to be gathering in Arnhem, digging in north of Velp, and requisitioning buildings and villas in town and up by the Burgers' Zoo and Openlucht Museum, and east in Rheden and beyond, all along the IJssel.

Word had it there were at least a dozen tanks of the II SS Panzer Corps in the Arnhem-Velp area—Audrey had seen a number of them parked in front of the Beukenhof before they rolled up the boulevard and into the woodlands.

There was a hint of autumn—*herfst* as the Dutch called it—in the air with cool evenings and a touch of orange in the edges of the leaves on the trees. The breezes carried conversations among the Germans of the Panzer Corps to Ella's ears as they discussed the joy of being in a peaceful place after the hell of their time in Normandy.

But the word *peace* uttered by anyone threatened bad luck, and sure enough, on 10 September the gun emplacements in Westervoort just to the south hit an Allied fighter plane that Audrey heard screaming overhead just before it exploded into houses on the Kerkallee, the street just a few blocks to the south past the railroad tracks. Five Dutch civilians were killed.

Then came yet another new worry. On the evening of Saturday, 16 September, after dark the Dutch Resistance set off a bomb that damaged a railway viaduct between Arnhem and Velp. It seemed to be just another random event in a series of random events—Deelen bombed repeatedly, Spitfires buzzing overhead as if looking for something, and now an act of sabotage by the Resistance. If only Audrey had known what was to come, that the events weren't random at all. Even Dr. Visser 't Hooft and the L.O. with all their connections had no idea about the bomb this evening or the plans for tomorrow. But really, what could they have done about it? There was nothing the civilians could do now as, far away in England, the Allies were setting their sights on Arnhem. No, the Dutch could do nothing but risk some precious plastic explosives to blow up the odd rail line. It was likely the Resistance arm known as the L.K.P., the Landelijke Knokploeg, the local saboteurs, that had set that bomb, and they wouldn't dream of letting the L.O. know about it. Such operations were need-to-know only.

Locals awoke on Sunday morning to learn that the Germans had reacted as the Germans always did, with posters nailed to the message boards of Arnhem, Velp, Apeldoorn, and other towns in the area: The saboteurs involved in this cowardly bombing must present themselves at Utrechtseweg 53 in Arnhem—the notorious headquarters of the SD—by this afternoon, or hostages would be chosen at random and shot. The pronouncement iced the blood in the veins of the women of the Beukenhof as it brought back those August days and the death of Otto, and Audrey could but sit alone and wonder: Would Opa be next?

The inhabitants of the Beukenhof had spent a restless Saturday night worrying about sabotage and reprisal. All Velp remained on edge through Sunday morning because the saboteurs did not surrender themselves. But the baron was not one for worry. All along he had remained civil to the German officers who tried to befriend him. He collected stamps, and so did they. So few gentlemanly pastimes remained in this violent world; surely the mutual love of collectible postage stamps that he shared with the Wehrmacht men must shield him from harm, mustn't it? No, of course not, because decisions on this scale were political and not based on who was friends with whom. They came from Seyss-Inquart himself, based on how the wind was blowing. Or they came from General

Christiansen, of whom Seyss-Inquart said, "We got along together very well in our work," or from the most evil decision maker of all, Rauter. Any attempt to arrest the baron would come out of the blue with a knock at the door, and so the logical thing was for him to go underground at once—the very last course of action the baron would ever consider.

The baron was above all a practical man and it was Sunday morning, which meant they must all dress for church. With thoughts of reprisals and death in the air, they pulled on their worship clothes not knowing that life for the village and for the country would change in an hour and never be the same again.

22

The Devil's Picnic

"There was a sudden, terrible noise," said Audrey. "Everything seemed to become a burning mass."

Despite the German ultimatum, the morning of 17 September had progressed like any other Sunday with the mostly Calvinist churches of Gelderland filled. But nothing would be usual in just a little while. This account by Greta Stephany from Wolfheze, the next village over from Oosterbeek, typified what Dutch civilians around Arnhem experienced this particular morning. "That Sunday we were in church," said Greta. "We started hearing noises above us, like planes shooting at each other, and flying low. We knew that meant we had to find shelter, but the minister kept preaching as usual. People became restless and there was lots of whispering. Then, all of a sudden, we heard bombs falling. Everybody got up and started running outside, to our homes and safety...."

Low-level Allied air attacks were taking place all over the area, from Wolfheze to Velp and beyond, causing people to spill out of churches to find cover. Near some houses of worship, the ground rattled and people toppled off their feet. The concussion accompanying the explosions wrenched breath from bodies and blew in precious stained glass.

Twin-engine B-26 Marauder and Mosquito bombers had come calling to hit German barracks, air defense cannons, and ammunition stores. The big Wehrmacht barracks across the street from Arnhem Centraal Station went up in a mushroom cloud. The Wehrmacht building and ammo dump in Wolfheze shot sky high.

Anti-aircraft batteries all about, in Arnhem, up by Deelen, in Wolfheze, and in Westervoort, answered the attack, only to come under fire themselves from British fighter planes guarding the bombers. The Nazi defense cannons in all the local Dutch towns sent shells continuously skyward. Every second the thump-thump-thump of the cannons could be heard, with flak bursts plainly visible above Velp as German shells exploded in the western sky. The Arnhem tableau as seen from Hoofdstraat looking west seemed like angry bees swarming around a picnic as the Marauders and Typhoons swooped and dove and climbed and circled, and British Mosquito fighter-bombers joined the attack in formations of six. Dozens of fast-moving dots filled the sky. Smoke rose from several places to the west, and heaven help the poor Arnhemsche civilians caught in so many deadly transactions. Audrey could only try to plot the location of the Dansschool in relation to the black smoke and fret over the safety of her ballet friends and their families and especially Mistress Marova in what had suddenly become the devil's own inferno. The sight of the columns of smoke billowing up from Arnhem in this moment simply terrified her.

The action over Arnhem continued from late morning into early afternoon. The poor place took such a pounding, and the air smelled of sulfur and burning wood.

Just when it seemed Audrey's village would be spared, the Velpsche air-raid siren sounded. The van Heemstras sought shelter in the small cellar under the kitchen in the rear of the villa. Down the baron shepherded his daughters and granddaughter. Audrey's ears were filled with the sounds of the alarm and then with the roar of Allied planes buzzing above the treetops of town.

Very close by, the Velp anti-aircraft battery opened up and cannons boomed every second. Then came the suspended moment when they knew the eye of the storm had found them, with the planes directly overhead and ready to drop their bombs. The air-raid siren had fallen silent and no one so much as breathed. All that could be heard now were aircraft motors and the occasional purring of German-made Spandau machine guns pointed skyward. Did the men in the planes know about the radio station upstairs? Would they go after that? There! There! The whistle of falling bombs! The four van Heemstras could but cover heads with arms and pray. *Onze Vader die in de hemel zijt...*

Explosions began to sound close by—much closer than Arnhem. The Beukenhof's walls and floor joists above their heads shook. The Allied planes must be going after the cannons down below Willemstraat. That was just a little ways off, across the railroad tracks in South Velp. More and more death rained down. How long did the attack continue? It seemed like hours but was only minutes, and then all grew quiet again. The van Heemstras allowed themselves a breath, but in their minds they wondered how many innocent Dutch didn't have any breath left at all. What would they find outside? In a village like Velp, everyone knew everyone and every structure was dear.

The air-raid siren sounded all clear and the four of them trooped upstairs and outside, where the clanging bells of the fire brigade testified that Velp had new troubles. All along the street, neighbors could be seen creeping out of the shadows in a day that had begun with worship until the air had been fouled by the arrival of war. Warily, homeowners inspected rooflines for damage and walls for bullet holes, while the German soldiers occupying the town had a very different reaction and could be seen running in all directions. German officers barked commands randomly, and on Hoofdstraat army vehicles sped along in both directions as if not knowing which way was best but understanding that a moving vehicle was harder to hit. Some of these machines careened by the Beukenhof and sped north in the direction of Rozendaal.

Sure enough, down toward the main thoroughfare past the activity of the Germans, black smoke billowed up with fury over the rooftops of the business district and into the hazy blue afternoon. It was unspeakable, unthinkable—innocent Velpenaren losing their homes and their lives just for being in the wrong place at the wrong moment, because they had been unlucky enough to see the Germans wheel an anti-aircraft battery into their neighborhood.

The van Heemstras' first impulse was to help, whether that meant fighting the fire or bandaging survivors or heading to the Ziekenhuis to offer aid there. By the time they reached Hoofd-straat, word had spread that a number of Dutch had indeed been killed down past Willemstraat, with many more wounded and several houses destroyed. But before the baron or Ella could decide what should be done in the way of helping victims, a new, deep, and foreboding sound could be heard off to the west. More planes were coming. Many, many more. The four van Heemstras turned to head for home, but shouts and pointing made them stop. Many in the neighborhood climbed onto their roofs to see over the tree line. Off to the west amid the rising columns of dirty brown and black smoke from Arnhem and the villages beyond, those in the streets beheld a breathtaking sight. Orderly formations of dots had appeared on the horizon, planes flying in rank and file and not terribly high. Then, oh! Something new—something spilling out of the planes filling the midday blue.

Fourteen-year-old Dick Mantel, Audrey's neighbor across the street, stood on his roof to get a view of what was going on in the western sky.

"Parachutes!" someone called with excitement. Parachutes? It took a moment and the people of Velp realized all of a sudden: Invasion! Allied invasion! Shouts of joy filled the air as, at long last, liberation was at hand. Their saviors would not be plodding along on the ground from the Belgian border to the south; they would drop from the heavens by act of God. Of course—deliverance on a Sunday!

Planes, planes, and more planes appeared on the horizon, some of them banking grandly as if part of an aerial ballet and easing into a landing somewhere west of Arnhem and Oosterbeek. So many parachutes! Hundreds, thousands maybe. Surely it would be enough to drive out the "rot moffen"—those hated Germans. Everyone wept from a wellspring of tears, years of them.

In Oosterbeek Kate ter Horst lived near the Old Church—a thousand years old—and watched the spectacle up close. "We can see the large bombers approaching from the west in marvelous formations," she wrote in her diary. "They seem to be towing something behind them; planes but without landing wheels, flat underneath and very long. Oh! They're coming down. Do you see that?"

Soon thousands of paratroopers of the British 1st Airborne spilled out of the gliders and unhooked from their parachutes. Green-clad Tommies in steel-pot helmets or red berets, each carrying everything they would need for a mission of short duration, began forming up into their units in the farm fields and then hurrying east looking for the roads to Oosterbeek. Just as British scouts had predicted, there wasn't much German activity near the landing zones, so maybe this would be a cakewalk after all.

A few miles away, the German command reacted to the invasion with veteran calm, although nobody quite knew why the Allies had chosen Arnhem for an attack. There had been no intelligence this might happen. Seyss-Inquart and Rauter imagined they might be the targets, so both packed up and headed east toward the German border. The Dutch SS commanders at the Hotel Naeff, located a few blocks from Audrey and the Beukenhof, knew they possessed years of top-secret documents recording actions that in no way aligned with the 1929 Geneva Conventions. As soon as parachutes filled the air off to the west, they decided there wasn't time to move their records out of harm's way. They doused everything with petrol and set the venerable hotel ablaze, loaded into staff cars, and evacuated.

Even a battle-tough Wehrmacht man like Field Marshal Model at the Tafelberg watched with mouth agape at the enormity of the parachute drop. He knew he was dealing with at least a division's strength of enemy troops and got on the phone at once. His calls to German units in the area and then a series of visits in his staff car set in motion a critical response. Then, he packed up his headquarters and headed out of Oosterbeek.

Just east in Velp, the air-raid siren sounded again, yanking the Rozendaalselaan neighbors back into the moment. It was past time for the van Heemstras to retreat once more to the cellar as Allied fighter planes could be heard again roaming over the treetops, and German cannons thudded and now frantic bursts of machine-gun fire joined the chorus. No one among the civilians could make sense of where the liberators were or where a battle might take place. All they could do was sit underground and wait.

By now the British paratroopers had started the journey toward Arnhem and made good progress eastward into Oosterbeek. They'd been able to bring some light jeeps on the gliders to carry machine guns, ammunition, and other equipment. Cheering Dutch citizens saw them coming and lined the streets as if viewing a parade, some waving Dutch flags grabbed from hiding, others sporting the Oranje armbands of the Dutch Resistance.

A young local girl remarked to herself that "a lot of the soldiers seemed small, with their squat helmets and laden with equipment. It is a memory I shall never forget, all those men...."

Capt. Tony Frank of Frost's battalion was impressed by "the incredible number of orange flowers or handkerchiefs that suddenly appeared like magic. The Dutch were very much in family groups, in staid clothing, out on this fine Sunday afternoon."

September blooms were presented to Lt. Col. John Frost, commanding officer of the British 2nd Parachute Battalion. Bread and fruit were offered to his 500 men as they passed single file—

wine, champagne, and everything else the ecstatic Dutch could find, especially flowers since the marigolds were in bloom.

Frost, a relaxed officer except in combat situations when he became a tiger, was a stern-looking man with a moustache surrounded by an oval face. He had already seen a lot of action in this war, enough to make him pass sharp orders now to ignore the adulation and by no means consume any alcohol! Yes the locals meant well, but distractions just now could be lethal.

He hurried his men eastward along the narrow little road designated by his commanding officer for the advance to the bridge. This road with an unpronounceable Dutch name a mile long—Benedendorpsweg, which meant Lower Village Road—snaked along the southern edge of this place called Oosterbeek that was as colorful and tidy as a picture postcard, with lush greenery and stone fences near the road, and old, well-kept houses with steep-sloping tile or thatched roofs. The men were conscious of their equipment, canteens, mess kits, weapons, shovels, and ammunition all clanking with every step, and their hobnail boots clomped like horse's hooves on the cobblestones of the street.

Frost wasn't enamored of this plan to drop his men nine miles from the main objective, the Arnhem Road Bridge, because it meant troops scattered all over the place in unfamiliar country, and they would be vulnerable to ambush. But there just wasn't a place closer to the bridge to bring in all the gliders and equipment. His column moved eastward into the dusk in enemy territory as fast as they dared. Up ahead on the right Frost found a landmark on his map: the ancient Protestant church called, fittingly enough, *de Oude Kerk*—the Old Church. He knew nothing of the van Heemstras or their patronage of this fine building in the 1930s. Frost cared only for the fact he was on course and making good progress toward Arnhem.

Two of Oosterbeek's leading citizens, Jan ter Horst and his wife, Kate, learned of the approach of Englishmen: "We rush out of the garden on to the road," said Kate. "Yes, there is the impossible, incredible truth. Our unknown British liberators, like a long green serpent, are approaching one by one, a couple of yards between each of them; the first gives us a jolly laugh from under his helmet...."

A short while later, Frost heard machine-gun fire to the north a ways and the explosions of grenades. He knew some of his mates had found the enemy and feared the Germans would soon run into his lonely single-file column. Frost had but one thought now as the sun set in the western sky behind him: He must reach downtown Arnhem and capture the road and railway bridges over the Rhine. He could see them occasionally up ahead, a tantalizing glimpse here and there as the road twisted and turned.

After what seemed like a lifetime of tense footsteps, off to the right Frost saw his first objective: the railroad bridge over the Rhine that he must capture intact. Once he had done this, his men could race over it and his unit would capture both ends of the Arnhem Road Bridge at once before the Germans understood or responded. He knew that if he didn't take the bridges, the whole grand operation involving 30,000 American and British troops could collapse. He would be answerable at that point, if he happened to live, to Field Marshal Montgomery himself.

More than six miles to the northeast, Audrey, Ella, and Meisje huddled in the cellar with Opa as explosions sounded in the distance. The bulb in the ceiling joists that lit the enclosure flickered, went dark, lighted again, and then died, and they sat in darkness. As planes roared overhead and cannon boomed trying to knock those planes down, bombs began to fall once again, and the van Heemstras could but muse that just this morning they had fretted for the Baron's life with the clock ticking on the German ultimatum for saboteurs to surrender themselves. With just a couple of hours to spare the Allied planes and paratroopers had arrived to save the day for many Dutch civilians. But such was the grim humor of this war that Dutch lives saved from a firing squad were taken by Allied bombs instead. Most likely the very last thing on the minds of the Germans this evening, as they fought to maintain their hold on Gelderland, was an act of sabotage at a lonely viaduct that had injured no one.

Now, in the dim light of evening, the van Heemstras had no electric service and ate by the glow of candles from supplies grabbed on the way down the steps. In the far distance they could hear the staccato beats of machine-gun fire, punctuated every so often by rifle shots and the heavier boom of an exploding grenade. It all sounded so angry, so deadly. There were shouts from the street, always in German, directing traffic and ordering faster movement. *Schnell! Schnell!* The desperation of the Germans revealed itself to the cellar dwellers by the speed of the trucks and tanks zooming down toward the Velperweg to join the battle, and those frequent shouts and raised voices and sharp exchanges of conversation.

Such a strange feeling to have Allied soldiers on the same parcel of earth, practically in the neighborhood. They weren't in planes flying high overhead on daily missions to bomb Germany; they were real foot soldiers close by and paying attention to Arnhem! Ella could but wish that she had received an offer in response to the classified advertisement in The Hague, but time had run out all too fast. And here she and Audrey sat in the one place they couldn't afford to be. The battle for Arnhem, the battle to free the people of the Netherlands, had begun.

23

Cakewalk

As a Hollywood star shining bright in early 1954, Audrey would sum up her little corner of the war very simply: "Arnhem took a bit of everything—the bombs, then the occupation, and finally the Airborne." The entirety of her description of the experience of Operation Market Garden would be summed up in two words: the Airborne—the British division of 10,000 men, nicknamed "Red Devils," who had been assigned the task of dropping near Arnhem and capturing the bridge. They dressed in drab green uniforms with a red Pegasus emblem on their shoulders, and those that didn't wear helmets sported red berets. They were bright, cheerful chaps despite the dirty work assigned to them. As would-be liberators, they marched into the hearts of the people of Gelderland in these few days, no matter how many civilians were killed, or homes destroyed, or lives disrupted. They were the Tommies, the liberators, and they captured Audrey's heart the same as everyone else's.

The man who would become the most famous of the liberators at Arnhem, Colonel Frost, kept leading his men on in the twilight. The shooting to the north had swept the locals off the streets and safely inside where they belonged. This was deadly business and finally the welcoming civilians had come to understand that. As Frost's serpentine column neared the railroad bridge, he received a report that his men had captured it intact. Then, BOOM! The southern end of the span went up with a heavy charge of German-laid dynamite. Frost could see his treasured objective shoot skyward in a terrific explosion heard for miles around, at which point he understood that the report of its capture was "a little premature." The Jerries had blown it at the very last instant—if they couldn't have it, no one would.

There was no course of action now but to keep moving on to the all-important main objective, the Arnhem Road Bridge, less than three miles farther on. Frost ordered his men along, burdened as they were by all their equipment. It was clear now that the enemy was close, and sure enough, in another moment the shooting began. Many of his men were hit but Frost kept them going and knew from constant study of his maps in recent days that he had entered Arnhem, which he confirmed when up to his left he could see a long, impressive, three-story building he knew to be St. Elisabeth's Hospital. By now he had the bridge in view ahead.

The Tommies clomped onto the streets of the city center and soon they stood at the deck of the bridge they had come to capture. Frost could see some buildings on the far side of the ramp leading off the bridge. There was a big white villa with the name de Nijenburgh at the top, a school with the name van Limburg Stirum, and a third building painted red. Past these three structures stood some sort of music academy. Off to the left, according to the map, was a theater called the Schouwburg. Frost couldn't know that all these structures were important to the history of a family called van Heemstra. The schoolhouse in the middle was the pride and joy of Cornelia, Countess van Limburg Stirum. On one side was her home, and on the other the villa that had been Baron van Heemstra's home for the entire time he had served as mayor of the city. Now it was painted red and served as a second school building.

Across the street from Countess van Limburg Stirum's villa lived twenty-two-year-old Piet Hoefsloot, who heard rumors of invasion and, anticipating trouble, had led his big family to the cellar of their row house. He was among the first Dutch to see Frost's men arrive at their prize, the bridge. "Late in the evening…," said Hoefsloot, "we saw the first English soldiers who were walking directly opposite our house on the far side of the boulevard to the van Limburg Stirum School. Immediately afterwards, we heard that the necessary windows were being smashed open."

It was almost dark now. As one of Frost's men put it, "The CO arrived and seemed extremely happy, making cracks about everyone's nerves being jumpy."

Yes, Frost was elated "to see that big bridge still intact and our soldiers getting on to it," he said, "not blown in their faces like the railway bridge." He looked about him at a number of beautiful homes and buildings near the northern end of the bridge and chose those to be occupied by his men. Among them was an office building that became his headquarters and the sturdy van Limburg Stirum School across the bridge ramp. There was no better place to set up anti-tank weapons and machine guns than the windows of that school.

Hunkered in another building near the bridge was Wilhelmina Schouten, a language teacher. "Someone opened the front door," she wrote in her diary, "and within a moment the ground floor and the basement were full of soldiers." She reported that these Tommies made little noise, were polite, and quickly told a little of themselves. "There were several wounded among them," said Schouten. "One Irishman had lost two fingers on the way; he did not want to stay behind because, he said, he could still fire with one hand. Another man had been shot in the eye and the thigh. Yet another had been shot in his stomach; he was the worst of all."

Night had fallen. Off to Frost's left a half mile, over the tops of the old-town buildings and the trees, fires in central Arnhem continued to rage brightly, with molten embers drifting into the sky. The firelight made the uniforms and dirty skin of the men glow orange. It seemed likely the big fire was the death throes of the Wehrmacht barracks up near the train station that had been knocked out by the morning's air strikes. Frost was a great one for studying the maps; he believed he couldn't know too much about the terrain he'd be fighting for in coming days.

Frost sent out some men to try to capture the bridge, but a German machine gun let loose at point-blank range on his poor men. The survivors scurried back to safety, dragging wounded with them. The battle grew more intense as German armored vehicles tried to drive across the bridge into Arnhem, and the paratroopers fired on them until all erupted in flame.

The great racket alerted every German soldier and civilian in the area exactly what was going on in downtown Arnhem, but the blackness of night held everyone in check, and Frost could do nothing but sit in Arnhem Centraal and wait. All over the area to his west as he sat at the bridge, he could hear stuttering bursts of machine guns along with occasional artillery explosions and grenades. Sometimes they were accompanied by ghostly powder flashes like lightning.

Before dawn on Monday, 18 September, along the Pietersbergseweg in Oosterbeek just three-and-a-half miles west of the bridge, another group of soldiers filed by under a window of a house just down the street from the baron's old Villa Roestenburg, the place where Audrey and her brothers used to play with such glee. The night in Oosterbeek had included gunfire and explosions that had terrified the citizens. The men seen by locals now in blackness of night tiptoed in hunched fashion single-file along the edge of the street. It was plain they feared for their lives. Oosterbeek teenager Anje van Maanen, who was just Audrey's age, watched ghostly figures pass by the window with her family, and they speculated whether these ghosts were the prayed-for Tommies or just the dirty moffen. If the latter, the van Maanens would be machine-gunned without hesitation. Finally, the curiosity of

Anje's Tante Auke forced her to fling open a window. She called brightly, "Good morning!"

"We get a fright," said Anje in her diary, "but then we hear them answer, 'Sst, Ssst! Good morning.' Whispering figures in the darkness, but they are Tommies and so we are free, free, free!" Yes, they were Tommies. They had been desperate to find a path to the bridge so they could join Frost; they had spent the night groping along trying to get through Oosterbeek with its winding streets, garden walls, hedges, shrubbery, and other symbols of the Dutch gentility. And behind any of these obstacles on a night with a new moon could be found a heavily armed German. Finally, with the sun was peeking over the horizon, the poor men were nearly frightened to death by an old Dutch woman wishing them a good morning.

An excited Anje grabbed what food she could from the cellar to present to her brave liberators out on the Pietersbergseweg. She said, "It has grown a little less dark and we can now see the street crowded with people in pajamas or dressing gowns, carrying all sorts of food, trays with cups of tea, coffee or milk, bread, pears, apples. All one can possibly eat is produced by a lot of very glad Dutch people as a welcome to our liberators."

On the Utrechtseweg running through Oosterbeek toward Arnhem, Anje saw a line of British vehicles representing the relief column meant for Colonel Frost at the bridge. She referred to them in her diary as "our Airborne." The citizens showered the liberators with love as morning brightened. Off to the right toward Arnhem, a battle was growing in intensity, and the Tommies didn't hesitate to push right on toward it.

Back at the bridge, the men of Frost's command battled against Germans attacking from all directions. German tanks were everywhere, and the paratroopers fought for their lives as central Arnhem was chewed to pieces by sprays of machine-gun fire and the blasting of grenades and cannon.

Finally at three o'clock in the afternoon, more Allied aircraft roared off to the west. It was the second wave of British Airborne paratroopers coming down in the drop and landing zones. Hundreds of brightly colored parachutes filled the air and a wave of gliders came in for lovely landings. But from positions at the bridge, the paratroopers could also see transport planes going down in flames.

In Velp, Audrey could see none of it in the cellar of the Beukenhof, but oh, the sounds of battle. Rifles and machine guns and grenades and artillery—constant, horrible, and every instant all in the cellar knew that humans were dying, torn to pieces no doubt, hour after hour. And poor Arnhem, what of that? Then this new sound, the drone of more planes was enough to rattle the teeth. Now came the distant boom-boom-boom of anti-aircraft cannon shooting at something in the sky, and overhead, the pitch of the engines changed as the armada of airplanes banked sharply and began to head west again. More and more planes did that very thing just above their heads, it seemed. This must be another grand event that was bringing liberation closer. It just had to be.

In theory it was. Another batch of British paratroopers had landed, their mission delayed for hours by fog in England. They attempted to join the battle and reach the bridge, but German troops were flooding into the area with tanks and cannon far bigger than anything possessed by the Tommies.

On this Monday afternoon, Steven Jansen of Oranjestraat in Velp wrote in his diary that he had finally witnessed the sight he had longed for on the streets of his village: the liberators! "We have already seen the first English," he wrote. "Unfortunately, as prisoners." Groups of British soldiers were moving along with hands up. They had been stripped of their steel-pot helmets and equipment, and most sported red berets—others were bare-headed.

Farther up Hoofdstraat, ten-year-old Clan Visser 't Hooft and her siblings—children of Audrey's friend, Dr. Visser 't Hooft—had found safety in their cellar and were peering out the window where they could see movement on the pavement past their broad lawn. Their cellar window was just about the best in town for observing German troop movements; they lived near the point where Hoofdstraat became the Zutphenseweg and ran straight into Germany. Mostly, the vehicles the children saw speeding through Velp were German and heading to Arnhem—troop transports, tanks, half-tracks, and motorcycles. But now the Visser 't Hoofts watched an amazing sight heading east.

Clan's younger sister Annemarth saw military men marching past and heard heavy boots. "Clonk, clonk, clonk," she said, "and these soldiers were whistling. Germans never whistled. They were Tommies! Big groups of prisoners of war marching and whistling, and behind them shuffled the German guards with their sinister guns." The six year old could make no sense of it—the prisoners were whistling—at gunpoint!

Medical orderly Cpl. Arthur Hatcher had been captured at St. Elisabeth's Hospital with more than fifty of his mates who also used music as a show of resilience. He said, "We were still full of confidence and thought we would be relieved any minute and we would be top dog again. The Germans didn't like it, but they didn't stop us."

For the residents of Velp, none of this made any sense. How could there be so many Allied paratroopers falling from the sky to the west, and heavy fighting all around, and Arnhem and parts of Velp burning to the ground, but now British soldiers by the score were being led off as prisoners? Even with telephone service cut, reports circulated around the entire area: parachutes near Heelsum and Renkum! A British column in Oosterbeek! Tommies on the Arnhem Road Bridge!

British Airborne trying to reach Frost at the bridge were stunned at the strength of the German opposition they met between St. Elisabeth's Hospital and the bridge area. Soon the Tommies found themselves in disorganized groups fighting for their lives in the residential streets of western Arnhem, with shocked civilians in every house. Cpl. Donald Collins of the 1st Parachute Battalion would recall that in the heat of this terrific battle, "to my amazement, I saw at different intervals Dutch ladies cleaning the inside of their front windows. I presume that their curiosity overcame their caution, and they were doing this as an excuse to see what was going on." But then Collins didn't know the Dutch; no matter the lead flying about, Monday was probably the day to wash the windows. And that was that.

The battle witnessed by those housewives was vicious and fought at close quarters, Tommies against tanks, arms and legs blown off, bodies everywhere, and nothing seemed to be getting better. Just to the east, the Velpenaren had a different view out their windows: More and more Germans were entering the village to join the fight one town over. Not only zooming down from Rozendaal and Zutphen but also rolling past on trains right through the center of Velp. Those first orders issued by German commanders Model and Bittrich had set off a rapid response to thwart the attack of the Allies, and the Airborne couldn't imagine what had become of their cakewalk.

By Monday night the battle sprawled from the business district of Oosterbeek eastward all the way through western and central Arnhem to the bridge, with pockets of confused paratroopers just about everywhere, cut off by swarms of Germans. British casualties were atrocious, food and ammunition were running out, and the radios worked only sporadically.

Piet Hoefsloot, in the family cellar for the third day with his many siblings and other relatives, reported, "On Tuesday 19 September it became very dangerous. During the day we saw from our rear garden that all other houses in our boulevard were burning like torches and the wind was coming in our direction." General Bittrich had decided enough was enough and it was time to end the battle at the bridge. He ordered the burning of all structures that might shelter enemy troops in the bridge area.

Colonel Frost's command had nearly run out of ammunition and his casualties were heavy. "New weapons came to harry us and all the buildings by the bridge were set on fire," he reported. "Toward evening heavy tanks appeared, incredibly menacing and sinister in the half-light, as their guns swung from target to target. Shells burst through our walls. The dust and settling debris following their explosions filled the passages and rooms."

Arnhem, medieval fortress of old, one of the most beautiful cities in all Europe and home of Audrey Hepburn-Ruston's dance career, was being destroyed brick by brick.

Left: The 1896 wedding photo of Aarnoud, Baron van Heemstra, and Elbrig, Baroness van Asbeck. Above: Four of their children, Ella, Geraldine, Meisje, and little brother Willem, pose in about 1913. (Both photos, Dotti Collection.) Below: Cornelia van Limburg Stirum's villa, de Nijenburgh, stands across the street from the Arnhem Muziekschool. To the left of it is the van Limburg Stirum School. Partially visible at far left is the home of the van Heemstras from 1910 to 1920. All would be destroyed in Allied efforts to take "a bridge too far." (Gelders Archief: 1584-1339, N. Kramer, CC-BY-4.0 license.)

Left: Ella, Baroness van Heemstra, in the early 1930s. Below: The dashing and mercurial Joseph Ruston, Audrey Hepburn's father. (Both photos, Dotti Collection.)

THE CALL OF FASCISM

By Baroness Ella de Heemstra

It is comparatively easy for those versed in politics to understand the ideas Fascism brings to the people of England: our loyalty to King and Empire, the Corporate State, and the revolt against alien domination of banking and trade.

It is quite another thing to point out to them that if we want our hands and feet to work freely and our brains to be delivered from the impressions of current falsehoods, and if we want to reorganise things material, we have to aim, first and foremost, at a reorganisation of our thought.

NOT ONLY MATERIAL

It is not our sole desire to get Empire bread and butter, homegrown vegetables and homespun clothes. We do not merely aim at bettering conditions for the body and easing the condition of humanity. Such amelioration cannot and will not be based on materialism or intellect, but on ideals and the spirit.

Too long has the world attempted to improve itself by self-destruction, to purify by a decimation of numbers. Too long have we thought that matter paid for matter, and that earthly things could improve the earth.

It is not so.

We who have heard the call of Fascism, and have followed the light on the upward road to victory, have been taught to understand what dimly we knew, and now fully

BARONESS ELLA DE HEEMSTRA

realise that only the spirit can cleanse the body, and only the soul of Britain can be the salvation of Britain.

THE ROAD TO SALVATION

Too long have we been fettered by the fetish of materialism. At last we are breaking the bondage and are on the road to salvation.

It is not by changing laws, not by breaking fresh political ground, not by laying down new rules, that we shall save this country.

It is not by forswearing all that Britain has stood by during this last decade, not by only material rebirth, not by just the facts contained in our programme, that we can reorganise the State. By the spirit that inspired them they shall bear fruit; by the spiritual meaning of the reforms we propose, by the light behind the veil which we shall draw aside, by the rebirth of the soul of our country.

And this rebirth is possible through Fascism. In this creed we find expressed all our hopes, all our desires, all our faith.

It is the spirit and not the letter, the creed and not its outward manifestations, that count. If to-morrow all words were washed away and all sentences became meaningless, if our language ceased to exist and the Ten Points became obsolete, their essence, the spirit that inspired them, would hold out.

THE FOUNDATIONS OF SPIRIT

The activities of a Corporate State are not in themselves our Faith. The Ten Points of our programme are an enunciation of our beliefs, not a dogma unto themselves. The growth of prosperity and the material ease of our people will be the result of our creed, not of material expectations. Only on the unshakable foundations of spirit can a new world be rebuilt.

And we who follow Sir Oswald Mosley know that in him we have found a Leader whose eyes are not riveted on earthly things, whose inspiration is of a higher plane, and whose idealism will carry Britain along to the bright light of the new dawn of spiritual rebirth.

"Britain dares to be great," said our Leader. Britain dares to have a soul!

Ella, signing with the Belgian "de" rather than the Dutch "van," makes a stir with her first article praising Hitler in the spring of 1935 (above) and then follows it up six months later with another (right) after visiting the 1935 Nazi Party rally in Nuremberg. Ella's actions here would cause lifelong problems for her daughter.

AT NUREMBERG

I recently visited Germany and went to the "Reichsparteitag" in Nuremberg, the yearly rally of National-Socialist Germany.

What struck me most forcibly amongst the million and one impressions I received there were: (a) the wonderful fitness of every man and woman one saw, on parades or in the street; and (b) the refreshing atmosphere around one, the absolute freedom from any form of mental pressure or depression.

These people certainly live in spiritual comfort and the inspiring conviction of creating good. By next year they will have solved the problem of unemployment; there will not be a single soul on the dole in Germany.

To watch their boundless enthusiasm as they march past in endless formations, hailing their beloved "Führer," Adolf Hitler, is one of the most inspiring sights on earth. Hitler has a magnetic and most charming personality, which fully reflects the spiritual aspirations of this mighty people.

From Nuremberg I went to Munich, and there it was most striking to behold the individual fitness of this new Germany, with its organised and controlled national health. All the time I was there I never heard an angry word, and yet, far from being sluggardly, the people are keen and alert and full of life. They are happy; they are content and fully satisfied to live to-day for the glory of an ever better future.

Well may Adolf Hitler be proud of the rebirth of this great country and of the rejuvenation of the German spirit. The Germany of to-day is a most pleasant country, and the Germans, under Nazi rule, a splendid example to the white races of the world —a mighty people, upright and proud, as, indeed, they have every right to be.

BARONESS ELLA DE HEEMSTRA. Brussels.

Above: Baron and Baroness van Heemstra, Adriaantje's grandparents, lived at Pietersbergseweg 44, Villa Roestenburg, in 1930s Oosterbeek. Next door sat the Hotel Tafelberg. Left: Adriaantje poses with Tante Meisje and Oom Otto during an extended stay in Oosterbeek while her parents meet with Hitler. (Both photos, Dotti Collection.)

Above: Adriaantje loves animals. Here she stands among the hounds of George Butcher, who looks on. Below: Near the end of her stay in Elham, Audrey (fourth from left) waves the Union Jack. (Both photos, Dotti Collection.)

Above: The chatty van Heemstras in 1937 on a Sunday in the backyard of Villa Roestenburg in Oosterbeek. From left, Meisje, the baron, Ian, Ella, Alex, Otto, and the baroness. Below: Adriaantje, seen here with Ian and Alex, experiences her first "Roman holiday" in June 1938 when Ella takes her children to Rome, and Adriaantje flies in a biplane piloted by Don Mario Colonna, Duke of Rignano. (Both photos, Dotti Collection.)

Above: Today, as in 1940, the elegant Park Janssingel separates main streets Jans-buitensingel (far left) and Jansbinnensingel (far right) in Arnhem. On 10 May 1940 Ella, Adriaantje, and Ian watched the Germans march down these streets. (Matzen Collection.) Below: Adriaantje at around the time the occupation of the Netherlands begins. (Dotti Collection.)

Above: The Stadsschouwburg Arnhem today. Below: A performer's view of the interior of the theater with its two balconies. From the front of the first balcony, in the "Queen's Circle," Adriaantje watched her first ballet performances. (Both photos, Matzen Collection.)

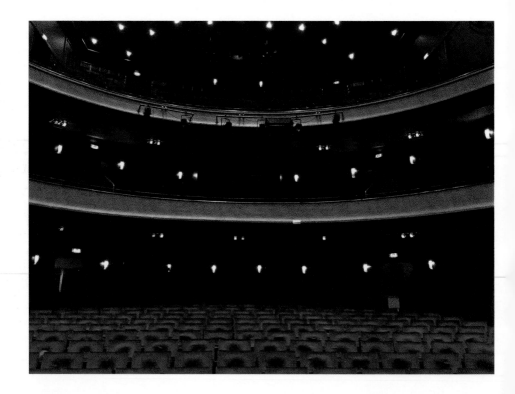

Above: Dress rehearsal for the Nazi-approved Mozart celebration of December 1941. Alex Quarles van Ufford is at left, with Adriaantje next to him and Ella second from right. (Dotti Collection.) Below: Huis Zijpendaal, where the baron, Meisje, and Otto rented rooms from 1939–42. On these grounds among the cats and geese, Adriaantje enjoyed some of her happiest Arnhem memories. (Matzen Collection.)

Above: Audrey's first public performance is in the nineteenth-century Arnhem Musis Sacrum, which had been renamed the Wehrmachtheim in 1940 and reserved for use as a recreation hall by the German military. (G.J. Dukker, photographer; Rijksmuseum Cultural Heritage Collection, object number 20025991.) Left: Audrey sits in the hilly Sonsbeek section of Arnhem in February 1942. (Dotti Collection.)

Above: Otto Ernst Gelder, Count van Limburg Stirum, mugs for the camera in Oosterbeek in 1937. Right: Meisje and Otto pose with Ella at Huis Zijpendaal. (Both photos, Dotti Collection.)

Above: The Sint-Michielsgestel complex held more than 1,000 "death candidates." Only the main building remains today. (Matzen Collection.) Below: In Arnhem four days after Uncle Otto's arrest, Audrey (standing, left) holds Annelies Bouma at a birthday party for sister Hilda (striped dress), who is Audrey's classmate from the Middelbare Meisjes School and dance mate at ballet school. A third Bouma sister, Maya, sticks out her tongue at the camera. (Van Rossem-Bouma Family Collection.)

Above: Five black poles and a monument mark the spot where Audrey's Uncle Otto, Count van Limburg Stirum, and his four companions were executed on the morning of 15 August 1942. Right: On 16 August, a British newspaper carries the story of the atrocity. Below: The graves of Alexander, Baron Schimmelpenninck, and Count van Limburg Stirum rest side by side at the execution site. (Both photos, Matzen Collection.)

Above: This artist's rendition of Villa Beukenhof at Rozendaalselaan 32 in Velp was based on original architectural drawings. The modest (by Dutch colonial-wealth standards) eight-room house with one-and-a-half baths would be home to the van Heemstras for more than three years; its small cellar would serve as refuge from the war. (Matzen Collection.) Left: Now known in Arnhem as Audrey Hepburn-Ruston, the ballerina is photographed in the summer of 1942. Not until the birth of her sons would Audrey experience anything to rival the joys of dance. (Dotti Collection.)

Above: Reichskommissar Arthur Seyss-Inquart (center) reviews a parade in Amsterdam. By 1944 Seyss-Inquart would commandeer a villa less than a block from the van Heemstras in Velp. (akg-images.) Right: The physicians at Ziekenhuis Velp lead Resistance efforts in the area. They are (from left to right) Dr. Haag, Dr. Visser 't Hooft, Dr. Scherpenhuijsen, Dr. Op te Winkel (sitting), Dr. Hartman, Dr. van der Willigen, Dr. Eykman, and Dr. Portheine. (Visser 't Hooft Collection.) Below: Audrey in 1943. (Dotti Collection.)

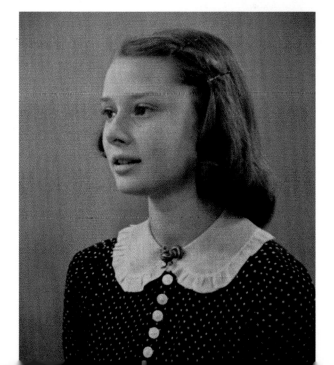

for my dancing grand-daughter

MR. A. J. A. A. BARON VAN HEEMSTRA
OUD-GOUVERNEUR VAN SURINAME

11 – 7. 42.

Bravo Adriaantje !

A. J. Baronesse van Heemstra

en Opi

Karel van Gelderlaan 5   Oosterbeek

Left: Inside the Dansschool, Audrey and Elisabeth Evers (center) practice for Winja Marova (right) in December 1943. Right and below: Costumes and poses from the January and February 1944 recitals are captured in the studio. These performances would be Audrey's last during the war. Below left: After each performance Audrey would be showered with bouquets. A calling card was attached to each, like the one from her opa, the baron, and another from Tante Arnoudina, youngest of her aunts, the baronesses. Audrey cherished them all her life. (All photos, Dotti Collection.)

Above: Audrey Hepburn's Arnhem revolves around the Lauwersgracht at right in the photo. Once part of the moat around the city, this small lake sits below the grand Musis Sacrum; to the left is the Stadsschouwburg; below is the Muziekschool. (Copyright Aviodrome Lelystad.) Left: Parachutes fill the sky of the Netherlands on a quiet Sunday. (U.S. Library of Congress image ww2-109.) Below: Prisoners from the 1st Airborne Division are marched through Velp for days. (Bundesarchiv, Bild 183-S73820/ CC-BY-SA 3.0.)

Kasteel Zijpendaal>

<Park Sonsbeek>

Sickeszlaan>

<Apeldoornscheweg 8A>

Musis Sacrum>
(Reception Helm)

To Velp>>

Stadsschouwburg>

van Limburg Stirum
School>

de Jayenburgh>

Muziekschool>

Right: Frost's men occupied these buildings during the battle, so the Germans pounded them with artillery before setting many ablaze. By the end of the battle for the Arnhem Road Bridge, all of central Arnhem is destroyed. (Spaarnestad.) Below: Audrey's beloved Muziekschool, which stands within the bridge battle zone, could not be saved. (Gelders Archief: 1584-1339, N. Kramer, CC-BY-4.0 license.)

Above: Castle Rozendaal, home of the van Pallandts. The van Heemstras spend many cordial evenings here—until the war comes calling.
(Gelders Archief: 1613-720, H. ter Hall, CC0 1.0 license.) Below: Nine
die the night of 27 March 1945 when a malfunctioning V1 falls on
Oranjestraat in Velp. The threat of V1s ratchets up the terror level for
months. (Brouerius van Nidek.)

Above: On the beech-lined Ringallee looking toward Rozendaalselaan, Canadian armored vehicles rumble through on 16 April 1945. (mevr. C.L. Bosma-van het Kaar.) Right: Wilhelmine Visser 't Hooft (left) chats with her neighbors while a Canadian soldier drinks from a bottle of wine offered by Dr. Hendrik Visser 't Hooft, who is smiling and looking at the camera. Another bottle of wine from his secret collection is stuffed in his pocket. (Visser 't Hooft Family.) Below: Canadian armor on Hoofdstraat signals the end of the occupation. In the right foreground is the Hotel Naeff, which the SS burned to destroy records during Market Garden. Past the hotel, damage from Allied fighter attacks on German columns can be seen in a building's wall and roof. (mevr. W.G. Matser-Wassink.)

Audrey returns to Velp for a 25 April 1946 dance recital to raise money for the Red Cross. That same day she poses for publicity photos at an Arnhem studio. (All photos, Dotti Collection.)

Above: At the Cambridge The-
atre in December 1949, dancers
Gillian Moran and Adele pose
with Audrey in a publicity shot
for *Sauce Tartare*. (Heritage
Images/Keystone Archivers/
akg-images.) Right: Ella and
Audrey take a stroll in London.
(Copyrighted material; Dotti
Collection.)

Above: On 5 November 1954, the last day of their whirlwind tour of the Netherlands, Mel and Audrey Ferrer step away from a wreath they laid at a memorial to the British 1st Airborne Division in Oosterbeek. (Nationaal Archief/Collection Anefo.) Below: In 1957 the stress of a day in Switzerland with "Fritzi" and Otto Frank is visible on Audrey's face. He had asked her to portray his daughter Anne in an upcoming film; she will tell him that, for a variety of reasons, she can't. (Eva Schloss, photographer; Anne Frank House.)

24

Aflame

"Arnhem was pretty much flattened" was the way Audrey described it. From her location in Velp, she couldn't see it happening but everyone heard it all day and into the night. There were booms, booms, a pause, then more thundering blasts that rattled the ground. Bursts of machine-gun fire and the smaller explosions of grenades underscored the tympani.

Bittrich's attack had raged so long that nothing remained in the area of Colonel Frost's position. The van Limburg Stirum School lay a pile of useless rubble. On one side de Nijenburgh smoldered in a heap, and on the other the red school had been flattened. All that remained of the Muziekschool were half-standing walls. Hundreds of Dutch residents had been caught in the crossfire of battle, praying they could ride out the storm, until finally, with fires burning unchecked and the central city in ruins, those still alive, like Piet Hoefsloot and his family, rigged white flags and made their way out as best they could.

Frost received leg wounds and was captured, but for the remainder of his life, when anyone around him mentioned the word *surrender*, he would snap, "We did *not* surrender." In his memoir he maintained, "No living enemy had beaten us. The battalion was unbeaten yet, but they could not have much chance with no ammunition, no rest and with no positions from which to fight."

His original orders in England had been to hold on for forty-eight hours until the relief column had arrived from the south. He held his position for twice that length of time, and he hurled curses at the relief column for letting obstacles get in their way—at the time that Arnhem burned, tanks of the British 2nd Army sat just a few miles south of the bridge waiting for the infantry to catch up. The American 82nd and 101st Airborne had done their jobs and captured or built bridges for the British relief column to use as it raced northward and fought its way toward Arnhem. But the grand plan for Operation Market Garden hadn't been thought through well enough, and time had run out not only for Frost but also for the center of Arnhem.

Bodies of Dutch civilians lay everywhere. Thursday morning an old lady was found by an air-raid warden lying in the garden beside the smoldering wreck of her home, de Nijenburgh. The lady was grand old Cornelia, Countess van Limburg Stirum, Otto's aunt. She lay scorched and covered in grime and ash. She had been dragged out of de Nijenburgh by her maid after the Germans had warned they were going to set a flamethrower on the villa as part of their operation to capture Frost. Cornelia clung to life by a thread. The air-raid warden and some of the Christian school students managed to get her up to the Diaconessenhuis, the hospital where Ella used to work. There the Countess died two days later.

Just across the way in Velp, the ongoing cacophony unnerved villagers who had lost their electricity that first day and then their water service, and neither had returned. After the Velpenaren had sat out the fighting for the better part of four years, the apocalypse had arrived. When asked if she could hear the battle next door in Arnhem, Annemarth Visser 't Hooft responded that it wasn't next door. "It was here! There was nothing *but* the battle of Arnhem." Her only solution when it grew too terrifying was to put her fingers in her ears as British and German forces slugged it out. The din carried every second eastward to the ears of the Visser 't Hoofts as well as to Audrey, Ella, and everyone else in Velp. The sights and sounds of this battle bored into the sensitive dancer's soul, and they would always echo there for what they meant to humanity and to, as she labeled it, "poor Arnhem."

It was at times like this that the fifteen year old leaned on the adults surrounding her. Said Audrey's son Luca, "My mother always told me that in the war, because her father was not there, Ella was her father figure, and Meisje was her mother, which is a strong statement. So I asked her, what do you mean by that? And she said Meisje was the one first and foremost with the kindness. She was the one teaching her how to draw, and to play, and to read—a motherly figure. It was really Meisje who made the magic come alive; you know, what mothers usually did. Ella was about rules."

As British paratroopers and Wehrmacht and SS troops battled for control of the city next door, Ella was the one to tell Audrey whether she could spend time upstairs or if she had to go to the cellar for safety. It was Ella dictating bedtime. But Meisje was there with cuddles and comforting words at the horrors they were witnessing and assurances that they would make it through. And it was Meisje who would have provided understanding when Audrey feared her career in dance was being bombed out of existence.

The battle they witnessed blazed in three dimensions. Increasingly, day by day, German fighter planes zipped over at treetop level to fire on British positions—the first of the Luftwaffe seen over Velp since before the bombing of Deelen Air Base. The Germans were loath to send their fighters out as ground support, not because they feared losing planes but because so few skilled pilots remained and each was precious.

But even with the danger of stray machine-gun bursts from planes, the battle was not so close by and so immediately dangerous that Audrey and the others had to remain in the cellar twenty-four hours a day. The toilet stood directly above, off the kitchen, so they would skitter up during a quiet moment and then back down again. When they ventured up on Tuesday evening, they had seen off to the west the red curtain of Arnhem burning. The sight of it tore at their hearts, at their stomachs. Grand old Arnhem a funeral pyre. The next day, word reached Velp that one side of Boulevard Heuvelink had been torched or blown to dust, and so Audrey knew the Muziekschool must be gone, and any hope of a career in dance along with it.

But there were more sights. Gazing down their own boulevard to Hoofdstraat, the van Heemstras could see refugees streaming from Arnhem into Velp, a human river at flood tide, unending. The wretched souls looked as refugees always looked, white flags, suitcases and multiple layers of clothing and overcoats and hats and dragging children and pulling hand trucks, carts, bicycles, toy wagons, and whatever else could be used to haul away possessions. Scores, then hundreds, filed by the Beukenhof on their way north through Rozendaal toward Apeldoorn. And streaming the other way, south on Rozendaalselaan and west on Hoofdstraat, the Germans rushed by in trucks and armored vehicles. There were tanks of various sizes including the really big ones, with everything heading in the direction of the poor Tommies.

As each day passed, more and more British soldiers could be seen, small and large groups of prisoners, each looking worse than the last. All the young, battle-scorched faces were visible as the defeated paratroopers shuffled through, many wearing red berets, their hobnailed boots clomping along on the sidewalks and cobblestone streets. These young men made a great show of bravado, group by group, as they passed by, as if captivity were a minor inconvenience, as if they knew they were better soldiers than the men guarding them, but this time the fates had not smiled.

The bravado was due in part to a surprising source: their guards. "It is striking," wrote Max Hastings, a British historian who studied the history of the SS, "that when the survivors of the British 1st Airborne Division at Arnhem found themselves in the hands of the SS, they expected to be shot. Instead, they were treated with the respect due to heroes. According to the SS code of chivalry, these were fellow knights worthy of their highest honor."

Frost himself confirmed this. "The SS men were very polite and complimentary about the battle we had fought," he wrote.

Words could not do justice to the sight left behind at the bridge. It was reported the bodies—British, German, and Dutch—lay all about the area, from the bridge to the Muziekschool. The mood in Velp grew hopeless, and the news got even worse. The entire city of Arnhem, every square inch, was in German hands, and the British liberators had been driven back into Oosterbeek village and were under siege, holed up in the houses, villas, and hotels with Dutch citizens again caught in the middle. Yes, the earwitnesses in Velp could confirm—the sounds of battle had indeed changed and grown a bit more distant, but still, as morning turned to afternoon on Thursday, 21 September, heavy explosions punctuated every sentence dictated by rifles and machine guns.

By afternoon that Thursday, four days into the battle, it seemed that all the Germans who had fled from Velp before and during the invasion had now returned. Green Police again roamed the streets and issued an edict that all able-bodied men of Velp must report for ditch-digging duty—those that could be rounded up were marched off to Arnhem to dig mass graves. Then Audrey saw a most unwelcome line of SS Tiger II tanks clatter down Rozendaalselaan and stop, one of them directly in front of the Beukenhof and seemingly as tall. There it sat through the day, as if there were already plenty of tanks in Oosterbeek to take care of the Tommies, and these were extras, placed here just in case of more Allied activity.

Later Thursday, past midday, confusion reigned when the air-raid siren yet again sounded and the heavy drone of airplanes once more rattled the windows of Velp. As had happened days earlier, the anti-aircraft batteries opened up, including some new groups of cannon just brought into the area. What did it mean this time?

Up to now, each unfolding of such events had unleashed hell on the Dutch people. This time, the Velpenaren watched a sky battle just off to the southwest, much closer than the previous Sunday, with bursts of flak amid the dozens of Allied transport planes with parachutes spilling out. Suddenly, one of the planes caught fire and fell out of formation, then another, and a third. It was horrible, but still the air was filled with brightly colored parachutes that seemed to be falling on the other side of the Rhine in the direction of the village of Driel. The effect of this new threat sobered up a German presence that had grown both talkative and jovial. Amid much excitement, the tanks on Rozendaalselaan rolled out and turned onto Hoofdstraat heading toward Arnhem, apparently to counter this latest threat. In fact, these paratroopers were Poles who arrived too late to support Frost by attacking the south end of the Arnhem Road Bridge. Instead, the Poles set out to cross the Rhine and join up with the Airborne in Oosterbeek—only 200 would succeed.

The din of the battle raging in Oosterbeek five miles away went on for days. There continued to be no electrical service in Velp, and no running water as about 3,000 men out of the original 10,000 made a last stand in the center of Oosterbeek. Audrey had two familiar points of reference in that village—the big, thatched-roof Villa Roestenburg where Opa and Oma lived next to the Hotel Tafelberg, and Villa Maria, the Monné's lovely home on Utrechtseweg. She wouldn't learn their fate until later: In the midst of the battle that engulfed the town, both the homes she knew so well were being cut through with bullet holes. The Hotel Tafelberg had been wrecked but still served as an aid station for injured and dying men. Years later, Audrey's cousin, Michael Quarles van Ufford, would report that there had been fighting on the family grounds in Oosterbeek.

How far the world had come since 1935 when Ella and Joseph had deposited the children at Villa Roestenburg in Oosterbeek so they could go meet Hitler. Nine years later, on that quiet, tree-lined street where the van Heemstras had once lived, the battle raged. Its cross street, the Utrechtseweg, saw German and British soldiers fighting for their lives, not just house to house but room to room until the resort town too had been chopped to pieces. Right near the intersection, Anje van Maanen's aunt had thrown open her windows just a few days earlier to greet the liberators—now all their windows had been shattered by gunfire.

Said one British soldier, "The Germans were spraying the houses; bullets were coming through the roofs and windows, whizzing around the rooms inside and hitting the walls behind us."

In Velp on Friday, then Saturday, and again Sunday—Audrey heard the air-raid siren, and then the anti-aircraft cannon would open up from batteries near and far. More batteries than ever, it seemed, as more and more flak guns were brought into the area. Then she would see or at the least hear Allied transports fly nearby and parachutes would dot the sky. The locals thought it was more paratroopers joining the battle, but the crews in the planes were trying to drop supplies to the surrounded Airborne troops already on the ground, men who had days ago run out of ammunition, rations, and medicine.

The refugees continued to trudge their way out of Arnhem. The greatest numbers were heading due north toward Apeldoorn, but many sought refuge in Velp or kept on walking up the Zutphenseweg toward Dieren and Zutphen. Some arrived at Velp's Ziekenhuis seeking treatment for wounds from bullets, flying glass, shrapnel, and splinters as well as cases of dehydration, undernourishment, and shell shock. As the fighting moved farther off toward Oosterbeek, Audrey hurried the three blocks to aid Dr. Visser 't Hooft and the other physicians as they faced their overwhelming task.

Each day Audrey watched captured Tommies as they clomped through town, audacious chaps who would sing or whistle, and as they passed they would wink at Audrey and other pretty girls of

Velp and flash V for Victory signs to the men. By Thursday locals calculated that a thousand captured Airborne had been marched up from Arnhem toward Germany. By Saturday, the estimate had risen to fifteen hundred.

It was clear that the battle to capture the bridge and free Gelderland was going badly and that the Germans were winning. The shooting was continuous and every sign, particularly the emboldened attitude of the moffen in green and gray uniforms as they roamed the streets, indicated that the status quo had returned.

Audrey faced a devastating new world without dance because the Arnhem she knew was simply gone. But in just a few weeks, circumstances would converge and the lack of dance instruction would be the least of her worries.

25

Champagne for One

"My grandfather, my mother, my aunt, and myself were living together to pool whatever we had," Audrey explained long after the war—a war that lived on in her memory, "food, heat, gathering around the stove to keep warm. If there were any rations, you'd do better if you stuck together."

The battles that sprawled from the Arnhem Road Bridge west to Wolfheze and Heelsum would claim nearly 200 Dutch lives and cause mass destruction of homes and buildings. So great and all-consuming was the horror of it that while the local citizenry lay prone on floors or huddled in cellars, another emergency had gripped the nation and they weren't even aware of it.

On the afternoon of Sunday, 17 September, as the newly landed 1st Airborne Division troops were marching on Arnhem with high hopes, the Dutch government in London took to Radio Oranje with a message to 30,000 railway workers in the Netherlands: Shut down all rail service nationwide. These rails moved German troops, equipment, and ammunition that would be responding to the Market Garden invasion. These same rails had transported tens of thousands of Dutch Jews to concentration camps and Dutch men to Germany where they served as slave labor in factories. And these rails conveyed V-weapons west to their launch sites near the coast—the V1 buzz bombs and V2 rockets that were raining down on London. For so many vital reasons, the trains must stop and they must stop that day.

There was just one problem with heeding the royal call for a strike: The rails served as the primary way food—such as it was—moved through the Netherlands to reach the civilian population. Shutting down rail service would mean famine for a people who had already lost so much.

German-run radio accurately advised the captive Dutch population that this strike ordered from London would hurt the Netherlands and her people much more than the occupier. The people would starve, they claimed, and yet more than ninety percent of railway workers heeded their queen and remained at home, and the strike was on.

Seyss-Inquart was furious at the audacity of the Dutch and asked for permission from Berlin to have any participating railway workers shot. But such a step could backfire and make the stubborn Dutch dig in their heels yet further, so his request was denied. All the while, the battle for Arnhem and then Oosterbeek raged, and all across the area, local citizens were helping the Tommies wherever they could. They had greeted them as heroes on the day of the landings and handed them flowers and food in the street. They hid them when the fighting turned grim, fed them from a family's own meager rations, and died beside them in the worst of the battle.

The Germans felt betrayed by their Aryan cousins the Dutch. How patient the Reich had been. How lenient. But now the truth revealed itself to be bitter. In four years or forty, these people would never agree to become partners of the Fatherland.

With the battle in Arnhem ended and the British and Dutch dead stacked like cordwood, the Germans faced a crisis they simply refused to deal with—they now controlled a city that had become a no-man's land, not worth defending, with a possibility that pockets of enemy troops remained to cause trouble in the days and weeks to come. It was a situation made much worse by ill feelings over the deepening railway strike. The two circumstances converged into the order issued Friday night, 22 September, that would break many a heart in Arnhem: Evacuate the city.

City residents had been hanging on for dear life for five days. They had ridden out the battle with bullets whizzing through walls and windows. The order stated that by eight o'clock in the evening of 23 September, the part of the city of Arnhem south of the railroad tracks must evacuate. By four the next afternoon the half of the city north of the railroad tracks, almost exclusively a residential area that had mostly been spared in the battle, must also be vacated.

All Saturday afternoon a population numbed by violence packed up and headed out of their city in advance of the deadline to be gone or be shot, because the order stated that after nightfall on Sunday, 24 September, those remaining inside Arnhem and all the way west through Oosterbeek to Ede would be assumed to be saboteurs.

Audrey said, "There were 90,000 people looking for a place to live." As a spectator in Velp, she witnessed the dark moment in Dutch history. "I still feel sick when I remember the scenes. It was human misery at its starkest—masses of refugees on the move, some carrying their dead, babies born on the roadside, hundreds collapsing of hunger." Everything with wheels became a precious conveyance of a family's entire history—all that could be loaded or borne. As always, a stick with a white flag propped on wheel barrows or tricycles or baby carriages communicated noncombatant status.

Said Steven Jansen, a witness on Oranjestraat in Velp, "Worry is stamped heavily on the faces of the evacuees. Worry for what they left behind, concern over the future."

With the sounds of battle constant in the distance, most homes in Velp opened doors to refugees that weekend. The baron accepted his responsibility as a titled Dutchman and welcomed friends and strangers alike. Audrey made note of the Wehrmacht radio operators in the attic when she said, "Not counting our uninvited guests upstairs, we eventually had thirty-seven people sleeping in our house as evacuees continued to arrive." Two of the faces that showed up at the villa caused tremendous joy: Alex and Miepje lost themselves within the crowd of displaced and sought out the Beukenhof at this most desperate hour. The reunion with Ella and Audrey brought momentary joy in the face of utter sorrow.

And at least one of the thirty-seven faces under the roof of the Beukenhof would have been especially grimy and battle-scorched. Audrey told her son Luca that the van Heemstras hid a British paratrooper in the cellar of their house in Velp.

"At first I remember my mother told me it was thrilling for her—it was risky, he was a stranger in uniform, a savior, and therefore a knight and hero." The war had literally come home to Audrey in a way a fifteen year old could never have expected, a way that knocked the pins out from under her. But with the excitement came deadly consequences. Luca added, "Then I learned about the German law that if you were caught hiding an enemy, the whole family would be taken away."

Years later, Audrey alluded to the fact that by this point in the war, people in the Netherlands knew the fate of the Jews whom she had seen crammed into cattle cars. She well remembered the news about Otto and the others taken out and shot. The consequences for hiding a British paratrooper, one of the brave Red Devils of the 1st Airborne, would be lethal.

As the combined and growing German forces in the area set about crushing the British attack, uncounted hundreds of these highly skilled Airborne troops had gone underground, many with the aid of Dutch civilians. In response the Germans had indeed promised death for any civilian aiding an enemy combatant. If shooting an entire family would teach the Dutch a lesson, so be it.

As a result, said Luca, his mother "said she had this mix of excitement and fear. But he [the paratrooper] definitely stayed inside the house, I don't know if for a week or even more."

Logistics would not be easy for the van Heemstras, with the Beukenhof full and now the vital living space of the cellar taken by an onderduiker—no matter that the Englishman would be polite, as they all were, as well as apologetic for what his mates had done to Arnhem. The simple fact was that the baron faced the challenge of keeping this Tommy not only hidden but also fed when supplies were already critically low.

The population of Velp swelled thirty- and forty-fold. Dr. Visser 't Hooft would have taken in refugees, but with now five children, a nanny, neighbors whose home had been confiscated by the Germans, and various family members sheltered there, his villa was full—not to mention that the ivy-covered carriage house behind the villa held fugitive Tommies in the upper floor. It was certainly Visser 't Hooft who asked the van Heemstras if they could manage to hide a British fugitive or two—through the course of the war he had been in charge of distributing and moving Jews through the village, and likewise it would have been his job to parse out the Airborne fugitives among trustworthy homes in the village.

The churches of Velp filled with refugees. And on Sunday, as the remainder of Arnhem emptied, and again on Monday, the battle raged on in Oosterbeek, with the British paratroopers squeezed into a sliver of town that they defended with their lives. Each rattle of machine-gun fire and explosion of a grenade or mortar round carried on the breezes into Velp and signaled fresh death. King Tiger tanks had been brought in to finish the job, and all the Tommies could offer in return were small cannons that were light enough to be carried in gliders—toys by comparison to the tanks. These cannon were set up all around the Old Church and the surrounded men fought on.

The home of Jan and Kate ter Horst by the church had been

serving as an aid station for a week and was crammed with wounded British soldiers in every room. Kate had marveled at their manners—and at their sorrow for the damage done to her house. More than fifty had already died and a steady stream of bodies were carried out for burial in her garden. She said to her liberators, "With death or imprisonment before your eyes you have, like all the other officers and men, found that marvelously pure comradeship and simple strength of mind which makes the life in this house, which is bleeding to death, rise to a mystery of human perfection."

Said a German officer trying to lead an attack on the British cannons at the church, "Reports and detonations followed almost without let-up, the earth was trembling and a curtain of fire and dirt of unprecedented dimensions rose over and between our positions. We ducked down and sought shelter, but still remained exposed to the blind raging of the shells."

By now, another new and terrifying instrument of death in this hell's symphony was reaching ears in Velp. First came a devil's cry that made no sense—a repeated series of howling sounds that carried for miles and signaled a series of impending explosions to follow. The Tommies in their Oosterbeek perimeter knew this terrifying howl all too well, as if prehistoric dinosaurs now roamed Gelderland. It meant that German *Nebelwerfer* rocket launchers, nicknamed "screaming mimis," had been brought into play to pound the Airborne at the church and houses nearby.

Incoming shells tore into the church's sanctified stone from the Roman Empire that had been laid a thousand years earlier. It had sat there so long; the high tower of the Oude Kerk commanded the entirety of Oosterbeek. Now the tower made a perfect target for enemy guns.

Then came a rumble of thunder from the south: Long-range Allied artillery from Nijmegen ten miles away started shooting at the Germans attacking the church. The 2nd Army was in radio contact with the 1st Airborne Division survivors and did their best to help from a distance. The Tommies welcomed the help from their long-range guns—even if those guns were aimed at Germans that crouched across the street, and even though any change in wind could nudge the shells down on British heads. It was that kind of battle.

Up the road a ways at the Beukenhof in Velp, it was banshee cries in one direction and rumbles like thunder in the other. The shells from Nijmegen whined northward on a blistering arc and fell less than five miles away with frightening explosions on the edge of Oosterbeek.

As evening arrived on Tuesday, 26 September, a gentle rain began to fall and still the thud of rifle fire and the rat-tat-tat of machine guns echoed in the blackness. But after one more fitful night of sleep for all in the van Heemstra villa now teeming with humanity, finally, at long last, the air grew quiet.

The baron would learn later that the British armored column moving north to relieve the 1st Airborne Division at Arnhem had been stopped mere miles south of the city, and there was no hope they could save their mates hanging on in Oosterbeek. Instead, the surviving paratroopers in the red berets, the ones fighting to the death on behalf of the people of the Netherlands, had been ordered by Allied command over the radio to withdraw south across the Rhine and retreat through a path that had been cleared to Nijmegen. They had sneaked out in the darkness and rain right past the Old Church, fewer than 2,400 of the original 10,000-man invasion force. The survivors crossed the river with the expert guidance of Canadian and British engineer units on boats brought up from the south. The Airborne Division, what was left of it, had vanished from Oosterbeek, leaving the worst of the wounded behind to be cared for by British doctors who stayed behind, and by German doctors as well, after all the wounded had been captured.

It was now nine long days since Allied fighter-bombers had roared over to hit German barracks and flak guns as a prelude to parachutes filling the skies over Wolfheze. Back on that bright and glorious Sunday, the word "Liberation!" was spoken freely and repeated every second. Now the citizenry saw what had come to pass from this invasion. They were demoralized, their towns destroyed, 100,000 Dutch now refugees, and their bellies increasingly empty.

Velp had accepted every refugee the town could hold. They filled vacated spaces in most homes and public buildings not occupied by Germans. Hundreds poured into the Openlucht Museum on the northern edge of Arnhem, with its series of structures from small huts to towering windmills that traced life in the Netherlands back centuries. It was outside the evacuation zone and now teemed with city dwellers who had once considered the museum only an afternoon's diversion. Still, refugees shuffled into Velp under white flags and dragging their belongings, this time displaced from Oosterbeek. But now Velpenaren could only point these latest souls to towns farther east.

Velp's hospital operated around the clock, with critical care and services supported by nine healthy young men, former soldiers and Jews, who were known as *de jongens in het wit*—the boys in white. All were onderduikers hiding in the attic of the hospital under the noses of the Germans. They had already proven invaluable to the running of the hospital and now became heroes for turning a car motor into a generator to provide electricity, and serving as ambulance drivers during the chaos of the battle for Arnhem and later during air attacks.

To ease the sudden medical crisis, schools were converted into hospitals; whenever it was deemed safe, Audrey continued her work in support of Dr. Visser 't Hooft. Conditions were deplorable: no beds or mattresses, and only what bedding and blankets the citizens could spare. With no utilities, the buildings weren't really hospitals at all. Like many, Audrey and Ella kept a pot of water boiling to sterilize old cloth and then tear it into strips for bandages. They also boiled dirty bandages for "second use."

"Cleaning bandages was a very important and necessary business these days," said Clan Visser 't Hooft. "There was a terrible shortage of materials. Used bandages were cooked on the stove as the only way of sterilizing them. Then after drying they had to be stretched by two people and put into rolls again for the next patients. This was daily routine as well at the hospital as in our own kitchen." For Audrey, it was a way to help.

The Germans, with wounded by the hundreds, were scrambling as well. They converted the Park Hotel to a war hospital and casualties streamed up from Arnhem and swamped the structure inside and out.

At the Beukenhof, the baron saw fresh ration cards offered in gratitude from those poor souls he had taken under his roof, and yet what good were ration cards when there was no food for miles? He had almost forty mouths to feed, including the Tommy in the cellar. But the shops of Velp stood empty a week. Everything on hand in every shop had been consumed, mostly by the moffen who had stolen it, and no deliveries were made because of the fighting. Food preserved in family cellars across town was all that remained now in what had become in so short a time a crisis. The crisis extended to the entire Netherlands, one signaled by Radio Oranje when an announcer admitted, "The weeks before us will be the most difficult in the existence of our nation."

With the battle ended and conditions primitive—no electricity or running water, with liberation a dashed dream, the enormity of the railway strike sank into the marrow of a citizenry gripped by the first frosty, foreboding nights of a winter to come. Posters placed by the Resistance mysteriously appeared all over town reminding of the strike and urging loyal Dutch railway workers to abide by it. As fast as the SD or Green Police tore down the posters, fresh copies appeared. But ambivalence reigned. Simply put, stopping the trains would hinder the Germans, true enough, and maybe slow down the rate of V1 attacks on London. But at what price would the English get their respite? Without trains, there would be no food or fuel to resupply the desperate Dutch. Freezing temperatures and snow were weeks away at most, and it seemed to many, including the van Heemstras, that the strike amounted to a death sentence.

On Friday, three days after the end of the battle for Arnhem, German troops pounded on the front door of the Beukenhof. The hearts of the van Heemstras must have stopped, considering the paratrooper in the basement. But the Green troops had purpose and dragged away healthy men from the ranks of the refugees to work as day laborers on general cleanup details for Arnhem's streets, which must be made passable for military vehicles. The men were handed shovels and told to remove debris and bury the bodies of British soldiers still littering gardens and alleyways in just about every block between the bridge and Oosterbeek.

On Saturday the news grew more grim. The Green Police ordered all Arnhem refugees—everyone taken into people's homes, everyone at the Openlucht Museum—to leave Velp by 4 October. The simple fact was that British paratroopers had slipped out of Arnhem alone and in small groups and had made their way into Velp. They were now on the run, mixing with the refugees and creating for the occupiers a situation that could not be policed. With the refugees gone, house-to-house searches could more effectively root out the fugitive British Airborne—like the one in the Beukenhof cellar and those hiding in Dr. Visser 't Hooft's carriage house.

The only exception to the order to vacate was for those too ill or grievously wounded to be moved from hospitals. The van Heemstras wanted to know whether this also meant that everyone in Velp must leave their homes. Ella, the baron, and Meisje could only wonder where they could possibly go in a country now gripped by the strike and still controlled by Germans in a murderous mood. Panic was close at hand for the village and for every surrounding community as rumors of a pending evacuation tore through like a virus. One said that two fresh German infantry divisions were moving in and these troops would be quartered in the homes of Velp. All knew what that would mean. It would be the end of everything with the moffen looting and destroying at will.

By now, hundreds of British prisoners from the battle were jailed by the Germans in villas on the Velperweg. Among them was Maj. Anthony Deane-Drummond, who would become Velp's most celebrated Tommy for his exploits, not so much during the battle as after it. While a prisoner at the Villa Bena Sita, he slipped into a cupboard and stayed there eleven days, long after the 300 other prisoners had been moved out. He then made good an escape past the German occupants of the villa and traveled the streets of Velp by night. He talked his way into in two homes, first at Laarweg 2 with the Broekhofs, and then at Schaapsdrift Overbeek 16, a rambling two-story brick home up the street and around the corner from the Beukenhof.

The Huisman family lived in this home, and although already hiding two onderduikers, they offered refuge to Deane-Drummond. It was here in early October that the emaciated English major became known to some of the Velpenaren, including Ella van Heemstra. The baroness likely learned of the fugitive Tommy from Dr. Visser 't Hooft, who was in communication with Deane-Drummond's contact in the Resistance, a man known to the English as "Pete." Like everyone else in the neighborhood, Ella was astonished at the story of Deane-Drummond's eleven days hiding in a cupboard, his reckless escape from the Germans, and his perilous journey through Velp looking for someone to shelter him. The British officer had quickly become a legend—the Houdini of Gelderland. The night before the Resistance was set to move Deane-Drummond out of town along with other Airborne outlaws, Ella sent him a precious bottle of champagne from its hiding place in the cellar with a note addressed to the "poor British officer who is so thin."

History doesn't record when the Tommy in the van Heemstras' cellar headed out into the world; the Resistance was conducting groups of paratroopers over the Rhine on a regular basis. The van Heemstras had contributed, for which Audrey would always be proud. And the villagers threw Deane-Drummond a going-away party that made good use of Ella's champagne. He said, "By the light of flickering candles they were soon singing patriotic songs in quick succession at the tops of their voices. Thoughts of war and Germans were pressed into the background. Here, at least, was a little piece of patriotic Holland trying to forget its worries and anxieties." Audrey was among those feeling especially patriotic: Her family had done the right thing, taken the risk of shielding a Tommy, and lived to tell the tale. For a time at least, she didn't have to feel shame that her mother had once been a fascist.

In the future, those dangerous days harboring an Englishman provided a direct, unbreakable connection between Audrey and Anne Frank. When Audrey said that Anne's diary "paralleled so much what I had experienced," prime among those memories was the constant anxiety that went with potential discovery by the Green Police of the British paratrooper in the cellar of Villa Beukenhof—the same anxiety that Anne Frank had lived with for two years in het achterhuis.

Said Luca, "My mother used this story to explain to us the meaning of war: Hiding somebody could take away your normal life, but, she said, 'For us it was the big reason. If we had been discovered, we would have all been shot.'" But they hadn't been discovered. They had, in fact, helped one of the liberators to avoid capture, which made it, according to Luca, "my mother's favorite story; one she always told us."

For the remainder of her lifetime, Audrey would remain taciturn about her part in the war, which was a very Dutch trait. After all, she considered her role insignificant. Had her mother Baroness van Heemstra not always taught that one must never boast?

Audrey was deflecting interviewers' attempts to draw out stories about Resistance work with a wag of the head even forty years later. She told one, "I'll never forget a secret society of university students called '*Les Gueux*,' which killed Nazi soldiers one by one and dumped their bodies in the canals. Now *that* took real bravery, and many of them were caught and executed by the Germans. They're the type who deserve the memorials and the medals."

Still, Audrey's war included running secret messages, helping downed fliers, dancing for the onderduikers, and doing whatever else Dr. Visser 't Hooft and his fellow physicians needed at the hospital. It also meant taking food to the liberator hidden in the cellar—on penalty of death. She may never have thought so, but Audrey did her part.

Part V: Toys

26
The Princess

In 1959 world-famous movie star Audrey Hepburn was six years removed from her Best Actress Academy Award for Roman Holiday and five years distant from a Tony Award earned for Ondine on Broadway. She had recently broken her back in a fall from a horse while making the western Unforgiven. She earned half a million a picture these days, and her career survived even poorly received films like War and Peace and Green Mansions—the latter directed by her husband since 1954, actor Mel Ferrer. The world saw the quiet, reserved Hepburn as an oddity. She lacked the curves and overt sex appeal of Marilyn Monroe, now the hottest star in movies. A debate raged as to whether Hepburn was beautiful or ugly, sexy or boyish. With a tall frame and twenty-two-inch waist, Audrey Hepburn had already gained a reputation as a clothes horse and her designer of choice was Hubert de Givenchy, but she didn't seek glamour or the spotlight. It found her despite serious efforts at avoidance. She longed for a quiet home life, wanted children, and didn't like to party. She rarely provided juicy quotes for gossip columns. Words often used to describe her personality were "distant" and "aloof."

Eleanor Harris, a writer and minor celebrity in Hollywood at the time, penned an article for Good Housekeeping about Audrey Hepburn just as prints of her new film, The Nun's Story, circulated to theaters around the United States. The forty-seven-year-old Harris was known for writing the original story that became the 1948 Cary Grant film Every Girl Should Be Married, as well as a few other film and stage properties. Now, in the summer of 1959, she used her inside-Hollywood connections to put Audrey Hepburn into the crosshairs.

The resulting article accused Hepburn of pretending she was a real-life princess like the one she had played in Roman Holiday. Hepburn was, according to Harris, a synthetic personality adept at portraying a long-suffering soul. She wasn't really too good to be true; she was just pretending she was, according to the author.

Examples abounded in Harris's piece. When Audrey convalesced from a broken back, she reclined in a white room with white appointments in a white bed. She wore a white dressing gown and a white ribbon in her hair. The nurse who tended Audrey said, "She refused all narcotics and sedatives, and despite her pain she never once complained. As a matter of fact, I never even saw her become irritated. She seemed more interested in other people's problems than in her own."

Another Harris example of Hepburn's disingenuous self concerned the making of her latest picture: "For the six months of shooting The Nun's Story," wrote Harris, "she seemed to be playing the role of the selfless nun whether or not she was near a camera. 'It's that princess bit again—be a shining example to the populace,' comments an acquaintance." And, according to Harris, at one point Hepburn "was stranded for many hours in the broiling African sun without drinking water. When it arrived, she poured cupfuls for thirsty natives, leaving none for herself."

A third example of Hepburn's oddness from Harris: On location in Rome for the same picture, Hepburn developed kidney stones and suffered pain that literally knocked her out of bed. But she refused to bother director Fred Zinnemann and his wife after hours, even though they lodged a phone call away in the same hotel. "This makes it clear that Audrey, having chosen her noble role, plays it to the hilt, as any superb actress should," wrote Harris's poison pen. She noted "the intense way she [Hepburn] goes about making everything perfect—from her performances to her household, to her marriage, to her opinion of others, and to her own princess-like view of herself as she thinks others should see her."

Harris noted with seeming disapproval that Hepburn and husband Mel Ferrer had never owned a home in their five years of marriage, instead renting in a variety of countries. "But I feel at home everywhere, never having had a permanent home in my life," she quoted Audrey as saying. "And beside, we move our home with us, like snails."

Harris said that "like an exiled member of royalty, she takes with her, wherever she goes, trunks packed with her own candelabra, flat silver, books, records, pictures."

Harris also attacked the world-famous waist of Audrey Hepburn. "As with everything else in her life, her elegant, bone-thin figure is the result of harsh discipline. She always eats the same breakfast: two boiled eggs, one piece of seven-grain whole-wheat toast from a health-food store, and three or four cups of coffee laced with hot milk. Her lunch consists of cottage cheese and fruit salad or of yogurt with raw vegetables. For dinner she has meat and several cooked vegetables."

In the world of Eleanor Harris, there was no room for a "too-good-to-be-true" creature like Audrey Hepburn. But Harris held out hope that someday Hepburn would "prove it by finally revealing herself to be like the rest of the human race, both good and bad."

How simple for freelance writer Eleanor Harris. Bang out 2,500 words, snag a $500 paycheck, and move on. But for Audrey Hepburn, the sentence was life long, written in blood, half British and half Frisian. The too-good personality had been pounded into her, not only by Mother but by merciless dance instructors, by ruthless German authorities, and by bombs manufactured in three countries. The mastery of self had been her means of survival in times that were blacker than black, when people she knew were dragged off, never to return, and when the food ran out and there was next to nothing to eat for weeks and months on end. No, there was never anyone quite like Audrey Hepburn, and there's no way of understating how wrong Harris had gotten her story. In fact, to meet Hepburn was to be in the presence of honesty, integrity, and genuineness. To see what remained after the war. All that was forged in the war. She was a woman who had survived. Yes, she carried secrets, and their burden was great. If a reporter strayed too close to any of these secrets, she would say, "I don't want to talk about that." But she would never dream of lying to you about anything. She had been brought up better than that.

Just fifteen years earlier she had ridden out the battle for "a bridge too far" and helped civilian victims deal with its aftermath. She would never go into detail about what she had seen—how much blood she had washed off her hands, how many souls in misery she had comforted; these were among the things she didn't want to talk about. While Eleanor Harris lived in the safety of the United States and wrote screenplays of adventure, the Dutch girl was experiencing adventures that were far too real. After the death of the baroness, Audrey opened up about the trials of being her mother's daughter: "I was given an outlook on life by my mother, a lady of very strict Victorian standards," said Hepburn. "It was frowned upon to bother others with your feelings. It was frowned upon not to think of others first. It was frowned upon not to be disciplined."

In October 1944 she brought fifteen years of her mother's training to bear in the hospital of Velp as she started down a path that would have at its end, forty-four years later, the role of UNICEF ambassador.

27

Hunters

"Our presence there [in Velp] was tolerated by the Germans, but just barely so," said Audrey of the tenuous weeks after the battle for Arnhem. It was a time when her village maintained its status as the most important spot to the Nazis in the whole of the Netherlands. Seyss-Inquart and Rauter, the ruling administration, moved back into their villas. The Dutch SS contingent, minus all their records lost in the panic-burning of the Hotel Naeff, returned as well.

British prisoners were processed through Velp and marched to prison camps in the east, and fresh German troops passed through on their way to Arnhem. Morning and evening, steady streams of tanks, half-tracks, and trucks loaded with soldiers headed west down the van Heemstras' street and main street as well, then on to Arnhem to reinforce the troops there.

The steady flow of military vehicles on Velp's thoroughfares quickly drew attention from the "hunters," Allied fighter aircraft that were the dread of both the German army and Dutch civilians. Photographs by reconnaissance aircraft noticed the situation first, then free-wheeling British fighter planes began patrols that sought targets of opportunity. The city of Arnhem and village of Oosterbeek might have been the prizes earned by Model and Bittrich, but the skies over all of Gelderland were, with the Luftwaffe now crippled by Allied bombing and fighter support, every inch British. The RAF Second Tactical Air Force, or 2nd TAF, had taken over the former Luftwaffe airfield at Le Culot near present-day Louvain-la-Neuve, Belgium, putting Allied aircraft just 100 air miles south-southwest of Arnhem and Velp.

All Velpenaren, including Audrey, learned fast lessons regarding the art of aerial warfare as practiced by the Allies in the days after Germany's victory at Arnhem. "I had gone into the village to do something," said Audrey. "I don't know, shop for my mother or whatever, and all of a sudden there was a German convoy going through the village. And everybody along the road sort of stopped. And then British Spitfires suddenly swooped down going dit-dit-dit-dit-dit, and I was pushed under a tank, which saved me—the German tank." It was the first time she had been in the direct line of hostile bullets, in this case fired by the Spitfire's Browning machine guns.

The sudden formations of fighters patrolling the length of the vital road from Arnhem through Velp and east to Germany caused the Reich's motorized columns to seek shelter during the daylight hours for fear of drawing a rocket attack. These hunters, as both the Dutch and Germans referred to them, would swoop out of nowhere, sometimes with a moment's warning from the air-raid siren, sometimes not. But German soldiers kept their heads on swivels to see what might be coming from above.

Armored vehicles were parked under the canopy of the beech trees along Rozendaalselaan every day and, invariably, in front of the Beukenhof. Neighbor boy Dick Mantel reported that the van Heemstras' residence was usually buttoned up tight at this point in the war, with very little coming or going from the occupants. But Audrey continued to help Dr. Visser 't Hooft tend the sick and wounded as a result of the battle.

"My father's time was completely taken up caring for refugees and wounded people pouring in from all sides to Velp," said his daughter Clan. "He was, apart from working at the hospital, a great deal of the day visiting private homes where refugees and sick people needed care. He was an overall doctor, pulling teeth, doing small operations like stitching wounds or removing shell splinters, delivering babies, and so on."

Through it all, Audrey could hear Allied heavy bombers flying over, the Americans by day and the British by night. As she had all year, on clear days she could take heart by looking up during her walk to work or out the hospital window at the dots in the sky four miles straight up and marvel at their brilliant white contrails. The German flak guns still blazed, but the bombers still flew, never ceasing their attacks.

On cloudy days the bombers couldn't be seen, but they always could be heard, and then, a while after they had passed overhead, the detonation of bombs rumbled in the east on the far side of the German border fifty, seventy-five, or even a hundred miles away. And on every surface inside every home grew a gritty layer of residue from the war. Bits of gunpowder, dust and fragments from flak bursts, ash from homes and buildings burned out in Arnhem—it all rained down on Velp and stayed there, with no spare water to clean anything. Not that it mattered, because even if the ever-tidy Dutch wiped and swept up the grit, which they did constantly, the war would just rain down again the next day, and the next.

Reminders of the 4 October deadline for refugees to depart from Velp came on the second of the month and again on the third. Announcements were posted on message boards and nailed to trees. Those poor souls taken in by the van Heemstras dutifully packed up and prepared to go.

"It was unspeakably hard to turn away family and friends into the cold night," said Audrey of that 4 October. "Even my brother, who was hiding there, had to leave."

The fourth was a Wednesday, and Audrey was at work in the Ziekenhuis, which the Germans had labeled "a center of illegal action." They knew it was Resistance headquarters in the village, but the facility was so well run that it couldn't be proven. Said Velp historian Gety Hengeveld-de Jong of the ever more sophisticated system of smuggling onderduikers through the village, "[Chief of Staff] Dr. van der Willigen and [head nurse] Sister van Zwol worked to assist 'illegal immigrants.' For example, a flight line for Jews, co-organized by the later publisher Geert Lubberhuizen, ran from Amsterdam and Utrecht via the Velp hospital to the 'hidden village' in the woods near Vierhouten; Velpsche Jew Mrs. Saartje Pik and husband spent the war in hiding in the hospital; and escaped French prisoners of war were temporarily taken care of and possibly medically cared for there." And of course the boys in white remained on the premises. All these activities went on in the building where Audrey assisted Dr. Visser 't Hooft.

It was on this Wednesday, deadline day for the refugees to vacate, that disaster struck at the heart of Velp. It began with the air-raid siren announcing the approach of a formation of British twin-engine Mosquito fighter-bombers following the Velperweg up from Arnhem. The eyes of the lead pilot must have grown wide at the sight of three Tiger tanks lumbering east up Hoofdstraat toward Germany in broad daylight. They were the Reich's finest, notorious both for their lethal bite and utter slowness. The "hunters" snapped into a dive after their prey.

On Hoofdstraat at the home of radiologist Dr. Bernhard van Griethuysen, no one even noticed the Tigers clanking past because tank activity was common on main street—except these tanks were careless enough to be moving during the day. Instead, all eyes were on Corrie van Griethuysen, who had just returned from the hairdresser with her two sons, Joost and Ben, in tow. The boys began playing with neighbor Annemarth Visser 't Hooft and other children in the garden.

Jan van Hensbergen, an accountant in Arnhem until the battle, sat reading at home on Audrey's street when the air-raid siren began to wail. The noise became deafening in seconds as the planes thundered over and plates flew from the cupboard in all directions. Van Hensbergen grabbed his dog in one arm and the child he was babysitting in the other and dove to the floor as bullets stitched the walls over their prone bodies. Rockets hit the house next door and shrapnel ripped through the walls. The Mosquitoes zipped over the van Heemstras' street still firing wing guns and sets of rockets. The next pair of rockets pierced the wall of the stately brick post office and exploded inside.

Up the main street, Corrie van Griethuysen had time only to turn and see a plane screaming toward her firing rockets. The van Griethuysens' home was located at a jog in Hoofdstraat. The road jogged to the left and the tanks jogged with it. The planes kept firing in a straight line.

Corrie shoved Joost, Ben, and Annemarth inside the glass patio door of their home as rockets exploded at intervals of fifty yards. Boom! Boom! Boom! Boom! Boom! Closer and closer and into the Griethuysen garden hit the rockets. A sixty-pound warhead exploded a few yards from the group of frightened civilians. Windows were shattered as far away as the Ziekenhuis.

When the smoke cleared, Corrie van Griethuysen, mother of Joost and Ben, lay dead. "She took the shock and we were safe," said Annemarth. Six refugees from Arnhem sprawled in death nearby. The wounded children were whisked away from the scene. All told, seventeen civilians died and forty were wounded in the day's air attack on those three tanks.

Craters stepped their way along Velp's busiest street and a geyser shot water skyward from one of the few pipes in the village that was still operational—connected to a German facility no doubt. Jan van Hensbergen hurried up from his damaged home to gather information for a report to the Resistance. He wrote, "According to our observation, no tanks were hit."

Allied bombs had again made innocent Velpenaren pay. It

was always the Dutch civilians who suffered and mourned while the fighter planes simply flew away, their pilots shielded from the moral ramifications of killing civilians. "You are not in immediate contact with the damage you've created on the ground with your rockets or whatever it was—your guns," said RAF fighter-pilot Sir Kenneth Adam, "because you're flying over at 500 miles per hour and you're not like when you are in an infantry unit attack. You see tanks being destroyed and you attack to concentrations, but you are still detached from what is happening on the ground."

In the wake of the British Mosquitoes, back in Velp Audrey saw wounded received at the hospital. For Dr. Visser 't Hooft and his fifteen-year-old helper, the attack that killed Corrie van Griethuysen was personal because of the close relationships among the doctors of Velp, like family. With great care little Ben was brought in; he had been too near the blast that killed his mother. He was deafened in one ear and suffered other injuries, and yet didn't know his mother was gone. He was told she was in the hospital and would be back in a few weeks. For Ben, the days passed with agonizing slowness, and as each went by he anticipated her return. Then with no mother in sight after what must surely have been more than three weeks, he asked his older sister what was going on.

"She told me the truth that my mother was already buried and not living anymore," said Ben. "And then I went to the hospital and there Audrey Hepburn met me and took me in her arms to calm me. I remember looking into her big, wide eyes." He would never forget the compassion in Audrey's face as this gentle teenager who had always loved children now sought to comfort little Ben.

For Audrey and all the van Heemstras, the war was hitting ever closer to home.

28
The Magic Stamp

"After living the long months and years under the Germans," said Audrey, "you dreamed what would happen if you ever got out. You swore you would never complain about anything again."

On 5 October, the day after the rocket attack had killed Corrie van Griethuysen and the others, the British fighter squadrons sought to repeat their luck finding German vehicles moving along the streets. Hoofdstraat had been identified by now as a wide-open, highly visible thoroughfare and, obviously, the main artery for military traffic moving from the German border to Arnhem and all points west.

Fighters attacked Velp three times that day, as Steven Jansen described from his vantage point just two blocks from the Beukenhof: "Majestically circling high above the village in the bright blue sky, then noses down they dive. One after the other they come rushing on the ground as their wings sparkle and crackle firing rocket bombs. The machine guns rattle. Houses collapse in ruins. Streets are ripped open. The fighters climb up, turn, and dive again."

The second Mosquito attack of the day hit Rozendaalselaan. Rockets detonated just yards from Audrey's home and blew in windows in the neighborhood. One house was set on fire, and a woman near the Beukenhof received a head wound and bled to death.

All grew quiet again—until a quarter to five, when the third and final attack of the day rained dozens of bombs down on Velp as the van Heemstras sheltered in their cellar and prayed. Homes were destroyed across the village and more civilians died. At dusk, the fires continued to burn. Agitation was high and families packed up to get out. Among them were the van Heemstras' neighbors, the van Hensbergen family. They gathered belongings and headed away from what had suddenly become the war's main street. The Visser 't Hoofts also moved away from Hoofdstraat. But Opa decided to sit tight and hope. After all, where was there to go that was any safer than here? Even the Castle Rozendaal, that mighty fortress of the van Pallandts with walls fifteen feet thick, had been hit with an incendiary and nearly destroyed. Death lurked in every corner of the Netherlands now, and no one was safe.

On Friday the fighters circled again, firing machine guns and rockets, and on Saturday South Velp was hit and more Velpenaren died. Every ear now strained to hear an airplane motor in time to find cover, and yet attacks from the sky were but one of so many evils plaguing the population.

More than 28,000 Dutch railway workers had joined the ranks of the onderduikers after 17 September when the Dutch government in exile had urged a strike. By 1 October, members of the Dutch Resistance were alerting London to the impending disaster of a Netherlands without the food that could be carried only by train. The answer received from London to these Resistance warnings: "Military interests demand that the strike goes on—till the day the enemy leaves the country."

Through October loyal Dutchmen followed the wishes of their queen and British Prime Minister Churchill; the trains did not run with the exception of a few moving from Germany into Velp and on to Arnhem as manned by rail forces from the Reich. These trains kept men and supplies flowing into Arnhem, but for the Dutch civilian population, there was no food at all.

Velp was surrounded on three sides by farms, and yet to journey out in daylight meant to risk death from those hunters above. The situation grew dire. The German military confiscated all the food it could find in town for its soldiers. Trucks that might carry food to the civilian population had no fuel, and those few that had been converted to wood-burning engines dared not drive about the roads. Allied fighter attacks couldn't be predicted; any movement on the ground, down to a civilian walking on a sidewalk, could draw attention. But of all reasons why hunger began to grow, the greatest was simple math: The Velpenaren had shared food with the vast numbers of refugees and they were gone now, leaving nothing. Rations resumed for the people of Velp but they had been cut, and then they were cut again. Bread, cheap and cherished foodstuff of the Dutch people, declined in quality when wheat flour supplies ran out. Pea and rye flour were substituted, but these wouldn't rise, and the bread was what locals described as "wet."

On 13 October the train station in Velp was bombed, as was the makeshift German military hospital at the Park Hotel. The tidy hotel was now a wreck and would never be rebuilt.

In mid-October, rumors started up again to the effect that Velp was about to be evacuated like Arnhem. The van Heemstras made contingency plans and rounded up supplies. By this time, with the daily fighter attacks, the desire among the battle-numbed citizenry to shelter at home was no longer as passionate. Then on 20 October nearly the entire population of a village to the southeast stumbled into Velp to report they had been ordered to evacuate with no notice. Again every manner of conveyance appeared, each sporting a white surrender flag. The road to the ghost town of Arnhem had been blocked, so Velp was the next logical destination.

"We enjoyed our few days' rest from the evacuees," said Steven Jansen, "until we learn we must accommodate their successors." Once again homes, including the Beukenhof, took in new boarders.

The German and Allied battle lines had solidified, with the Germans galvanizing their positions in the ruins from Oosterbeek through Arnhem and into the area of Velp. The British reinforced the city of Nijmegen to the south. Long-range artillery exchanges became a regular occurrence, usually in the evenings, and after a deep, booming launch to the south, and the arcing, whining passage of a heavy shell north, a home in Velp might simply, suddenly cease to exist along with the people inside it. Just gone. Between the air strikes and the shelling, it remained a sad, inarguable fact that most Velpenaren were being killed by the Allies, not by the Germans.

Not that sympathies toward the occupiers had changed. Since the battle of Arnhem and the railway strike, German high command reacted to every Dutch offense with an especially ruthless fury. When the Resistance attacked four German soldiers in the remote village of Putten, northwest of Velp, at the beginning of October, General Christiansen ordered executions and those who were not shot were rounded up and shipped to Germany as forced labor—589 men in all. To conclude Christiansen's day of terror in Putten, ninety homes were burned to the ground. Of the men taken away, fewer than sixty would ever see home again at war's end. Later in October, a massive Green Police raid in Rotterdam netted 50,000 men for shipment east to work as forced laborers in Germany.

The Germans were taking everything even vaguely useful out of the Netherlands. Food was of prime importance, from grain to livestock. It also became a common sight in Velp to see trucks piled high with loot stolen from the homes in Arnhem and Oosterbeek being driven toward the German border. Especially needed there were beds and bedding, but fine Dutch furniture was prized and anything of value left behind by refugees—from dishes to clothing to picture frames—was soon pilfered.

Everything that could be stolen from the area was stolen—

like Velp's beautiful fire engine and the trams in Arnhem. Most of those not destroyed in the battle were dismantled and taken to Germany. It was maddening.

Then came those damn rumors again. Velp would be evacuated next because the military didn't want useless civilians around. Some families kept a hand cart always packed with essentials for the inevitable order to get out of town. Everyone in Velp had seen the looters' cars and trucks heading for Germany, and these sights made the Velpenaren intent on digging in their heels and staying in their homes, come what may.

On 21 October came word: Velp must evacuate. Villagers knew this was fact and not rumor when they learned that Velp's Mayor Kalhorn, who was in the know if anyone was, had begun packing. And so everyone in the village followed suit, including Baron van Heemstra and his family. They had no idea where they would go; they knew only that seventy-three-year-old Opa would be leading his two forty-something baroness daughters and his malnourished granddaughter on an odyssey by foot. *They* would now be the specters trudging through the countryside under a white flag, like so many before them.

The next day came a surprise reversal: Audrey and her family and all other villagers learned that they didn't have to vacate after all. The relief was enormous and no one ever knew exactly why a reprieve had been granted.

Velpsche historian and author Gety Hengeveld-de Jong attributed the reversal to the infrastructure needs and practicality of the Germans. The local office of the Dutch National Office for Food Supply in Wartime was run by Paul Roelofsen and Jan Koens of Velp, who, according to Hengeveld-de Jong "worked to assure that there would be enough food: meat, potatoes, chickens, and vegetables from around the province, not only for the inhabitants, but for all the Germans fighting in and around Arnhem. [At this time] hundreds or perhaps thousands of Germans were sleeping, eating, and relaxing in Velp, where there were shoemakers, black-smiths, and other craftsmen they needed. Soldiers could go shopping and to pubs. If Velp were to be evacuated, the Germans had to organize all that in little villages nearby."

Seyss-Inquart may have realized that he would be creating headaches for all involved by evacuating the village where he had set up shop, along with Rauter and other key Nazi officials—not to mention the fighting men who had flooded into Velp. It was, after all, the only functional business district for miles around.

Another story has circulated to account for cancellation of the order to evacuate the village. In this version, a certain rare postage stamp (the 1934 Dollfuss Austrian ten schilling) was coveted by a stamp-collecting German general who knew that one such stamp existed in Velp. When the stamp was brought to him, he rescinded the evacuation order. Whichever story is correct—and perhaps portions of each have merit—the van Heemstras did not have to march out under a white flag to points unknown while their home was looted behind them.

It proved to be an isolated piece of good news. Across the Netherlands, electricity to the civilian population was cut back, and then cut back some more; in Velp it had never returned since the Airborne. In all ways, the people of the Netherlands had descended into darkness.

Even now, Audrey still managed to give private and group ballet lessons here and there, whenever relative calm returned to the village. She operated in any room that could be lit by daylight and used a hand-cranked record player.

"We had no light, no heat, no water," said Audrey. "We had no food, because all the shops were closed. We ate what we could find."

Many Velpenaren were too enterprising to sit in their homes and wait for the situation to improve. With the weather growing colder but snow not yet falling, the fittest took to bicycles with patchwork tires or no tires at all and ventured into the countryside. They would make their journeys at sunrise or after dusk to avoid the hunters circling in the skies. Some ventured into the Veluwe north of the village to visit farms for any food available. Others paid to be ferried across the Rhine or the IJssel in rowboats. Food was obtained in trade for real Dutch money or jewelry or clothing and brought back for those with the muscle and know-how, always at the risk that Dutch SS in *zwartjassen*, the dreaded black coats, would confiscate the food as it was brought back to Velp and arrest those carrying it and worse, forward them to the Reich. In many cases children were sent to find food because the Germans didn't bother with children or consider them a threat. But the Beukenhof was home to neither fit men nor energetic children.

With the steady stream of wartime casualties, Dr. Visser 't Hooft kept Audrey busy at the Ziekenhuis, and each day she completed that brief but intense walk from the Beukenhof, head down to avoid scrutiny by the moffen.

Among her duties was the situation with little Ben Griethuysen. "In November I had just lost my mother," he said. "I would go every afternoon to the hospital, to where the bandages were washed and had to be rolled, and Audrey was my oppas, my buddy. And she would roll the bandages and I sat in front of her. So she took care of me a little bit."

Visser 't Hooft also had unorthodox requests of his young volunteer aide, like calling upon Audrey to deliver the local Resistance newspaper, *Oranjekrant*. With paper pulp in extremely short supply, the *Oranjekrant* packed its volume of critical information into a surface area about the size of half a paper napkin. Audrey described having "to step in and deliver our tiny underground newspaper. I stuffed them in my woolen socks in my wooden shoes, got on my bike and delivered them."

Audrey wasn't alone. Visser 't Hooft's daughter Clan and her older brother Willem delivered messages to addresses in Velp under the pretext that they were carrying medicine to patients on behalf of their father the doctor.

"Wim and I were always sent out together," said Clan, because these were, she said, "rather tricky expeditions." Later, Wim and Clan would be recognized by the Red Cross with a medal and certificate for their clandestine work.

While the Germans paid no mind to children running about, the danger and worry for the parents was real. But for Audrey and the Visser 't Hooft children, outsmarting the Germans could at times be a grand adventure, and they never knew the significance of what they were delivering. "Messages about the refugees, the onderduikers," supposed Annemarth with a shrug, thinking about the papers carried by her brother and sister. "We were never told."

The situation in town remained tense, with the occasional *razzia*, or raid by the Green Police to find able-bodied men to work in Germany. The curfew to clear the streets was moved up to six in the evening, meaning there was even less time for outdoor activities for civilians and more hours to be sequestered at home with no electricity or heat.

On 7 November deep rumbling explosions were heard to the northwest. Villagers in Velp would learn through the grapevine that the moffen had blown up the interior of the Diogenes command bunker at Deelen Air Base rather than let the facilities fall into enemy hands. Diogenes was a massive building with walls several yards thick. Inside was the nerve center where all radar information filtered in about Allied bomber formations and was displayed on a state-of-the-art glass map twenty feet square. Those in Velp considered its destruction to be significant; it was the first hopeful sign in months. Perhaps the Germans were expecting another major attack? Another invasion? Hope made a minor comeback, yet the air was turning very cold, and coal for the furnaces was fast becoming a precious commodity.

November brought the worst autumnal rains in generations;

rains so constant and so dismal that the Dutch began to wonder if the weather now favored the Nazis. Radio Oranje reported that the advance of the Allies on the western front was now checked, not by the Germans but by mud.

To the west in The Hague, food had run out. Still, the Dutch sought not to suffer but to act. "City dwellers left their homes by hundreds of thousands to descend like locusts on the farmers," wrote historian Henri van der Zee. Some farmers cooperated, but others did not, arguing that they couldn't feed everyone. The farther west one went, the worse the situation grew. Hunger had the Netherlands by the throat. And winter lay ahead.

29
Streaking Evil

"My childhood in Arnhem and in Velp was the most important part of my youth," said Audrey. "I was ten when the Germans invaded the Netherlands and I was fifteen when it was all over. They were very delicate, precious years. I experienced a lot then, but it was not all misery. The circumstances brought family and friends closer together. You ate the last potatoes together."

Intrigue ruled the country's most important village in the latter half of November. First, the Resistance managed to free all twenty-two political prisoners who had been placed in the Rotterdamsche Bank for the purposes of confinement and torture. While the daring rescue had probably been pulled off by the more violent and radical arm of the Resistance, the Knokploegen, or K.P., the hospital's corps of physicians was immediately suspected. Six days later Green Police cordoned off the entire building and conducted a search room by room looking for the missing prisoners. The officer in charge of the moff went chin to chin with the head nurse and Audrey's boss in the hospital, Sister van Zwol. While the nurse gave the Germans an earful, all nine boys in white used their escape hatch behind the bed of another nurse, Sister Fenna, and crawled up to the safety of the secret chamber in the attic above the operating room.

Perhaps like never before, the traditional arrival of *Sinterklaas* bore special meaning on 5 December 1944 in a Velp shaken by war, darkened by lack of electricity, and wracked by a deepening hunger. The uniquely Dutch secular celebration of Sint-Nicolaas Eve preceded a 6 December feast that could not properly come, at least not this year. But the celebration would be held nonetheless.

According to tradition, Sinterklaas sailed into a Dutch port from Spain in November accompanied by Zwarte Piet, his helper, who was a Moor and carried Sinter's bag of toys and candy. Then, mitre on his head and staff in hand, Sinterklaas would mount his white steed and head to his round of appointments on 5 December, which included a sit-down in each home in the Netherlands. As Ella described it, "Sint-Nicolaas comes on the 5th of December and puts sweets and presents in children's shoes. He rides on a white horse over the roof tops, dressed in the long red cloak of a bishop, with a mitre on his head. He has a long white beard and is accompanied by a little black boy, his servant Pete." Pete carries the sweets and presents in a large bag—the same bag that bad children are placed in when they're carried off to Spain.

When Ella had been told at age eight that Sinterklaas didn't really exist, she rebelled, saying "one cannot give up one's beliefs just like that! They become part of one's life, especially in the very young." As a result she always held the Christmas traditions dear, and passed this soft spot for Sinterklaas on to Audrey.

By some strange twist of fate, the Germans had looted all the toys from a store called Perry Sport in Arnhem and moved them to a building in Velp, perhaps intending that they would be taken to Germany in time for Christmas. After a certain time, it became clear that the idea was forgotten, perhaps because of the hunters and their attacks. And yet the toys remained. With Sint-Nicolaas Eve at hand, Dr. Visser 't Hooft asked Audrey to see to distribution of these toys to the children of Velp. Audrey and children had always been a match made in heaven. "I loved them when I was little," she said. "I used to embarrass my mother by trying to pick babies up out of prams at the market and, you know, that kind of thing. The one thing I dreamed of in my own life was to have children of my own."

On this evening, nearly every child in the village became Audrey's own. They converged on the building of the N.H.V. on Stationsstraat, where the toys were taken. It was the place where Audrey had conducted her dance lessons for village children, and now it became Toyland for a teenager as grateful for the opportunity to distribute presents to children as the children were grateful to receive them.

A makeshift Sinterklaas, portrayed first by one of the boys in white and later by a member of the Red Cross, wore a false beard but not a mitre on his head. A white helmet would have to do. On his arm he wore a white armband, both helmet and armband designating the saint as a Red Cross noncombatant. He had arrived in an ambulance with its markings covered instead of on a white steed. The children delighted in the toys they received from Sinterklaas via Audrey this evening; they loved even more the opportunity to be out among their friends and breathing fresh air after weeks spent cowering in cellars while the battle raged and later while the bombs, shells, and rockets rained down. If the small ones had ventured out in the past couple of months, it was to gather food, or firewood, or to deliver a message from one member of the Resistance to another. The children were so very much depended upon, their missions life or death in some cases, and now they could merely *be* children and celebrate a grand old Dutch tradition.

For adults like the baron, Ella, Meisje, and even Audrey, since she had long outgrown a belief in Sinterklaas, there was still a celebration to be had—the night of the surprise. This tradition involved the drawing of a family member's name and then the selection of a gift, with the point of the tradition being to praise or call attention to the recipient in clever and loving verse as the gift is presented. It was an evening of celebrations across Velp that was free of both British artillery and German raids and a brief respite from the relentless gloom of war.

Gallows humor, a Dutch specialty, ruled at the Beukenhof. Audrey would remember later, "It actually was a marvelous time because people needed each other more than ever and depended on each other. And you borrowed each other's books...and you sat around the table eating a *hutspot* (stew) made with everybody's potatoes, you know? And I have a family with a wonderful sense of humor. Both my grandfather and my aunt, my mother and friends. In many ways it was quite a wonderful period."

By the beginning of December, people in Velp began to notice on clear days, up in the sky, a single white line tracing its way across the blue. "Slowly they blow away," said Steven Jansen of the vapor trails. "Now the lines appear in the east, then in the west or north. Only in the southern sky, the areas liberated, do you not see these stripes in the sky. They resemble condensation trails from planes, but that's not what they are. Then the solution comes. It is the mark of the new German weapon, V2."

These "vengeance weapons" were rockets forty-five feet in length and carrying a one-ton warhead. They were remarkably machined and well tested, with a range of up to 200 miles. They had been stationed on the western coast of the Netherlands, but now with the Allies in control of the coastline, all the artillery units had moved their mobile platforms to the eastern part of the country. Dozens of V2s were launched every day toward the most important target within range: the docks at the port of Antwerp in Belgium, where tons of Allied war supplies were landing by the hour. "Nobody hears, nobody sees this monster weapon," wrote Jansen from his home not far from the Beukenhof, "as with staggering speed it drops from the stratosphere onto tortured humanity."

The December weather grew ever colder. When Audrey wasn't working on behalf of Dr. Visser 't Hooft, she continued to occupy herself, and many of the children of Velp, with dance lessons. Then on the night of the 15th, a strange new sound carried on the air. At first it seemed to be a truck that was down-shifting on a steep hill. No, no, it was a motorcycle speeding along Hoofdstraat. No, that deep grinding sound, half machine gun, half jackhammer...

Every time the sound went away, it came back again a little later. Finally, the answer was revealed that night, flying low in the sky. Said Jansen, "Velp has been introduced to a new horror: V1."

"All day long, V1s are flying over in a southwestern direction," wrote Audrey's neighbor Jan van Hensbergen who had returned to his house on Rozendaalselaan. "You can't see them by day, but in the evening you can see a fiery glow in the sky."

The German V1 flying bombs that would become a part of the lives of everyone in Velp had first been launched from the coasts of the Netherlands and France, so many that this region had become known as the "rocket coast." About 10,000 V1s with a range of 150 miles each had been launched at London, beginning days after the Normandy landings, with 2,419 making it to target and killing more than 6,000 British subjects in just four months. It was another "vengeance weapon" justified by the mass killing of German civilians in British bomber raids that had gone on night after night throughout the war. By now, millions of Germans had died under Allied bombs.

Each V1 was twenty-seven feet long, with a distinctive jackhammer thrum produced by a pulsing jet engine. The V1 was catapulted off an inclined ramp thirty feet long and carried a 1,750-pound warhead—roughly equivalent to half the payload of a U.S. B-17 bomber in a single death missile.

As more of the western coast of Europe became threatened by Allied advances in the summer of 1944, V1 launch sites were moved east, like the V2s had been. Now, London sat out of range of the flying bombs, but the Germans believed this weapon was too important to sit idle, and so, as with the V2, the Reich pointed V1s at the port of Antwerp. As luck would have it, the Luftwaffe had established V1 launch facilities in Eefde and Gorssel, less than twenty miles to the northeast of Velp, and Audrey and the others in the village were hearing its maiden launches.

For those in Velp, the V2 was just another weapon of war flying high overhead, like the bombers they had been seeing and hearing for years now. But the V1 became a real concern and a deadly menace when one of these flying bombs malfunctioned and fell in the Veluwe just outside the village. Then another saw its engine quit and down it came even closer to town. Soon the pattern became clear: After launch, the V1 would reach altitude and the autopilot would take control just to the east of Velp, if not directly overhead. But on many of the V1s, the controls were faulty, and the bomb meant for Antwerp might just fall from the sky or fly crazily and menace the village. There was no way to predict what was going to happen when the V1s were heard throbbing in the sky, and they flew over several times every twenty-four hours, every day and every night. It was always worst late at night with no other competing sounds, just the "snoring in the fog," as Jansen phrased it. The snore of a streaking evil that could kill at any moment. And the Germans were producing V1s at a rate high enough to launch them continuously.

Audrey, along with everyone in Velp, shared these troubles, not just the threat of the V1s but also of disease as the lack of nourishment, water, and cleaning products and the high number of citizens and onderduikers packed into town brought an outbreak of typhus. In December, Audrey received three typhus inoculations along with other Velpenaren. Diphtheria also broke out, and scabies developed among people who for centuries had prided themselves on cleanliness. One member of the Airborne who ventured into an Oosterbeek cellar to treat a wounded civilian at the height of the battle noted, "The men were surprisingly neat, in good suits. They were very quiet and courteous, and there was no excitement or fuss." Comportment, even in the most trying conditions, meant everything to the Dutch.

Conditions now as winter deepened were trying indeed. The population was growing weaker as the supply of food decreased. The bread ration was cut from 900 grams per week, already a pitiable amount, to 800. Bread was counted upon because so many other foods had already run out, and now the slices were paper-thin, even for children.

The shortage of coal drove Audrey and others in Velp outside to find wood to burn in stoves for warmth as winter's grip tightened. Fences and railings that had survived the desperate search for fuel in previous winters disappeared around town as if by a sudden termite infestation, and trees fell to midnight axmen. Bombed-out homes were picked clean of every decent scrap and splinter. The Velpenaren found ways to keep going day upon day as they listened to Radio Oranje for the latest news of the war on the Western front.

One day they learned of a German attack across a broad front only 120 miles south of Velp, down in Belgium. Massive formations of German Tiger II tanks had broken through Allied lines in the Ardennes Forest, and with this latest development following soon after the British defeat at Arnhem, with V1s and V2s relentlessly pounding the Allies, it looked as if the entire course of the war might be shifting in Hitler's favor. If that were to happen, and with the lack of food and fuel, with disease on the rise, there was little doubt that this would be the end of life for Audrey and every other Dutch citizen who called Velp home.

30

Peace on Earth.
Yeah, Right.

"Food was very scarce, especially in the last few months of the war," said Audrey. "In the area where I was living it was particularly serious because [of] the battle of Arnhem, one of the bloodiest of the war...."

But there was bloody, and then there was bloody. The latest bloody battle raged in the Ardennes region of Belgium, with the Germans pushing hard to puncture Allied lines and make a mad dash to recapture Antwerp. Such a calamity were that to happen, with the Reich restocked with supplies, all of Belgium falling for a second time, and the war dragging on for years perhaps, by which time Hitler might unleash more of his terror inventions.

Across the Netherlands, all attention focused on the latest word delivered by those critical fifteen-minute broadcasts from Radio Oranje. Nearly a half million German troops were fighting in the snow in Belgium, pressing forward behind more than a thousand Tiger II tanks, the kind Audrey knew so well from seeing them parked in front of the Beukenhof, steel monsters ten feet high that were so heavy they tore up cobblestone and paved streets with equal ease. Now they were tearing up the lines of American soldiers who found themselves cut off in the forest and facing their own starvation diets.

Tensions increased in Velp as events in Belgium played out;

243

each day for the van Heemstras centered around Radio Oranje broadcasts. Opa couldn't be seen trudging over to Jan Mantel's house four times a day, so he most often waited until nightfall and caught the eight o'clock broadcast. The German radio operators clomping up and down the steps at irregular intervals only increased anxiety as any suspicious activity after curfew could mean immediate arrest.

In Velp, conditions worsened. The British army pushing north from Nijmegen threatened the Germans in Arnhem, so the moff had blown dikes in the Betuwe, flatlands south of the Rhine, to stop any troop movements. Heavy rains and floods cut Velp off from Rheden to the east. With that way closed, a vital source of food went with it. Then a deep cold snap signaled the dead of winter, and the skies were low and cloudy. Houses froze on the inside, even the one room that theoretically could be heated—but wood burned faster than coal and left behind less residual heat. Overhead, V1s shot through the sky from east of the IJssel toward Belgium in support of the Ardennes offensive. They flew over at all hours, their throaty growl unnerving everyone in earshot, and after dark when there wasn't low cloud cover, the fiery exhaust trails provided a fascinating and horrific sight. Worst of all, enough were malfunctioning and dropping from the skies that the Velpenaren held their breath until each had cleared the village and continued on its deadly sojourn.

Most nights, artillery boomed off to the south and across the vast flat expanse could be seen muzzle flashes like lightning in the distance. Was it the Ardennes battle moving closer? Was Gelderland again to become the front lines, and was the combat going to be street to street, house to house, and hand to hand?

Day after day, the Germans pounded Americans in the Ardennes. The Velpenaren wondered if this would be the end of everything. Said Steven Jansen, "For the first time in months the moffen go singing by the village." In his diary he captured the renewed bravado that Velpenaren heard from the occupier: "Now that the new weapons are ready," he quoted them as saying, "you will experience something! No Anglo-American will remain alive in Europe. Hitler wins the war!"

Radio Oranje said that the brave American troops in the Ardennes were dying by the thousands and that relief couldn't reach them because of the same bad weather that had been plaguing Velp. Worse still, Germans were wearing American uniforms and speaking fluent English, then infiltrating the lines and murdering Yanks. Everything was going wrong at once.

Five days after the first announcement of the German attacks, the Americans were pushed back into France and surrounded near a town called Bastogne. That same day, Audrey heard a number of distant thumps from the south, down Nijmegen way. That sound always made hearts stop because of what it could mean. In seconds shells whistled through the air and rained down on Velp in a series of explosions that tore up the earth and blew houses to splinters.

Several shells hit near Stationsstraat. The ambulance bell clanged and rescue personnel scooped up victims. The dead were lying on the main street and its sidewalks alike. After a quiet period more thumps sounded from Nijmegen and there was nothing for Audrey to do but seek shelter with others at the hospital where she was working and ask God for mercy. In came the heavy shells in booming explosions that knocked people off their feet a quarter mile from the impact site. On it went for two more hours until after seven in the evening. Then Audrey was among those caring for civilians injured in the attack.

Worst of all, there was no way to know what the Allies were trying to hit in poor beleaguered Velp, which remained the most important village in the entirety of the country. Were they going for Seyss-Inquart at his home on Parkstraat, or Rauter in his on the Velperweg, or a barracks or anti-aircraft battery? None of it made sense anymore, and there was nothing to do but light an oil lamp, if one could be found that worked and if there was fuel to power it, or light a candle, and sit huddled together for warmth. On nights like this one, it was just the four of them—Audrey, Ella, Meisje, and Opa.

"We entertained each other," said Audrey, "and it helped carry our minds away from the horrible life we were leading. We could do it, too; we lived in another world during those nights around the fire." Meanwhile, overhead, the V1s continued to grind their way west toward Antwerp.

Jan van Hensbergen captured the mood on Christmas Day in wartime Velp in his diary entry written just down the street from Audrey: "*Peace on earth*. Yeah, right. In the wonderful weather there are a lot of planes up in the air. Attacks with bombers in the direction of Dieren. Heavy artillery fire during the whole day. Is this going to be the last Christmas during war time? You would lose your optimism. Also the V1s are flying over peacefully."

The dawning of 1945 brought snows and deepening hunger that was worst in the west, where in places like The Hague and Rotterdam the ration had been cut to just 500 grams of bread a week—not enough to keep people alive with the cold and outbreak of disease. Yet it was also bad in Velp, where the pitiful ration was holding, but even potatoes were in short supply for more than a month, with no new orders being filled. The River IJssel had frozen over meaning no boat traffic could bring food. Velpenaren could be seen digging through the snow into frozen earth in potato fields desperate to find anything the farmers may have missed. Those who had hoarded potatoes now put a high cash price on them or traded for clothing or blankets that were needed to keep the cold at bay without adequate heat in the homes. And that was another problem: The Germans had stolen so many coats and sweaters and blankets for the people in their bombed-out fatherland that the Dutch had too little left with which to keep themselves warm.

The only constants through January were Germans on the

streets of Velp, snow, and hunger. The SS Panzer offensive in the Ardennes had ultimately failed. Hitler had risked everything on this attack against the Americans—all he had remaining of his army. He had never respected those Americans as fighting men, but they had held out. Then the weather broke, and Allied air power turned the tide and broke the German army.

Now the moffen in Velp were more desperate than ever for food and equipment, including even the few bicycles that had remained operational. More homes were confiscated to quarter reinforcements moving into the area to shore up the defensive line in Arnhem—by now German boys as young as fourteen or fifteen and men as old as sixty were showing up; this time it was Kerkstraat in South Velp near the railroad line where families must evacuate, although a villa was commandeered just a street over from the Beukenhof as well. If it could happen so close by, then Opa knew their home could be next.

Tempers grew shortest toward the end of the month after what had proven to be the most brutal winter weather in generations—every winter during the war had been worse than the one just past. Lack of food and fuel and the incessant passage of V1s over the heads of the Velpenaren drove many to the brink of madness. The sentiment expressed by Henri van der Zee, then age eleven, represented the experience of Audrey and everyone else who lived under the V1s: "We always listened tensely for the rumbling sound overhead to stop—which could mean disaster."

In Ede, ten miles west of Velp, Brig. John Hackett of the Airborne had been hiding out since an October escape from St. Elisabeth's in Arnhem. Hackett had been seriously wounded in the September fighting and now spent his time recovering in the care of a Dutch family. In the evenings in December and January, he had seen the V1s launched from Eefde and Gorssel paint their way west over Velp and then Arnhem. However, said Hackett, "Quite a large number were falling soon after launching. I watched several wandering crazily about the sky until their fiery tails went out. Then, after a breathless pause, there would be a rending crash we had now come to know so well. Others seemed to motor straight into the ground still going full blast." And it always seemed to be happening in and around Velp.

Velp's V1 problem was a constant threat and just too much to take given the snows and hunger. Then, finally, on the last day of January, the weather broke and a warm front ripped through the area, bringing spring winds and rain that divested the landscape of the snows in a couple of days. Still there was no food. Still the V1s flew over, and the sudden change in temperature seemed to cause more malfunctions in the buzz bombs than ever. On 2 February a V1 sputtered and fell just east of Velp; five days later another came down just a few blocks north of the Beukenhof and four days after that a bit south in the Velpsche Broek. The next day just north again, this time frightening half to death the van Pallandts at Castle Rozendaal, a V1 took off the top of the Rozendaal village school and then slammed into the van Pallandt castle garden and orangery. A week later twenty V1s malfunctioned and fell from the sky in a single night. One of them careened out of control just after launch and blew up a house full of German soldiers in the nearby village of Ellecom. Another fell in Rheden, the next town over from Velp, and injured fifty civilians. It seemed inevitable to Audrey that sooner or later a V1 was going to come down on the Beukenhof—everyone in Velp shared this thought about their homes as the Nazi death machines continued to fly overhead and so often plummeted to the ground.

But, oh, the hunger was worst of all and becoming desperate. "The last winter, the so-called 'hunger winter,'" said Audrey, "was the nearest I could come to saying I've seen starvation. It was not on the scale of Somalia, but it was pretty bad, too, you know. Children were always rummaging in the dust bins and people were dying of hunger and cold."

Six-year-old Ben van Griethuysen was one of the children Audrey described—sent out to farms and told to bring back dust from the mechanisms in the harvesting machines. Ben said what he and his friends found represented "the only thing we got to eat. We didn't have anything from the outside." In earlier months scavenging and trading had yielded results for enterprising families, but now there was next to nothing left to supplement the meager ration of bread. Potatoes were gone and now sugar beets were substituted. These coarse root vegetables were despised even by the starving Dutch. Said one, "Until I saw the first load of those monsters lying on the kitchen floor, I never knew that this wood in the shape of a turnip could be eaten." The only thing that seemed to work was to chop at it until it was more or less mashed and then form it into pancakes or porridge.

Lines formed at any store where rumors said food could be found. "Sometimes I didn't even have time to go home and let them know where I was," said Cornelia Fuykschot, who lived in Utrecht. "If you saw a line, you first joined and then asked what you were standing in line for. Sometimes the people ahead of you didn't know either."

In Amsterdam it was worse. Much worse. "Water rats, which normally stayed in the canals, now climbed the vertical brick walls of apartment blocks in search of food," said twenty-one-year-old Art Bos. "One sometimes saw a dog's head and skin in the gutter, people having eaten the dog, either their own or someone else's. Cats were long gone."

It was indeed total war in the Netherlands. To Audrey the sounds of battle, once distant, now didn't seem quite so far away. It was mid-February and artillery exchanges rattled the earth. She would describe it as "constant shelling." Tanks rumbled through the village heading toward Arnhem, their bulk often shearing off curbs, street signs, and low-hanging branches of trees. American P-47s and British Typhoons and Mosquitoes zipped low over the rooftops looking for moving targets or attacking German cannon. Often they hit Westervoort just across the IJssel to the south of Velp. Yes, the weather had broken, but the war hadn't. The war, the dying, the agony went on and on. All the van Heemstras could do was hang on for tomorrow, and then repeat the process and hope for a miracle. Through it all, Audrey's spirit was unbroken: "We would have great fun talking about what we were going to eat after the war was over," she said of those dark days of February 1945.

Part VI: Pursued

31

A Tree

Mogadishu, Somalia
September 1992

Under the protection of United Nations peacekeepers, Audrey stood with her man, Robbie, in the hot sun gaping at a cityscape of bombed-out buildings. Walls were rubble, roofs were missing. The devastation was vast—worse than anything she had seen in the Netherlands. She scanned the blocks for a building that hadn't been marred by bullet holes or worse, and she couldn't find even one. Civil war had broken out a year earlier, and the Somali government of Mohammed Siad Barre had been toppled. Audrey had called him "the most cruel despot imaginable." Into the void rose factions. Gunmen. Thugs. Two warring tribes now fought for control of the vast city and Audrey's delegation tiptoed inside that fragile peace.

The nation's agricultural sector had been destroyed, and she and Wolders were here to witness the resulting humanitarian crisis. And keep witnessing it. It wasn't safe to be here, but that was one of the reasons she needed to come—because it wasn't safe for anyone, especially the children.

Flying in from Nairobi to Kismayo, she had marveled at the parched red earth. Terra-cotta red. As she saw when the plane came in for a landing, the earth looked like a vast dry lake bed, that blood-red dirt puckered and lying in mounds, and she just knew the sights ahead were going to be bad.

At a child health care center in Kismayo, she looked about at the starving children of twelve and fourteen. It was only after she left that she realized: There were no small children. No infants. They were the first to go, and there were none left.

From Kismayo they set out on dusty paths that barely qualified as roads, where graves had been clawed out of barren soil for all the dead. This was why the terrain looked like it looked from the air: There were graves everywhere. It was said that a quarter of a million people had died since the civil war broke out, and now she had proof.

At Baidoa they arrived in time to see bodies being loaded into a truck, "most of them very small," she said. At a feeding center there was a courtyard with one tree, and the delegation saw small forms under the shade of that tree, being fed with delicacy by the nurses of the relief agency Irish Concern. Of these children Audrey said, "They were being more or less force-fed—a spoon of something every few minutes—because they can't drink or eat or don't want to any more. And what amazes me is the resilience of a human being, that they were still alive, still sitting."

She watched a boy of about fourteen fight for breath after breath, and then he just curled up and died. All about her there was profound silence. "Silent children," she said. "The silence is something you never forget."

Sights like these made the war come back in a flood of memories. The bombed-out buildings, the suffering, the starvation. She knew what it was like to be hungry because she had survived the Hunger Winter and so, oh yes, she knew.

She was tired, and everyone was concerned about her because she seemed especially thin and fragile these days. Sean and Luca had each called before the trip and begged her not to go, something they had never done on any of the other UNICEF excursions—and there had been many visits to dire situations. For some reason her very intuitive sons had sensed something about this trip in particular.

On the ground in Somalia, it was easy for the memories to yank her straight to the Netherlands, to those final days, to the sheer agony of the bombs and the hunger that ravaged her body and the cellar closing in until she could scream. When she thought about how those days felt, living them from the inside, she knew her duty. She must tell the world about Somalia and make the world listen. Step-by-step as she walked along in the heat and the dust with death all about, she fought the voices in her head that wondered if she had found a situation that qualified as hopeless, if this time there wasn't any answer at all. "You really have to wonder if God hasn't forgotten Somalia," she would dare to say later.

She thought back to '45, and that evening when Meisje had said they should stay in bed the next day because there was nothing to eat. Just stay in bed and sleep. But what had happened next had been a miracle, and she had to keep her heart open for miracles. And she believed people can't just wait for a miracle; sometimes they have to go out and work like the devil and make a damn miracle. So she had resolved to see what there was to see, all of it, and then go invite the media to press conferences in Nairobi, London, Geneva, and Paris.

At these press events Audrey tried to find words for the unspeakable. But there weren't any words to depict what she had seen—at least none that did it justice. "Somalia is one of the worst tragedies ever," she said. "It has gone over the edge." But Audrey being Audrey, she felt compelled to speak of the good, of the sailors on the USS Tarawa who had passed the hat and collected $4,000 and given it to Audrey for the children. Or the "oasis in the desert," an Oxfam settlement composed of people from different Somalian clans who were pulling together and working the land again using tools and seeds from Oxfam and UNICEF. "They all look well," said Audrey, "and they're all living together. They have a common purpose: They're surviving together. Now, is that just a dream? No, it's fact. It's there. I think that sort of thing can happen more often."

Said Audrey's biographer Barry Paris, "More than any other, this round of interviews generated an unprecedented amount of international coverage and captivated the world."

But the old war was chasing her. The war had been tailing her for the past forty-seven years, a relentless pursuer. She gave energy to eating too much and too little because of the war. She gave energy to keeping the secrets of her mother. She had started smoking to celebrate war's end and never stopped. Above all, she felt it was her duty as a van Heemstra to walk with children who today faced what she had once faced when cruel warmongers had decided the fate of innocents.

The war was catching up now and the long, black shadow of its hand reached out. "I'm running out of gas," she said. And there was still so much more to do.

32

The Race

"I went as long as three days without food," said Audrey of life in the first quarter of 1945, "and most of the time we existed on starvation rations. For months, breakfast was hot water and one slice of bread made from brown beans. Broth for lunch was made with one potato and there was no milk, sugar, cereals or meat of any kind."

It was now more than four years since Audrey or any of the van Heemstras had enjoyed a full meal unaffected by rationing and shortages. Up until Market Garden, times were lean and stomachs always rumbled. After the one-two punch of a failed invasion and the railroad strike, the country's food supply dwindled to nothing. Now, four full months later, Audrey and her family were suffering horribly from malnutrition.

One official report said that by February 1945, more than 500 Dutch people were dying of hunger each week. Across the Netherlands, but particularly in the west, people were succumbing at such a rapid rate that morticians couldn't keep up. The harsh winter temperatures became a blessing because the weather was so cold that it kept bodies of the dead from decomposing, and they could stay around for a while without fear of epidemic. That, in turn, was all right as there was no wood with which to knock together coffins anyway. The wood was too important as fuel to heat homes for those still living now that coal supplies were gone. Families buried loved ones in a bed sheet when they could spare one, but more often wrapped in paper, like a giant fish, or not wrapped at all.

At the Beukenhof, Meisje and Ella passed their rations on to the baron because those advanced in age were the most vulnerable, and Audrey attempted to pass hers on to her mother and aunt. Once again Audrey gave up the ballet classes that had meant so much to the children of Velp, and to herself, this time because of weakness brought on by malnutrition.

"I was very sick but didn't realize it," said Audrey, who came to appreciate later how her mother must have worried. "She often looked at me and said, 'You look so pale.' I thought she was just fussing, but now I understand how she must have felt."

Her biographer Barry Paris, said, "She was also having problems with colitis and irregular periods—possibly endometriosis, common among women dancers and athletes with little body fat—and her metabolism would be permanently affected."

When Alex returned to Velp to lend a hand in the desperate situation, Audrey described that she and her brother "went into the fields to find a few turnips, endives, grass, and even tulips." Her diet was so limited to endive during these months that "I swore I'd never eat it again as long as I lived."

Tulip bulbs became food, and Audrey would mention eating them in descriptions of life at low ebb under Nazi rule during the Hunger Winter of 1944–45. "It sounds terrible," she said in a 1992 interview. "You don't just eat the bulb. Tulip bulbs actually make a fine flour that is rather luxurious and can be used for making cakes and cookies," the only problem being that the remainder of the ingredients didn't exist to make either cakes or cookies.

Audrey said that by now she suffered from "acute anemia, respiratory problems and edema—swelling of the limbs.... I still have stretch marks on my ankles from where the skin was stretched by the edema."

In situations of extreme hunger over a long period, the body lacks proteins and minerals needed to regulate the amount of water retained. Water begins to collect first at the wrists and ankles. The fact that this happened to Audrey confirms the seriousness of the food situation in Velp.

"We all had it," said Annemarth Visser 't Hooft of hunger edema, "all the children." But older sister Clan fared worst of all by the end of the Hunger Winter, and her situation became life threatening.

Later studies would simulate the hunger conditions of this winter and paint a bleak picture of its effects on humans. Ever dignified, Audrey would not repeat stories of the darkest family times when it was likely there were outbursts of temper and an intense desire to suffer alone, away from others in the villa. Volunteers in one famous study said, "It was their minds and souls that changed more than anything else." They snapped at others close by, hoarded possessions, and suffered extreme bouts of depression. Physical symptoms included scaly skin, brownish pigmentation about the face, and blue lips and fingernails. The number of healthy red blood cells plummeted, triggering anemia and contributing to the edema experienced by so many.

A report sent from the Resistance to the Allies in London stated, "As long as hunger and cold rule, those who are in need will follow the law of life, i.e. the urge to stay alive and try to defeat every obstacle in the way. This has to be done by means which are in conflict with normal standards of morality."

Ella had always bulldozed all obstacles in front of her daughter, and now even she ran out of ways to help. For a while she had been able to trade her possessions for food. Audrey said, "There were no shops, no nothing. Everything was closed. The farmers were not taking any money. The money had no value. It was printed by the Germans. So you paid for things with linens, with a little bracelet, or a ring. That's how you got turnips or vegetables." But by now,

Ella had nothing left with which to barter.

Audrey looked at herself and knew the seriousness of the hunger edema. "It begins with your feet," she said, "and when it reaches your heart, you die." By now it wasn't just the Dutch who had run out of food. "The German troops, those that were there, were also starving," said Audrey.

Spring came early in 1945 and with it, finally, the beginnings of a break in the famine gripping the nation. For months the Dutch government exiled in London had been using every means possible—demanding or, as necessary, begging—the Supreme Headquarters of the Allied Expeditionary Forces, or SHAEF, to somehow get food to the people of the Netherlands. But the effort was mired in red tape, and besides, General Eisenhower had a war to fight on a front that stretched hundreds of miles; the Dutch would have to wait it out.

As far back as November when it had become obvious where this situation was going, Queen Wilhelmina and her prime minister, Gerbrandy, had sent appeals to many foreign governments asking for help for the people. It was neutral Sweden, cousins of the Dutch, who responded with enthusiasm.

After months working through red tape that included persuading the Germans to permit a flow of food into the Netherlands, on 28 January the first Swedish ships laden with food reached the northern port of Delfzijl bringing flour, margarine, and cod liver oil. But with 4.5 million desperately hungry Dutch citizens to feed, and with the Germans gumming up the implementation process organized by the International Red Cross, more precious time passed before a second shipment reached Delfzijl at the end of February. Due to German interference, this one wasn't even unloaded until later in March. At best it would take weeks for the food to begin to move as far south as Velp. But did the van Heemstras have weeks to spare? Audrey's once-plump face had grown thin by now, her eyes dull. Her wrists, knees, and ankles were swollen.

She couldn't sit comfortably because her buttocks had withered away, and she couldn't get warm no matter how many blankets she wrapped herself in.

The seriousness of hunger edema in children across the Netherlands made the Red Cross effort a race against time. And yet the lack of food was only one part of the suffering of the nation.

"It is impossible to describe what radical and dire consequences the lack of coal is having for the Netherlands," wrote a Red Cross official, "and how incredibly primitive life has become."

For the van Heemstras, the lack of heat and electricity exacerbated an already dire situation. But for Audrey, hunger and its consequences overrode everything else. And for all, the war had never left. Audrey lived exclusively in the cellar now with her mother, Meisje, and Opa, their mattresses moved down there. They would make mad dashes up to the toilet off the kitchen or, during heavy shelling, resort to use of a bucket. There was no other choice but to live this way as a war that could not possibly grow more hellish did exactly that.

Audrey would later talk about a particular evening in early March 1945. She said, "We had no food whatsoever, and my aunt said to me, 'Tomorrow we'll have nothing to eat, so the best thing to do is stay in bed and conserve our energy.'"

But Audrey loved to tell this story not because of the privation, but because of what happened next, thanks no doubt to Dr. Visser 't Hooft: "That very night a member of the Underground brought us food—flour, jam, oatmeal, cans of butter." For Velp, the famine was breaking, and for Audrey, the timing of the food's arrival after Meisje's gloomy statement gave the young girl a belief in her own personal luck that she would keep close at hand through a lifetime of struggles. "You see?" she said. "I've had black moments, but when I hit rock-bottom, there's always something there for me."

Other Gelderlanders would not be so fortunate. After dark on the evening of 6 March, ten miles north of the Beukenhof, between Arnhem and Apeldoorn at a country crossroads known as Woeste Hoeve, four members of the Dutch Resistance lay in wait to hijack a truck they could then use to distribute food supplies to Dutch civilians. When headlights approached, the Resistance men flagged down the vehicle, which turned out to be not a truck but an SS staff car.

The driver rose up over the windshield of the BMW convertible and barked, "Don't you know who we are?" He drew his luger and the Resistance men opened up on the vehicle with British-made Sten guns. More than 200 bullets shattered the windshield, tore up the doors and fenders, flattened the back tires, and killed the driver. Now the vehicle was of no use for a food heist, and the Resistance fighters fled into the night on their bicycles.

They didn't know that left behind was SS Gen. Hanns Albin Rauter, head of the Dutch security police and the most feared German in all the Netherlands. This ruthless officer with the dueling scars was on his way toward Apeldoorn from his office in Arnhem when the car came under attack. His aide joined the driver in death, and Rauter lay an hour in pools of blood until finally discovered along the lonely stretch of road. He had bullets in his lungs, shoulder, thigh, jaw, and hand and was scraped off the floor of the car and taken to Apeldoorn. The SD from Arnhem investigated immediately as Rauter, one of the men instrumental in the death of Uncle Otto and his four companions not to mention a mile-long list of other innocent Dutchmen, clung to life in the hospital. Heinrich Himmler, head of the SS in Berlin and Rauter's boss, ordered 500 executions, which Seyss-Inquart thought might set off a general revolt.

Two days after the ambush, 116 political prisoners and captured Resistance fighters from Arnhem and Apeldoorn were trucked to the spot where Rauter's car had been hit, Woeste Hoeve. All 116 were machine-gunned in reprisal for what had been done to Rauter. But that didn't end it. The Green Police ran rampant through

Velp and spread "moffenterror," in this case roughing up civilians, making arrests for the most minor offenses, and holding those arrested to act as forced labor. The moff also stole anything of value, particularly food and bicycles. For the Dutch, this was just another cruel act by the occupier because now more than ever, bicycles were needed to reach the food now arriving in town.

It was during this time that Audrey got caught up in the SD's hostility and retributions for Rauter's ambushing. She said in a 1988 interview for Dutch television, "I did once witness some men being *tegen de muur gezet* (set against the wall) and shot for some kind of reprisal. You know how they used to make people stop, and you couldn't walk on." She said after the executions the street was opened again.

During these days of Nazi payback she also came closest to entering a nightmare situation that might have killed her. On the streets of Velp, she walked into a Green Police roundup of Dutch girls and women to work in German kitchens. It was the occurrence that always had worried the baron and Ella: a teenage girl walking about during the day in wartime. Green guards herded Audrey and others into the back of a truck at gunpoint.

"I was picked right off the streets with a dozen others," said Audrey. The truck began to move but then made another stop during the roundup. By now, such German police weren't the cream of the crop—they were teenagers and old men, the bottom of the barrel. "When they turned to get more women, I nipped off and ran," she said. Hepburn lore would claim that Audrey hid in a bombed-out building for a month. In fact, she ran straight home to the Beukenhof "and stayed indoors for a month." Now, even volunteer work at the hospital was out of the question.

No one could guess in what direction the winds of war would blow next. The British had made their way north from Nijmegen through the Betuwe and now sat on the southern shore of the Rhine where they could gaze on the jagged skyline of a destroyed

Arnhem. Their shells blasted the city from close range and snipers picked off Dutch citizens forced to dig slit trenches for the Germans. Above, Allied fighters crisscrossed the skies looking for targets of opportunity, including the chance to shoot down V1s headed for Antwerp.

By the day, the final death gasps of war drew closer to Velp. "There was a lot of shooting and shelling from across the [Rhine] river," said Audrey, "so constant bombing and explosions. And this would go on all night and most of the day; there would be small moments where you'd go up for fresh air and see how much of your house was left, and we'd go back under again."

The Americans had crossed into Germany to the east. Patton's Third Army was rampaging through the German countryside and had reached as far as Ludwigshafen. Suddenly, the Tiger II tanks stationed in Arnhem were heard rumbling up Hoofdstraat in the dusk of evening on their way east to answer desperate calls for defense of the fatherland.

Tuesday, 27 March, passed like all the others, to the sounds of war: fighters and bombers overhead, artillery in the distance, occasional bursts of machine-gun fire, and a smattering of thumps from the anti-aircraft batteries. But after midnight it grew quieter.

In the Beukenhof cellar, Audrey could hear only the hum of a fighter plane overhead taking advantage of the clear sky and bright moonlight to look for moving targets. Then came a chilling sound but one all too familiar to the citizens of Velp: A V1 had launched off to the east. As with all such launches, she listened intently for the puttering motor to carry the death machine on past Velp.

Directly overhead she could hear the fighter firing its machine guns; who knew what might be the target? Then, dear God, the evil pulsing of the V1 motor stopped. The plane had been shooting at the V1 and had hit it! But where was the explosion? All knew at once: The buzz bomb was going to come down in the middle of Velp—instincts were keen after so long at the front lines.

Breathless seconds followed in the cellar as the V1 spiraled earthward in a building scream of high-speed flight. Was this the end?

The explosion rocked the earth. Attached to it, the roar of smashing glass sounded all around. Screams joined the cacophony. There had been so many moments like this, where afterward Audrey wondered if the villa still stood above their heads, or if it was ablaze, or if those that had been killed a second ago were friends or family. Out the small cellar window in the sliver of world that could be seen, there were no flames. There was just the deep blue velvet of night. About them grew stillness. The only sound was the lone fighter plane, the villain in this aerial play, heading back toward England in the distant night sky. Yes, that pilot had perhaps saved a detonation in Antwerp, but, oh, what had he done to Velp?

As a leading citizen of the community, the baron rushed out of the basement with the women trailing behind. Yes, there was a curfew but it meant nothing at a time of such desperation. They rushed down Rozendaalselaan and in the night could see a blazing fire beyond the rooflines on Hoofdstraat. It was so close and they were heading right toward it. By the time they reached the village center there was glass everywhere, blown out of every window and storefront.

People ran toward the fire from all directions, and the van Heemstras followed the flow of traffic, rushing across the main street and down Oranjestraat, where they found a scene of utter devastation. As they approached, they saw that all the houses on the right side of the street were gone or reduced to rubble and blazing. Bodies intact and in pieces could be seen littering the street in the firelight. As Audrey took all this in, another V1 puttered over. Everyone ducked on instinct. This one malfunctioned and fell some distance away. The Velpsche fire engine, the one stolen by the moff, would have come in handy this night—except there wasn't running water to fight the flames anyway. Instead, rescue efforts centered on recovering the dead in the houses not burning, including several children of the family van Remmen.

Steven Jansen lived just a few doors up from the V1's point of impact. In his diary he wrote, "Searches are conducted for victims under the heaps of rubble. Several are saved. For nine people, no help is possible. The night is endless. However, thirty V1s fly over. At least eight crash down in the surroundings.... Finally, the day breaks."

But it's another day of war, with planes menacing the village and artillery exchanges punctuating every hour. And of course there are V1s. But wait...

On 29 March Allied planes flew over Velp with what seemed to be ferocity—fighter-bombers at low level. Waves of them. Then, a ways off to the east came the sound of booms, booms, and more booms, so many and so heavy that the ground trembled. The citizens of the village could only thank God that this time, they had been spared.

Later came word: The V1 launch sites east of the IJssel had been flattened, and at long last the menace of the German terror weapon was at an end, not only for distant Antwerp but for the Dutch in Velp who had lived for three-and-a-half agonizing months under its curse.

Then came more good news. Food! A new wave of shipments from the Swedish rescue missions poured into Velp along with more generous ration coupons: for a two-week period, 2400 grams of bread, 4 kilograms of potatoes, 125 grams of meat, 200 grams of cheese, and 80 grams of oils. It arrived in quantities generous enough, as per the Swedish plan, that no one would have to wait in a line hours long.

The van Heemstras ate a rare meal of substance, and the baron crept across the street after dark to listen to Radio Oranje on the Mantels' radio set. Allied forces were blazing through Europe and the Germans were desperate—hanging on by a thread. Fear now centered around the possibility of a final battle for Velp that might lay waste to everything, as had happened in Arnhem and Ooster- beek. The German presence in Velp remained strong, and with the tanks rolling through, the planes flying over, and the rockets and shells falling, it seemed likely to the Dutch that nobody was going to make it through alive.

33

Gates of Hell

"When I could afford it," said Audrey, "I went to a doctor and he told me I was very anemic and must eat a pound of red meat a day." That physician was Dr. Adriaan van der Willigen, Jr., chief of staff at the Velp hospital, who had been consulting medical journals on the topic of edema because of its prevalence in the village. But the doctor was dreaming—the ration was just a small fraction of a pound, and for two weeks, not a day. But the van Heemstras pooled their resources, and their youngest ate all the meat available. "Very soon," Audrey continued, "I began to look and feel like a different person. I have great respect for how closely your appearance and vitality are related to diet."

March drew to a close. Reports on Radio Oranje described the Allies closing in on Berlin, the Yanks and Brits from the west and the Russians perilously close on the east. The bomber stream seemed endless as American planes of the Eighth Air Force flew over Velp in formations a thousand strong to deal final blows to German cities. Then sometimes would come the deep and distant rumble of detonating bombs.

Much lower, fighter planes continued to prowl the streets of Velp looking for German targets. Unfortunately for the van Heemstras, enough leaf cover had sprouted that the armored columns once again called their street home. German vehicles were parked in every possible place of concealment on the streets of Velp due to its abundance of hundred-year-old trees. Because of the hunters above and Allied ground forces at several points in Germany and the Netherlands, the tanks and half-tracks had nowhere to go at the moment. Their operators were frozen in place.

On the last day of March, the Saturday before Easter, a fighter dove against a luxury convertible driving down the Hogeweg just four blocks from the Beukenhof. Pilots knew that only German staff officers would be driving around these days with the shortage of vehicles, tires, and fuel. The fighter flying east to west strafed the car as it drove along the Velpsche street, but the pilot kept his finger on the trigger a second too long and when he pulled up over the treetops, the spray of bullets ripped into the Ziekenhuis and then over its roof and into the houses beyond, straying perilously close to the home of the van Heemstras. Fate had been unkind to Velp of late, but in this instance at least, no one was killed.

The next evening another British fighter plane screamed earthward over Velp, and as villagers gasped in anticipation of impact, the pilot managed to keep his plane airborne and came down in a farm field behind the centuries-old Castle Biljoen just to the east of town. The brave pilot who had avoided the houses below him died on impact. Explosions from his gas tank and ammunition sounded in the night.

At four the next morning grenades began to explode in Velp, killing and wounding several. Radio Oranje reported that the Dutch town of Enschede northeast of Velp near the German border had been freed and the liberators, said to be Tommies, were marching southwest toward Zutphen. That would put them just twenty miles from Velp and so they must arrive by nightfall. And if not today, then tomorrow for certain.

Excitement grew when a distant boom revealed that the Germans had blown the Westervoort bridge over the IJssel just to the south of town, no doubt to stop the British advance. It was wonderful news and meant that the Tommies must be closing in. And then from prime vantage points the Velpenaren could see the red, white, and blue Dutch flag flying over Westervoort, which indicated the Tommies were already there, just five miles away!

Then came word that a Canadian army pushing toward Velp from the south had been repulsed by the Germans. With this reprieve, the Wehrmacht and SD used their newly won time to lay mines in the roads and gardens along Hoofdstraat in Velp and cut down the beautiful trees lining the street from the wreck of the Park Hotel eastward all the way to Rheden, more than a hundred trees in all, the pride of the village, to block the advance of the Tommies from Zutphen. All the while, Allied fighters roared over, and grenades exploded with brutal ease from one end of Velp to the other.

Audrey told a story to magazine writer Kirtley Baskette in 1953 about a moment of terror at around this time, early April, when there had been a lull in the action, and she had pulled on a sunsuit and crept into the garden. Baskette paraphrased it this way: "She breathed deeply and, because she hadn't sampled any fresh air for weeks, she found it intoxicating. Then she stretched out on a pad in the sun and the bees in the orchard blossoms buzzed her to sleep. But she dozed fitfully because in her dreams the 'whump, whump, whump' of artillery seemed to march up the Rhine right to her garden, which was smack in the Nazi battle lines. Only when the earth shuddered beneath her and a blast tumbled her off the pad did she wake up and realize this wasn't her routine nightmare. It was real. Bits of gravel peppered her skin and shell fragments whined wickedly past her ears." Baskette wrote that Audrey lay flat on the earth as shells burst around her. "Finally the barrage moved on and she crawled back to her cellar door, shaking. She never wanted to try that again."

More days passed. Overhead roared British Spitfire and Typhoon fighters who turned their attention on Arnhem and pounded German positions in the poor destroyed city. Artillery was coming in all around, most of it hitting Arnhem but some straying into Velp. More grenades fell. More villagers perished.

Audrey and the others had now spent what seemed to be endless stretches in the cellar of the Beukenhof.

"During the day we merely existed," she said. "At night our only diversion was gathering around the fire. That was the only light we had—whatever wood we could find nearby. We couldn't talk about the day's happenings, because nothing had happened to us. So we sat around and made up stories, invented things. We entertained each other, and it helped carry our minds away from the horrible life we were leading."

In the midst of battle, it was a miracle the villa hadn't been reduced to rubble or set ablaze, although, as she recounted, "Parts of our house kept being shot away." She described Velp as "a shooting gallery between the two armies. Day and night the din continued until we grew so accustomed to it, we paid no attention even to the biggest noise."

Two blocks away, Steven Jansen wrote on 13 April, "If it remains quiet a moment, one crawls from the cellar. One does not venture oneself far from home. The stores of water must be replenished however.... Velp looks a sight. Stones, sand, scree, and fired branches lie on the street. Burned houses. Houses with direct hits and, most of all, houses without glass."

Later that day came a report on Radio Oranje that the president in America, Franklin Roosevelt, had suffered a stroke and might be dead. The people of Holland had always considered Roosevelt one of their own because of his Dutch blood. It was another bad omen, with liberation so close at hand; the world needed this American president now more than ever before.

The relentless shelling and shooting of grenades went on day and night. As soon as the sounds died out, another round began. By Saturday, 14 April, small-arms fire could be heard on the air mingling with the larger explosions. The sharp crack of rifles and rattle of machine guns raised hopes of impending liberation because it had to mean that ground forces were getting near enough to Velp that they were being shot at.

Shells landed all about the Beukenhof and then a thunderous, heart-stopping explosion sounded very close by. From the cellar they could smell smoke and wondered if the villa above them was ablaze. During a lull Opa and Audrey left their shelter to try to make sense of what was going on, one of those occasions when Audrey said she would venture up to "see how much of your house was left."

They stepped outside into daylight. While the Baron surveyed the latest bullet holes and shrapnel damage to the structure and property, Audrey looked about her. Down the street toward the center of the village, a building blazed. It was somewhere around Thieles book shop—perhaps the shop itself. The other way, up the street toward the north, one house on each side of the street was burning, and farther up, somewhere around the intersection with Ringallee, a building was fully engulfed with black smoke billowing skyward. The magnificent old beech trees lining Rozendaalselaan had not been felled to block the way because the Germans needed those trees for cover. But great limbs had been sheared off by shells and lay on the pavement and sidewalk. Here and there could be seen small flags marking unexploded shells in yards and gardens. Some had even burrowed into the pavement without detonating, and these too were marked. Fighter planes circled in the sky above, like vultures above carrion, six, no, eight of them banking high in the blue. Somewhere off to the south a little ways, anti-aircraft guns thumped and shells exploded in puffs of black cloud above the planes.

Other civilians began to appear to inspect their homes or the neighborhood.

To a fifteen-year-old girl it was, more than ever before, with the flames swirling, with the hunters above and cannoneers below looking for anything to kill, as if she and Opa had been transported inside the gates of hell. Velp had been such an idyllic place, and the Villa Beukenhof had been but one beautiful home in a beautiful neighborhood. Now look at it. Some houses afire, others already bombed out. All within the breadth of her sight was eerily still as the structures burned, because who would dare to venture out among flying bombs to fight the flames? In their ears were the drone of aircraft engines and the occasional snap of burning wood.

Just then grenades began to sizzle nearby and explode and, as was standard practice for everyone in the village, Audrey and Opa rushed back inside and down to the cellar to try to stay alive a little while longer. Into the evening the pungent smell of burning wood filled the room where the van Heemstras gathered by lamplight, and the exploding grenades sounded the irregular heartbeat of a war that would not die. It was worst near midnight, when the grenade fire came fast and furious in the darkness. And then it grew quiet and for a little while, sleep could come.

All over Velp there was but one thought, one utterance repeated over and over: The Tommies did not arrive today; surely the liberation will be tomorrow.

But the dawn came to the accompaniment of exploding grenades. Then it grew quiet. Then a grenade. More quiet. They were few enough in number and distant enough in location that breakfast could be consumed upstairs in the kitchen, away from the confinement of the cellar.

As they sat there into the afternoon luxuriating in moments of life above ground, they began to hear the far-off mechanical hum of what sounded like Tiger or Panther tanks and the squealing, puttering of other tanks or half-tracks. Were they in the south? To the west toward Arnhem? Who did they belong to—the Germans? Or was it the Tommies?

Jan van Hensbergen heard them from his home just a matter

of yards from the Beukenhof: "You can hear the humming of the engines and the rattling of tanks now from not that far away anymore."

And Steven Jansen also noted: "You hear already continuous noise in the distance. Seeming tanks coming from the southern direction."

Once in a while there would be the punch of a tank firing its cannon and a quick muffled explosion as the shell burst, then more maneuvering. All the people sheltering in their homes in Velp could feel they were living a moment of history, the death agony of the Reich. And once the heartbeat of the beast was finally stopped, its grip would fall slack and the Netherlands would be free.

The moments passed so slowly. A distant grenade. Stillness. A squadron of planes cruising through. Stillness. It was a time to reflect on almost five years of life under Hitler. Not that they had ever listened to his speeches or obeyed, but it had been life under the oppression of his terrible will and his twisted soul that they had endured.

For Audrey, there had been moments that would live with her forever. Otto's arrest, first and foremost. The dark days when Meisje had fretted for her man and traveled to be near him. Then that moment when they learned that dear Otto had been murdered, and Schimmelpenninck too. But there were so many more nightmares—the sight of Jews fleeing for their lives and herded along the street at gunpoint. And memories of the train station, the blank faces peering out of cattle cars. The closing of an Arnhem street for an execution and the crack of the rifles. The screams coming from the Rotterdamsche Bank. The refugees from Arnhem and other places. Poor little Ben van Griethuysen crying for his mama and so much suffering Audrey had seen at the hospital since the battle. And, oh, the hunger of the winter just past and how awful to watch her own young body betray her and fall apart.

Yet as she herself had said, "Five years of your life can't all be horrifying." There was the ecstasy of dance. Learning from the wonderful Mistress Marova, whom she hadn't seen since before the battle. Audrey could look back on her days at the Muziekschool and the discipline of the barre. Performances at the Schouwburg and perhaps the most wonderful night of all at the Musis Sacrum when she had begun her life as a public performer. Did it matter that the audience was made up of soldiers from the Wehrmacht? That it was the official newspaper, the Nazi newspaper, that praised her? No, because their assessment meant nothing anyway. She knew she wasn't yet a praiseworthy dancer—Mother had told her that often enough. She had more work to do, and more and more, but still, the lights, the costumes, the music: These were the things, elements of the dance, that made life worth living. More than anything else, this shy soul, this girl who had been so wounded by lack of a father that she had nothing to say to anybody, had found a way to express herself through dance. And it was so glorious a feeling. All of this had happened during the years of the occupation, despite the occupation.

At half past one in the afternoon, a thunderstorm of grenades made the van Heemstras grab food and water and rush back into the cellar. The blasts had been close enough that screams could be heard in the distance. Even the strongest could break down and cry at such savagery, but what was the point? Something even worse lay ahead—save your tears for then.

As the cellar window revealed light thinning to night, nearby German artillery opened up with salvos that took the breath away. The Allied response sounded immediately and almost as close, as if to say, *Oh yeah? Well take that!* The night sky lit up as the shells exploded with flashes like lighting from a summer storm. Then came a sharp bang of something hitting too near the villa. Later there came the rat-tat-tat of machine guns, not only the German Spandau but what the ears of the Velpenaren had come to know from the battle for Arnhem as the British Sten gun.

275

For hours the din of battle sounded all around, grenades, tank blasts, machine-gun fire, and a new sound—the dull thud of the hand grenade. It was deafening, terrifying, and it lasted through the night. The imagination tried to keep up with and make sense of every sound. One moment it would be a tank right outside on the street. Then shouts in German. Machine guns. The pop-pop of rifle fire.

Audrey said that in these late hours, gallows humor once again took hold in the cellar of the van Heemstra home. "I can tell you what that was like," she said, "lots of giggling and laughing. It's all we had, sleeping on mattresses and sitting there waiting for the shooting to stop."

Jansen said on Oranjestraat, "There is a nervous tension that dominates in the cellar. They must be very near. Whoever ventures above to look can see the flames of the shooting tanks between the trees."

Near the Beukenhof, a deep explosion rocked the quartet of van Heemstras, and another and another, renewing worry for the structure directly above. Sleep was impossible and, anyway, they thought bravely in their punch-drunk stupor, why would you want to sleep through your last moment on the earth?

34

First Cigarette

"Early in the morning, all of a sudden it was total silence," said Audrey, who gave a little gasp at the memory. "Everybody said, '*Now* what's happening?' because it was sort of frightening. You know, we had gotten used to the thumping of the shells."

They had just experienced Velp's longest and most violent, night-long thunderstorm of bombs and rockets. Now, nearing dawn on 16 April, the storm seemed to have passed, but life under occupation had instilled in Dutch minds the discipline to await the next terrible thing, for it would surely come.

Audrey crept to the window, with inky night opposite the pane, and put her ear to the glass: "I could hear the sound of shuffling feet—very strange, because at such an early hour, no one ever went out onto the streets."

She could make out the sounds of what seemed to be a great number of people moving outside, and she began to catch a whiff of something in the air. "The very first thing I smelled—I didn't see, because we were in our cellar where we had been for weeks because at that point our area was being liberated practically house to house."

What she smelled was the aroma of cigarette smoke. They were real cigarettes made of tobacco, no mistaking it. There hadn't been such an aroma in Velp for most of the war; only ersatz cigarettes made of oak and beech leaves had been available. These smelled awful and did smokers next to no good at all. And now she smelled genuine tobacco.

What happened next became one of her favorite stories to tell in interviews for the remainder of her life. The four van Heemstras tiptoed up the steps from the cellar to the first floor of the Beukenhof and then dared to poke their heads into the morning air. Instead of the jaunty Tommies she remembered from the battle for Arnhem, she ventured out to a horrifying moment facing soldiers pulling back bolts on Sten guns and ready for a fight, "their eyes glittering and their guns pointed straight at me," she said.

She blurted out some words in elegant English and "the instant they heard me speak their own language, they let out a great yell."

One of them bellowed, "Not only have we liberated a town— we have liberated an English girl!"

For the first time in five years the men with the guns weren't German. It was the moment the people of Velp had expected 211 agonizing days earlier on 17 September when British Airborne parachutes had filled the air. "Liberation!" they had shouted expectantly on that bright autumn Sunday, only to have the dream shattered.

This time the soldiers looked like Tommies and wore their uniforms, including some not in helmets but in those lovely red berets. Their shoulder patches did not show a Pegasus in white on a red field. These patches showed a white polar bear. They were in fact Canadian First Army troops, and the vehicles passing slowly by on Rozendaalselaan belonged to the 5th Canadian Armoured Division. Just a day ago German Tigers had been parked there.

"The guns, the tanks, the trucks, the jeeps, and the men came rolling into town," said Audrey. "Cecil B. DeMille could not surpass the spectacle."

Street by street they cleared out the Germans and Green Police. "I inhaled their petrol as if it were priceless perfume and demanded a cigarette, even though it made me choke," said Audrey. For the girl not quite sixteen, smoking suddenly became a delight that connected her to the incredible feeling of liberation and that first cigarette began a lifelong habit, one central to her personality.

Neighbors poured out of every house. Onderduikers who had been in hiding for weeks, months, and in some cases years tumbled outside to breathe free air.

Jews of all ages began to appear for the most unlikely of re-unions; people thought to be long dead in concentration camps had gone into hiding, aided by brave Velpenaren who for years had shared risks and rations. Even the closest of friends and neighbors in the next house over were shocked to discover that individual Jews or whole families had been concealed just yards away through the course of the war. Now these people too breathed in the free-dom of liberation.

Red, white, and blue armbands imprinted with a single word, ORANJE, designated members of the Resistance. They brought rifles into view and became an impromptu security force. Citi-zens donned any piece of orange clothing that had survived the war. Red, white, and blue Dutch flags waved proudly, hung here, draped there, tacked to tree trunks and telephone poles. Bottles of wine and brandy and champagne set back with great determi-nation in 1940 were dusted off and uncorked now. The citizens shoved precious bread and cheese into the hands of the soldiers, who handed out cigarettes and candy in return. The euphoria of the moment made everyone in sight drunk, with or without spirits, and before long every single person on the sidewalks and in the streets and gardens, equal parts Canadian soldiers and Velpenar-en, had broken out in laughter. Joyous, tension-shattering laughter gripped the village like a sudden spring madness. For all of them, whether from this side of the Atlantic or the other, there was one ultimate realization: I have lived to see this day!

"Oh, God, I could scarcely believe it," said Audrey.

A block away, Steven Jansen and his fiancée joined the celebration. "From all side streets one runs to Hoofdstraat. A flag! There a flag hangs. We are free! Congratulations! Congratulations! Embracing each other. The traces of the misery still on the face, but also the happiness to experience this moment. We are free! With tears clouding our eyes we see the long-hidden fluttering tricolor flying proudly."

But yes, the misery did hang on the air. The people let loose even more welled up emotion as they remembered those who could not celebrate this day because they had been shot by the Nazis, or killed in a bombing raid, or carted off to a concentration camp, or felled by typhus, or diphtheria, or starvation in the winter just past.

When the laughter receded, the anger welled. It was time to reckon with the collaborators—those who had been in league with the Germans or too cooperative to the Reich. These people were rounded up and pushed along to the center of town by the Oranje Resistance men with rifles. The accused were forced to run a gauntlet of their neighbors—the great majority of the population who had remained loyal to the queen. At the police bureau on Stationsstraat, women who had fallen in love with German soldiers or otherwise helped them over the long years of occupation were punished by having their heads shaved. Fists of Resistance men clenched the shorn locks of Dutch women who had been sympathizers and held them high on the balcony like Iroquois holding scalps. Below, the crowd cheered.

To Audrey's shock, a Canadian security officer accompanied by members of the Resistance asked Ella to go with them, and the Baroness van Heemstra was led away. In an instant the most wonderful feeling, breathing free air, became a sensation of not being able to breathe at all.

At Canadian headquarters, Ella sat for questioning by an officer identified only as Captain James, a field security man. During their conversation, Ella claimed she had done work for the Allied intelligence services; James duly noted her assertion. She listed her accomplishments on behalf of the Resistance, most notably her family's sheltering of a British paratrooper along with work tending the wounded of Velp. There was also the period during which she participated in the zwarte avonden—the secret dance performances—with her daughter.

On this day of retribution from the Oranje Resistance when Dutch women collaborators were being scalped right and left, Ella van Heemstra walked out of headquarters with her hair attached. For Ella it must have been vindication that she had finally been accepted as a supporter of the Allied cause, which she most certainly had been for three years now. Captain James noted that, to him, the baroness was neither dangerous nor suspicious. Instead, he—or perhaps the Resistance men at his shoulder—found her to be *onnozel*, an old Dutch word meaning "silly."

To the relief of the Dutch girl, her mother returned unharmed as tanks and armored troop carriers continued to roll down Hoofdstraat, kicking up great clouds of dust, spent gunpowder, and ash that coated every surface, especially the pavement. The fine grit got into mouths and nostrils and eyes and yet it didn't matter at all: *Liberation!*

In the afternoon, military bulldozers appeared and swept out of the way the giant felled trees of Velp, which the Germans had believed would keep the Allies at bay for weeks. The mechanical monsters pushed all of the trees aside in just that afternoon.

Men with mine detectors then swept every inch of town for buried explosive devices and booby traps planted by the Germans in previous weeks. There were so many mines along Hoofdstraat in the eastern half of the village that "the Germans had told me where it was safe to walk," said Ben van Griethuysen. At this stage of the war with defeat likely, they didn't want their mines blowing up children.

The center of Velp seemed to be the center of the world on

this day, with all citizens dressed in their Sunday best and walking about simply because they could. For the first time in five years they were free to be seen out of doors without a purpose, and without an Ausweis. The Canadian soldiers were everywhere, "millions of them," it seemed to Audrey, and all morning and through the afternoon the military vehicles rolled through, on their way to liberate the next town over.

"I stood there night and day just watching," said Audrey. "The joy of hearing English, the incredible relief of being free. It's something you just can't fathom."

But for some of these marvelous Polar Bears, it would be a last happy day. "Many would be killed in the battle to free Deventer," said Dick Mantel, who experienced Liberation Day as a boy of fifteen. Deventer sat twenty-five miles to the northeast, and the Germans fought there to the death, as they had in Velp.

At the intersection of Hoofdstraat and Rozendaalselaan, a military policeman with white sleeves directed the buzzing flow of Canadian Armoured traffic. It was breathtaking, all those tanks clattering past the Beukenhof and on up toward Rozendaal and beyond. The men of each one smiled and waved and gave the V for victory sign. They threw chocolate bars and cigarettes to villagers who applauded and shouted blessings in return. But by now Audrey no longer rejoiced. Soldiers had handed the shy girl chocolate bar after chocolate bar and she ate them all. Soon, a stomach that had not known chocolate for years sent the foreign substance back up. And yet, she said, "Filled with such happiness, I could not stay sick for long."

35

Sorting

"Unfortunately, people basically learn little from war," said Audrey. "We needed each other so badly that we were kind, we hid each other, we gave each other something to eat. But when it was over, people were just the same—gossipy and mean."

The gossip in the days after liberation, and most of the meanness, was produced by those among the Dutch who had resisted the Nazi regime and now turned on those who had not. All along Ella had been watched, beginning when she first set foot in Arnhem in 1939, a year before hostilities had commenced. At that time the Arnhem police had been tipped off that she was a Nazi operative, and they began secretly monitoring her mail. People noticed that she had had an NSB boyfriend before occupation began, and after. They saw her staging celebrations for Nazi-endorsed composers at the end of 1941. Those who visited the apartment on Jansbinnensingel witnessed Nazi paraphernalia on display. Several stepped forward to say that Ella and her Nazi boyfriend were inviting people to a cultural evening similar to the Mozart celebration, this one in Düsseldorf. Everyone who read the Resistance newspaper *Oranjekrant* had seen her name listed as being "Gestapo." Once the Dutch noticed such things, they weren't going to forget, even when the suspected collaborator was a Frisian baroness and daughter of a beloved figure like Baron van Heemstra.

Yes, Ella had worries, among them her daughter. Audrey had begun adding weight to her eighty-pound frame even before liberation when the Hunger Winter was broken by the Swedish food shipments. Just a day after the Canadians arrived to free Velp, the food trucks came, "and there were UNRRA crates," said Audrey of the United Nations Relief and Rehabilitation Administration efforts. "There were boxes of food that we were allowed to take home, blankets, medication, and clothes. After a few days I remember going to a huge classroom where we could pick out clothes, sweaters, and skirts, and they were so pretty, and how they came from America. We thought, how could people be so rich that they could give away things that looked so new?" After all, she was a Dutch girl, and in and out of wartime the Dutch wore every garment until it had been rendered threadbare. She would always remember the feeling she had when she laid her eyes on those UNRRA crates, and benefited from what was inside them; the experience inspired her participation in UNICEF forty-five years later.

As Audrey was marveling at American clothing, Meisje was retrieving her husband's beloved Renault from the Besseling family barn, where it had been hidden for the second half of the occupation. In gratitude, Meisje presented Frits Besseling with the 1933 volume *Arnhem, zeven eeuwen stad* (*Arnhem, Seven Centuries Old*) adding, "From my husband's collection." The vehicle had been important to Otto; now his widow could see it every day.

Across Velp, the healing had begun. Audrey ate and ate and ate. The bloom of health returned with the tulips in May and the ballerina once again danced. "My dream was to wear a tutu and dance at Covent Garden," she said, "but I never thought I'd make it. I was too tall, and I was far behind because of the war."

One day past her sixteenth birthday, 5 May, would become known as Liberation Day in the entire Netherlands. By this time all but some of the northern islands were free of Nazis.

Audrey began once again to give ballet classes for local children, among them Annemarth Visser 't Hooft, whose lessons with Audrey so enthralled her that she embarked on a ten-year career in dance.

For Audrey herself, any ballet career would by necessity be pursued away from poor wrecked Arnhem, but that was for the best anyway. Ella set to work writing letters to one of Europe's leading ballerinas and ballet instructors, Sonia Gaskell, to see if she might take on Audrey as a pupil. It didn't hurt to include years of clippings from the *Courant* praising Audrey's performances. Gaskell was a Lithuanian Jew who had spent the war as an onderduiker in Amsterdam but after liberation was resuming her full schedule of teaching.

Probably because of the baron's connections within the hospital community, Ella had been appointed as a manager at the old Royal Dutch East Indies Army Invalids Home, just down the Velperweg toward Arnhem. The large facility had begun accepting British war wounded on a temporary basis—there were so many new wounded because of the final battle to free the country—and Ella took part in their care. Working here was another way she could contribute to the cause, yet she felt oppressed in Velp with the lingering hostile feelings of some of her neighbors.

It was, however, a happy summer for Audrey, who continued to volunteer for Dr. Visser 't Hooft. Mother and daughter received the best surprise of all in May: "We had almost given up," she said, "when the doorbell rang and it was Ian." Her half-brother had survived life in a Berlin factory and constant allied bombing raids to make his way more than 300 miles to reach Velp, most of it on foot.

Alex and Miepje returned to Velp for a joyful van Heemstra reunion, and Audrey became an aunt in July when Miep and Alex had a baby. The dancer was in heaven with a baby to hold and feed and cuddle. "It always boils down to the same thing of receiving love but wanting desperately to give it," she explained.

But Ella couldn't be affectionate with a grandchild any more than she could with a daughter. Ella remained single-minded in trying to get Audrey's entertainment career off the ground by whatever means possible. When a film unit arrived in Gelderland to recreate the battle of Arnhem and Oosterbeek, the production staff naturally stayed in the only fully functioning town in the area—Velp.

"The last time I saw Audrey," said fellow Velpenaren David Heringa, "was in August–September 1945 when her mother brought her to our house to see if we could introduce her to some bigshots of Gaumont-British, the Rank Organization. We had staying with us the scriptwriter Louis Golding and the director Mr. [Brian Desmond] Hurst."

The production of the feature documentary that would become *Theirs Is the Glory* was taking all the time and energy of filmmakers coordinating more than 200 veterans of the 1st Airborne who came back to relive their experiences in the streets of Arnhem and Oosterbeek, aided by war surplus armor, both British and German. The veterans simulated fighting amidst the ruins that were everywhere. Heringa said the production team "could only suggest to Audrey and her mother to continue ballet lessons, and then when things were more normal, to come to England."

Heringa added, "We all thought Mother van Heemstra a bit pushy about Audrey." But Ella was only half stage mother; she was also the same stifled performer who had been forbidden by her father from following her dream to act or dance. With the war out of the way, she wanted to do everything in her power to help along her daughter's aspirations. The talent was there, no question—too many people had been vocal about the fact that Audrey had a certain something and commanded attention on any stage.

But Ella had another reason to approach the movie producers staying in Velp: Her funds had been frozen as an initial investigation was begun about her activities during the war. A quick influx of cash could help fund a move to Amsterdam, where Sonia Gaskell had accepted Audrey's application to become a ballet pupil.

At age sixteen and a half, Audrey was beginning to sort out her life even as Ella's remained a tangled mess. There was lots of sorting going on all across Europe; for example, figuring out what to do with Arthur Seyss-Inquart, who had been arrested in Germany on 7 May, and Hanns Albin Rauter, who had miraculously survived Woeste Hoeve only to be arrested by British officials while still in the hospital. Justice would be swift for the former, who was condemned at the Nuremberg trials and hanged 16 October 1946. SS man Rauter would never leave the Netherlands. He was tried in a special court in The Hague and shot by a Dutch firing squad on 12 January 1949. Such a fitting end for this one in particular, considering the executions of "the five" and the murder of 100,000 Dutch Jews on his watch.

The restless slumber of those five Dutchmen at the southern edge of the Netherlands would end shortly after liberation when head gamekeeper Marinus van Heerebeek led Dutch authorities to the spot of forest where Otto and the other gijzelaars had been shot in 1942. A search of the surface area revealed only a tattered cloth that, judging by the way it had been tied, had served as a blindfold. Test holes dug at the site quickly confirmed that this was indeed the place of execution.

A doctor from St. Elisabeth's Hospital in Arnhem examined all five bodies. They had been sprinkled with lime to speed decomposition, but the sandy soil had limited its effectiveness, and the doctor saw that each victim had been shot from seven to nine times. Identifications were made, and the families of Robert Baelde, Christoffel Bennekers, and Willem Ruys claimed their loved ones for reburial in Rotterdam.

Not so for Otto Ernst Gelder, Count van Limburg Stirum, and Alexander, Baron Schimmelpenninck van der Oye. Their widows knew that these wonderful men were now with God and felt their earthly remains should stay where they had fallen as a symbol to the Dutch people. On 15 August 1945, the third anniversary of the murders, a service at the site unveiled a large marble monument. Now, finally, the families of the five, including the van Heemstras, could grieve. Long after the war, the five bullet-riddled poles to which the men had been tied, each painted black, remained planted in the earth at the site as a reminder of the men and their fate. More recently, reproductions have taken the place of the original poles, which were moved to a museum. Every year family members and patriotic Dutch men and women troop to the lonely spot by the Belgian border to remember the "death candidates" who had departed the world to shouts of "Long Live Oranje!"

36

Crossroads

"When the liberation finally came," said Audrey, "I took up my ballet lessons, [and] went to live in Amsterdam. Housing was very, very short at the time; it was a country that lay in ruins. I lived in a room with my mother, in a house which we shared with another lady, a writer." This was, in fact, the publishing house editor who was working on Anne Frank's diary.

Ella and Audrey finally made the move from Velp at the end of October 1945. Mother took a job in the recovering food industry, first as a produce buyer and then as a caterer. Daughter began dancing with Sonia Gaskell in her new, state-funded dance school. These were the leanest times of all, the period with Ella's funds frozen in Arnhem as she still managed to provide for Audrey and herself.

Sonia Gaskell accepted Audrey as a student knowing that the young dancer couldn't afford to pay for lessons but thought she deserved a chance as yet another hopeful who had been derailed by the war. Not that Gaskell was soft-hearted. She wasn't. She was a tough, disciplined taskmistress who in Audrey's case built upon the relentless work ethic that had already been instilled, first by Ella, then by Marova. As Audrey expressed it, the Gaskell way reinforced the dancer's iron will: "Don't complain, don't give in even if you're tired, don't go out the night before you have to dance.

Sonia taught me that if you really worked hard, you'd succeed, and that everything had to come from the inside."

Annemarth Visser 't Hooft would later make her way to Gaskell's studio and confirm Audrey's assessment. "I remember she was an extremely strict teacher," said Annemarth of Sonia Gaskell, "austere and very disciplined and close to the rigid traditional classical forms of dance. She was not easy to please."

Ella and Audrey would make a return visit to Velp in spring 1946 for the purposes of dance. At the invitation of Dr. van der Willigen and Dr. Visser 't Hooft, Audrey headlined a benefit for the Red Cross at the N.H.V. building on Stationsstraat. The date was 25 April 1946.

Audrey Hepburn-Ruston's first public performance since the days of the zwarte avonden was accompanied by pianist Willem Goedhart, who provided music by her old favorites Bach, Chopin, and Debussy.

Rosemarie Kamphuisen attended the recital with her parents. "I remember it was all solo," she said. "I remember that she made a tour around the limits of the stage, and I see her going around in very elegant positions."

Rosemarie also remembered the other act on the bill with Audrey, none other than Dr. Visser 't Hooft and his comedy troupe, for this occasion composed of his fellow doctors and some nurses from the Velp hospital. The doctor himself had written the script and created the act. It was, recalled Rosemarie, "a hilarious presentation of a 'leg amputation' on stage. The doctor was in a leading part with an enormous saw, with a separate underleg that fell on the floor and a lot of flowing blood!"

The next day, the *Velpsche Courant* newspaper reviewer had eyes only for Audrey and remarked on the way the sixteen year old expressed herself through interpretive dance, describing this as "her great gift." The reviewer likened her performance to "a fresh, bright spring morning" and said, noting that the great Sonia

Gaskell was now Audrey's instructor, "We can expect a successful future for this artist." At the end of the performance, Audrey was showered with bouquets from all quarters.

One month later Gaskell chose Audrey to appear with another dancer in a performance at the Hortus Theater in Amsterdam. A reviewer said Audrey's technique wasn't the best but noted that "she definitely had talent."

As 1946 gave way to 1947, and 1947 to 1948, Audrey continued to study with Gaskell while on the side she employed her fit dancer's body as a photographer's clothes model to make extra money. She also finally got herself a part in a movie. To Ella's delight, Audrey was cast in a low-budget travel homage to the Netherlands called *Nederlands in Zeven Lessen*. So dear was film stock to the project that the filmmakers cut Audrey's impromptu screen test into their feature. They asked her to begin the test on the far side of a busy Amsterdam street, make her way toward the camera while dodging traffic, stop under the camera, which was perched in a second-story window, and smile. The footage, which exists today, shows Audrey gliding with a dancer's grace, showing just enough leg in her slim skirt to impress the filmmakers and land the role of a KLM stewardess. Her roughly four minutes of screen time in the feature were shot at Schiphol Airport in Amsterdam, and the experience convinced the dancer that "I am not an actress." She was wearing her hair curly these days and her weight was up—facts preserved for posterity in *Nederlands in Zeven Lessen*.

By this time, the Dutch police in Arnhem had opened a full investigation of Ella's pro-German activities up to 1942. It was part of a countrywide purge of the ten percent of the adult population that had sided with the occupier, and everyone in all corners of the Netherlands began scrambling. It wasn't a matter of the ten percent maintaining their innocence; all Dutch citizens wanted to prove their loyalty. Friends asked friends to verify every act of defiance against the Reich large and small, from sabotage to stealing food to tearing down a tacked-up German edict. Members of the Resistance sent requests to the United States for letters of reference from American airmen they had fed or sheltered. The worst thing one could be in the post-war Netherlands was a verified Nazi collaborator.

Ella's vulnerability began in 1935 when she had traveled to Munich with Ruston and met Hitler, then had written about the experience in not one but two British Union of Fascist newspaper articles. Another damning fact was that she had worked for Pander and Zonen, which sold furniture, yes, *and* made aircraft and other equipment for the Reich. Witnesses against Ella included the director and staff of Arnhem's war hospital the Diaconessenhuis, as well as Arnhem civilians, plus the police detective in Arnhem who had inspected Ella's mail in 1939.

Finally, on 25 June 1948, Ella was called in to testify under oath, and gave a lengthy statement defending herself against several serious accusations that had been presented to police through sworn statements and also in writing. She admitted to National Socialist activities from 1934 to 1936 but only as influenced by a husband later proven disreputable; their marriage ended shortly after the trip to Germany. She denied having a flag with a swastika in her apartment, as had been charged; she denied any intimate relationship with secret police officer Oestreich or association with German nationals working at the hospital. Her cultural activities came under scrutiny as well, and Ella denied her pro-German activities. She was steadfast in stating she had done nothing against the Dutch at all. In her statement she claimed she had quit her job with Pander as soon as she learned they made German military equipment when in fact she had held that job for two more years. She claimed there was no Nazi paraphernalia in the apartment on Jansbinnensingel other than a paperweight in Ian's bedroom that may have had a Reich emblem on it, but that symbol meant nothing to anybody. She denied any association with German officers even though she had been seen in their company in public settings. She explained that she had taken the job at the hospital as a favor to her father to improve relations between the German workers and Dutch staff. Her mission had been to improve care to patients, not to further the German cause. Her most significant misstatement claimed that the Mozart celebration she directed had taken place in January 1940 before the occupation, when in fact it occurred seventeen months *after* the Germans marched in and was very much a pro-Nazi evening for an artist "claimed" by the party.

As always, Audrey lived and breathed dance. Now age nineteen, she faced a crossroads in Amsterdam when funding cuts at the Gaskell school necessitated the dancer be removed from the roster. But she remained "eager to become a prima ballerina" and applied to the Marie Rambert School of Ballet in London. An endorsement from Madame Gaskell helped to secure Madame Rambert's interest, but an audition would be required.

Sonia Gaskell herself spent endless hours preparing Audrey for the audition. "You know," said Audrey, "I always tell this story when people ask about turning points in my life. This Russian ballet teacher worked and worked with me, preparing me for my audition, going through such paces, training, sweating. And on my last day we went through it all again, and she gave me a big hug and said, 'Now, you forget everything I told you. From now on it all has to come from inside you.' And this has got me out of any amount of scrapes. I've been constantly in situations in my life and career where I've had no technique, but if you just feel enough, you will get away with murder."

For the first time in nine years Audrey separated from her mother (and her mother's legal troubles) and traveled to London—the fact that she was the daughter of British citizen Joseph Ruston and therefore British herself made this action possible. It didn't matter that Ruston had been considered a traitor and was imprisoned during the war. An Englishman was an Englishman, and his daughter was also English.

Audrey passed her audition and began instruction under Marie Rambert in a London still cleaning up from five brutal years of air raids and V1 and V2 attacks. Destroyed blocks and neighborhoods still marred the urban landscape—a constant reminder of where she, and the world, had just been.

According to Hepburn biographer Barry Paris: "To describe Rambert is to describe the history of British ballet. Agnes de Mille called her 'Queen hornet, vixen mother.' By age sixty, when Audrey met her, she was legendary, her credentials dating to the days when she coached Vaslav Nijinsky in *The Rite of Spring*."

Said Audrey as she was about to begin at the prestigious school, "Suddenly, I faced a problem: I could get no money from home." Ella's funds were still tied up in her legal defense, prompting Rambert, an empty nester with two adult daughters living on their own, to become the second ballet mistress to befriend the waif; she invited Audrey to live with her as Ella endured legal scrutiny in Arnhem and The Hague.

Which is not to say that ballet mistress Rambert had mellowed. Audrey said of Rambert that when she "would catch us folding our arms or slouching our shoulders, she'd give us a good rap across the knuckles with a stick."

In London, a male dancer noticed "this very pretty, strange Dutch girl who suddenly arrived at the Rambert School...." But here and now, Audrey faced a shock. After practicing under Marova and then under Gaskell in a Netherlands where ballet had just begun to take hold, Audrey was in the presence of a "queen hornet" who had trained the founders of the Sadler's Wells and Royal Ballets. The "strange Dutch girl" took her place at the barre next to "girls who had had five years of Sadler's Wells teaching, paid for by their families," said Audrey, "and who had always had good food and bomb shelters." The Dutch girl had had none of these things. Quite the contrary; she had lost well over a year of instruction due to battles, shelling, malnutrition, and illness. Most horrific of all, in a line of dancers each the ideal height of 160 centimeters, she towered at 170—an inelegant five-foot-seven.

The writing was on the wall; the dancer was devastated. But she remained her mother's daughter: tough, hungry, and above all, practical. A crowded ballet roster and her own gangly height required a strategy shift, which she made on a dime based on her experience back with Marova designing her own dances. "I wanted very much to become a choreographer," she said, "and Rambert was known for developing young choreographers. So I wanted to be Margot Fonteyn and a choreographer as well."

She salved the trauma of her foundering ballet career with a new best friend: food. For many who had endured starvation conditions in the Hunger Winter, the once-normal relationship with food would forever be altered. Taste buds changed, as did appetites. The sensation of being hungry became elusive, and what did it feel like to be "full"? When was enough enough? For some, food that had been deprived for so long now represented security and with so much of it around, those who had once nearly starved couldn't help themselves. Audrey shared these new challenges with millions of Dutch survivors. She admitted to a reporter in 1959 that after the war she "began to overcompensate and eat everything in sight."

"I went on an eating binge," she admitted. "I would eat anything in sight and in any quantity. I'd empty out a jam jar with a spoon." As a result, she admitted, "I became quite tubby and put on twenty pounds."

Audrey remained with Rambert because she still loved ballet and couldn't give it up. At the same time, she said, "I had been told that my height was a handicap in ballet and that I might have to slave for years to achieve only limited success. I couldn't wait years; I needed money badly.... I chose the stage."

London was returning to life, literally. With all the servicemen

back, there were babies everywhere, it seemed. Bombed-out buildings were being removed brick by brick, some becoming car parks.
The new communications medium of television appeared. The
rationing of bread, begun in 1946, finally ended in July of 1948
just in time for the Summer Olympic Games, which were held in
London despite shortages and rubble. It was a grand place to be,
London, and Audrey remained determined to work and prosper.
She could only hope that sooner or later her mother would be free
of obligations in the Netherlands and join her, and Audrey must
be ready for that day.

37

Completely Nuts

"[The war] made me resilient and terribly appreciative for everything good that came afterward," said Audrey. "I felt enormous respect for food, freedom, for good health and family—for human life."

"It was a simple deduction that my best way was to take on a job as a dancer while continuing to study ballet. I found that what everybody did in these circumstances was to audition for a job in some London revue. I liked the idea."

The Hunger Winter survivor continued her on-again, off-again love affair with food. Now it was time for a crash diet in preparation for auditions for a London show, something a girl with a will of iron could manage. "You can't turn your back…on temptations or worries," she told a reporter some years later. "You've got to face them head-on and reject them."

Of the actual crash diet that saw a loss of almost thirty pounds in two months, she said she accomplished it "by merely watching my diet and cutting out all starches and sweets."

As she changed her body, she also adopted a stage name better suited to the country in which she now worked: Audrey Hepburn. There was never a question that she could retain the surname Ruston after her father's hateful participation in fascist activities and imprisonment through the war. But the Hepburn name had character and history and worked beautifully. Audrey Hepburn it was. In another few years, Ella would file papers in Britain to officially change her name to Ella Hepburn as well.

The revue offering auditions was *High Button Shoes*, and Audrey, thanks to three years of intense ballet training that had produced athleticism and stamina if not perfect technique, was chosen as one of ten dancers out of the thousand who applied. *High Button Shoes*, with music by Jule Styne, lyrics by Sammy Cahn, and choreography by Jerome Robbins, had been the sensation of Broadway in 1947. Now it would open in London's West End in December 1948.

"I got my first job as a glorified chorus girl with bits and pieces to do," said Audrey. "This suited me fine. I was given a chance to express myself on one stage at least, while I didn't seem to get anywhere as a would-be principal dancer in the ballet."

The lead dancer of *High Button Shoes*, Nickolas Dana, ascertained Audrey's financial situation by her clothing as rehearsals began. He told biographer Barry Paris: "She had one skirt, one blouse, one pair of shoes, and a beret, but she had fourteen scarves. What she did with them week by week, you wouldn't believe. She'd wear the little beret on the back of her head, on one side, on the other side...."

The plot of *High Button Shoes* concerned two con men and a family in Atlantic City and featured the raucous "Bathing Beauty Ballet" number and hit songs "I Still Get Jealous" and "Papa, Won't You Dance With Me?" all with Audrey among the troupe of dancers. She had one line in the entire show: "Lou Parker, the star, stood in the middle [of the stage]," said Audrey, "and I went tearing across holding another girl by the hand and said, 'Have they all gone?' Believe me, I was nervous every single night. I used to repeat it to myself over and over before going on."

The bawdy show, loaded with charm and energy, ranged far from Audrey's comfort zone in the type of short programs she had performed for Winja Marova at the Schouwburg in Arnhem. But she had a dancer's soul if not training equal to other girls around her. She also had pizazz thanks to that deep performer's instinct to feel her way through performances. She was a natural chameleon who could give the people in any audience what they wanted. Her style drew the eyes of many, including actor-turned-theatrical-producer Cecil Landreau, who came to see *High Button Shoes* and thought Audrey perfect for one of the five chorus girls in his new musical revue in development, *Sauce Tartare*. The show would open in May 1949 and mean a raise in pay for the dancer—all she had to do was leave the show that had been her stepping-stone. And that's what she did.

Except for a few hops across the North Sea to England in 1947 and 1948, Ella had remained close to home in the Netherlands as the investigation into her wartime activity dragged on. With Audrey away Ella had moved from Amsterdam to Offenberglaan 1 at the northeastern tip of The Hague. In February 1949, finally, it was determined that her sympathies were definitely pro-German into 1942 and her actions may have been suspicious, but insufficient evidence existed to convict her of any crimes against her country other than, perhaps, bad judgment. But according to P.J. de Vries, inspector of police in Arnhem, Mrs. van Heemstra was and always would be "politically unreliable."

Ella was officially off the hook but now faced the red tape associated with leaving the country to take up residence in London, and as the months passed, Audrey began work in *Sauce Tartare*, and then in a second, shorter floor show at Ciro's nightclub, which was then billed as "the famous London rendezvous of smart society."

The Ciro's show was also the brainchild of Cecil Landreau. According to Audrey, "He said one day that anyone who'd like to make an extra shilling could be in cabaret. So after *Sauce Tartare*, at 11:30 at night, I'd be at Ciro's again at midnight, make up and do two shows. All dancing. I made £11 for the first show and £20 for the second. So I was doing eighteen shows weekly and earning over £150 a week. I was completely nuts."

She said on another occasion, "I worked like an idiot. It was work, work, work, work.... I did anything to earn a buck so that my mother could come over and join me." Under this brutal schedule, all traces of baby fat were long gone and her face had developed the sleek patrician look that would, before long, help to make her famous. By now "anything to earn a buck" included continued modeling work for the still camera and occasional bits on television. Among her gigs was a shoot for photographer Angus McBean. Soon Audrey's face appeared in advertising for the moisturizer Lacto-Calamine.

Finally, Ella shook free of the oppression of her native land and arrived in London determined not to live on her daughter's income. She tried various positions, as a cook, beautician, and flower saleswoman, before becoming manager of a stately three-story brick apartment building just east of Hyde Park. Her position included a flat for mother and daughter, and just then, according to Hepburn biographer Alexander Walker, Ella began a romance with sixty-one-year-old Dutch business magnate Paul Rijkens, founding chairman of Unilever. Rijkens had spent the war in England with Queen Wilhelmina and possessed the wisdom to stay away from any European investments for his Rotterdam-based company. Instead, he focused on building businesses in the United States and Britain. By war's end he had bought majority interest in Lipton tea, Birds Eye frozen foods, and Pepsodent toothpaste and sat poised to ride the wave of the baby boom.

According to Walker, Rijkens "now became the Baroness's benefactor. Audrey was devoted to him; if any man replaced her father at this stage in her life, it was he. He had an apartment in Berkeley Square, in the same part of central London as the Baroness's residence. Thus, for the first time in years, Audrey felt she had security."

Not that the dancer would ever dream of taking it easy. She kept earning money at a frantic pace, dancing in another Landreau burlesque show, *Sauce Piquante*. Ivor Brown of the *London Observer* was one who took notice of the *Sauce Piquante* dancer. "I suggest that the names of Joan Heal and Audrey Hepburn will some day be illuminated over theater doors," he wrote on 30 April 1950.

Life in the footlights kept her striking face, big brown eyes, and shapely legs on display night after night. Dance was getting her places—just not the places she expected to go as a twelve year old dreaming of life in the Royal Ballet. Time and again the sweat and toil of life in the chorus line provided a showcase where her innate charm and unique look could be noticed. Then would come auditions for parts in movies or television.

She would boil it down for the *Washington Post* in 1985 as, "I remember being very involved with the classical ballet and the movies were really not serious. To earn an extra buck, I did bits in movies but that was to earn an extra buck. That wasn't going to be my career." But to earn that buck, she needed some vague notion of moviemaking; she had none. "I didn't know what a camera was. I didn't know what was going on. It was still new to me. I had no idea how to play a scene or anything."

She wasn't a real actress, but the fates had seemingly decided she must become one. She joined the acting class of sixty-year-old character actor Felix Aylmer, a veteran of British stage and cinema. There, finally, the girl with no background in theater learned some basics of elocution, projection of her voice, and reaction to the dialogue of others—at least enough that she could fake her way through. "He taught me to concentrate intelligently on what I was doing," she said, "and made me aware that all actors need a 'method' of sorts to be even vaguely professional."

She landed a recurring role in the BBC television production *Saturday Night Revue* that she recorded around the time *Sauce Piquante* opened in May 1950. She earned a few lines and close-ups in a scene as a hotel clerk in the feature *One Wild Oat* for Coronet Films, then two scenes as a cigarette girl in the Alastair Sim comedy, *Laughter in Paradise*, then a funny short scene as a bought girl with Alec Guinness in *The Lavender Hill Mob*.

When MGM came to town looking for a fresh face to play Lygia in its latest epic, *Quo Vadis*, Audrey earned a screen test. "At the time Metro tested me they were forced to test a certain percentage of English actors," said Audrey. "They had to test so many English girls. I'm sure they intended to use their own [American-based] girls." She was right—the part went to MGM contract player Deborah Kerr.

It was never the career she wanted; it was the career that came easily to her—she had grown into an exotic face that responded to makeup and lighting. If she gained a few pounds that week, her face looked one way. If she lost a few the next, her face looked a different way. Given her personal history in the war, those dark days when she hated her looks and thought herself too ugly to ever marry, seeing herself as an actress in motion pictures led to life-long bewilderment.

In 1965 she said, "I can safely say that unlike others I simply stumbled into movies. And from one thing came the other. Suddenly I found myself acting. It's never been I who said, 'I can act.' Instead, mine has been a meek and curious, 'What is this thing you are giving me now?' I've been offered and given things to do, and in return I've given them what I have—which I know I have. Which is a capacity for hard work and a lot of instinct I've been born with."

In 1988 she addressed the subject again: "I didn't have the drive because I had the great luxury of not needing it. Once I did *Roman Holiday* the offers came in. It was not in my nature to be terribly ambitious or driven because I didn't have the confidence to be so. My confidence came and went with each movie; once I'd finished one, I didn't know if I'd ever work again."

And once more in 1991: "I never was the ideal performer, because I suffer so terribly from fear." She analyzed herself and went on. "An actress is not something I ever became. I think actresses are people with a very high level of professional technique. I act now the same way I did forty years ago. By trying to sense, feel. I am never backed up by anything professional. I did no Shakespeare at school, none of that. It's not like a great musician who has worked at his instrument, none of that. I've had to skip all that and do it with feeling."

Or as Ella phrased it to her daughter during the period when Audrey Hepburn shot to international stardom in 1953 and 1954, "Considering that you have no talent, it's really extraordinary where you've gotten." Her mother's attack of friendly fire became a source of pride for Audrey, and a story she repeated often enough that in 1989, news writer Angela Fox Dunn of the *Rochester Democrat* asked if it were really true.

"She did say that, oh, yes," recalled Audrey with a chuckle. "She said it in the middle of all the lovely successes I was having. And that's what I really believe to this day. I've always been self-conscious about interviews, about my thinness, my tallness, my unattractiveness. My success—it still bewilders me."

38
Peace

Audrey said late in 1964, just as *My Fair Lady* premiered, "If I have become a movie star, it's despite my childhood, not because of it. I grew up in Holland under the Nazi occupation and this was my world from my eleventh to my sixteenth birthday."

Audrey expressed the idea on many occasions in many different ways that experiences before and during the war affected her psychology; war made her introverted, but also tough and disciplined. It sharpened instincts that would form the foundation of her acting and philanthropic careers.

War also altered her physiology, and her "thinness" as the Hollywood years went by would become a much-whispered-about topic for friends and fans alike. In an October 1951 newspaper article about the new star of *Gigi*, reporter Norton Mockridge of the *New York World Telegram* said, "Miss Hepburn, who never drinks but smokes a little, is always hungry. And after being starved for years for a taste of fresh meat, she eats almost nothing else over here.

"'Look,' she'll say to a waitress, 'The tenderloin steak, please, but very rare. You know what I mean? Raw rare. With the blood in it. Dripping. Very rare. Almost raw.'"

At this point in her life she still channeled Dr. van der Willigen of the Ziekenhuis in Velp, the doctor who had seen her for edema near the end of the war and prescribed a pound of red meat a day.

In an 11 September 1953 sit-down interview with Hedda Hopper in Hollywood, she admitted, "I've put on a little weight—on my holiday in England. When I'm not working I put on weight."

By the end of the 1950s, her regimen would be very different—boiled eggs, wheat bread from a health food store, fruits, vegetables, and yogurt. This coincided with the beginning of the "bone-thin" period that would last for the remainder of her life. By the 1980s she was defending her lack of heft in interviews and saying, "I eat everything I want," which included at this time of her life lots of pasta. She claimed she lost her appetite in time of stress, and many things did indeed make her nervous. When nervous she didn't eat; she smoked somewhere between six and sixty cigarettes a day—official and unofficial estimates varied by a wide margin.

In 1944 into '45, an experimental program in the United States asked for volunteers to simulate the Hunger Winter of the Netherlands. The idea of the Minnesota Experiment was to understand what famine-plagued Dutch civilians would need after the war to regain their health. The results were troubling as they showed the dire psychological consequences of long-interrupted nutrition. The relationship of humans to food, once automatic, became after some months a love-hate experience for the volunteers that dominated and in some ways engineered every waking thought. Personalities changed, and what once was normal never quite returned to normal again.

Audrey was one of millions of Dutch males and females to survive the Hunger Winter. "I had gone through the war years deprived of food, dollars, books, music, and clothing—all the ordinary needs," she said. "Now I began to overcompensate by eating everything in sight, particularly chocolates. I became as swollen, and as unattractive, as a balloon.... My mother and I had seen too many unhappy things in Holland...."

She did survive Holland, and even thrived afterward; in the

long term, that last long, cold winter of the war may have caused irreparable damage to her digestive system. And yet it was *her* system, and she could clam up about anything she considered off-limits. Her rule: Keep the interview to under thirty minutes because "after that, the questions become personal," and personal was not okay.

As a young star of twenty-six, she spoke defiantly of her label as "aloof" for not answering some reporters' questions. "People who would rob you of your dearest possession—your privacy—aren't worth having as friends," she told *Cosmopolitan* writer Martin Abramson. "I'm a person who needs time to be alone—time to refuel. And I don't like to talk about my personal life, because I feel each individual has the right to keep some things to himself."

Kirtley Baskette, a veteran of Gable and Lombard and one of the first Hollywood writers to interview Audrey in 1953, nailed her right off the bat: "She takes you in but holds you off," he reported. "The Dutch treat with the English accent talks well but tells nothing. If you ask a personal question she smiles sweetly and is as silent as the sphinx."

Thirty-five years later she hadn't changed a bit: "I am a very reserved person. When I did *Gigi* and *Roman Holiday*, I was twenty-four with the mentality of a twelve year old. I was very green and naive, not a bit worldly."

She remained a little girl in some ways who had never gotten past the abandonment by her father. But she was a survivor, and in that respect very much like Joseph Ruston, who was arrested in June 1940 as "an associate of foreign fascists" and spent the duration of the war in British prisons. He wasn't released until April 1945, at which point he headed for Ireland because of its neutrality during the war. He believed that there he would not be judged for his beliefs or his actions, and he was right. Ireland became home.

Time passed. He got a job and married a much younger woman. He didn't make an attempt to contact his daughter after the war. Despite even this slight, as her star ascended in 1951, Audrey nurtured her connection to this man. Or, rather, she held close the pain of the severed connection. It stayed with her every moment through every career advancement. Magazines and newspapers mentioned Audrey Hepburn's mysterious father the fascist, and she never denied what he had been. She simply didn't address it.

The war, however, had a way of jumping out of the shadows at the most unexpected moments and oppressing Audrey Hepburn. She couldn't predict when it would happen, but it kept happening and always would. It happened during the screen test for *Roman Holiday*, shot at the Pinewood Studios in London on 18 September 1951. Paramount thought this unknown English/Dutch girl so fresh and unique for the part of Princess Ann that they tried to ensure the success of her test by handing it to British director Thorold Dickinson, who had just directed Audrey's major supporting role in the 1951 thriller, *Secret People*. Plus, Audrey's audition consisted of scenes from the *Roman Holiday* script with two actors whom she already knew and had worked with—another way to make her feel comfortable.

"Paramount also wanted to see what Audrey was actually like not acting a part, so I did an [on-camera] interview with her," said Dickinson.

In that piece of film, Audrey first appears with hands in pockets standing nervously on a stage and appearing very thin. Dickinson, who is heard off-camera, orders her to remove her hands from her pockets and move to a chair and sit down for a close-up. He then begins an informal interview, asking, "Seriously, Audrey, tell us about the war. You spent the whole war in Arnhem. Was it pretty awful?"

She had been smiling, feeling at home with this director, but the question rocked her and she tensed. Her face froze and the smile along with it. "Yes," she managed. "It was very bad."

"Did you entertain the people there?" he asked. "Is that how you began?" These were just general questions to assess the quality of her face and voice and reactions on camera; Dickinson had no idea how loaded this particular question was. Yes, of course that's how she began, in July 1941, dancing publicly at the Wehrmach-theim for an audience of German soldiers in an Arnhem under Nazi occupation. Then five months later she appeared onstage with Ella, Alex, and Ian for the pro-Nazi Mozart celebration. It was the beginning of several public performances in wartime.

Sitting there looking at Dickinson, she thought quickly and with the considerable control of a survivor. She said, "No, not quite how I began. I went to ballet school once I knew I was settled there for quite a while [in Arnhem]. I didn't know how long the war was going to last so I went to a ballet school and learned to dance." She paused, then said, "And in about," another pause, and she said slowly, "...1944, about a year before the end of the war, I was quite capable of performing, and it was a sort of...some way in which I could...," long pause, "...make some sort of contribution. I did give some performances to collect money for the Underground, which always needed money."

She didn't lie; she was careful about that. She simply sliced three years out of her own résumé—and how that must have hurt because they were the dancing years, which filled her with pride.

Dickinson said later, "We loaded a thousand feet of film into a camera and every foot of it went on this conversation. She talked about her experiences in the war, the Allied raid on Arnhem, and hiding out in a cellar. A deeply moving thing."

For Audrey, Dickinson's question represented more than a screen test; it was a test of her will to succeed because whether she knew it or not, and likely she did, a publicity storm lay just over the horizon. She had appeared in bit parts in 1950, and already in this year of 1951 she had completed important roles in *Secret People* and the comedy *Monte Carlo Baby*. And that role had changed her life when playwright Sidonie-Gabrielle Colette, author of *Gigi*, spotted Audrey as she worked on location in the Monte Carlo Hotel and declared her perfect to portray *Gigi* in the soon-to-open Broadway production.

The day of the *Roman Holiday* test, Audrey was planning her first trip to the United States to begin *Gigi* rehearsals. The surviving film of this test shows the extent to which Ella and Audrey had already worked out what she could and could not say about her life during the war years. Yes, Audrey could talk about the zwarte avonden and dancing to raise money for the Resistance. Yes, she could talk about delivering the Resistance newspaper *Oranjekrant*, helping a downed flier, and escaping from a German press gang. She could certainly discuss the famine, her illnesses, and the deaths of her uncle and cousin. But she must never, ever talk about her debut at the Wehrmachtheim or the Ella-directed Mozart celebration of 1941. Audrey also must never discuss her performances at the Schouwburg of 1942 through '44—even though the dancer held these performances so close to her heart; they were the greatest accomplishments of her life. They always would be. But the post-war world was black and white due to Nazi atrocities. You were either for or against the Nazis. There were no shades of gray, and the post-war public would not understand how Audrey could have danced before audiences that included the German military. It didn't matter that Audrey had been a twelve year old and then a teenager who despised the Nazis and all they represented. Nor did her need for self-expression matter. It was simply too much of a risk for Audrey's career.

Ella and Audrey had been a team since 1939. Yes, Ella had strayed. She had been foolish in the '30s, but she had also seen things more clearly and corrected her course. Now it became imperative as her daughter sailed toward stardom that Ella be seen as a Dutch patriot in the war. As luck would have it, she had a cousin, Ernestine Theodora Johanna, Baroness van Heemstra, who had indeed worked heroically throughout the course of the war on behalf of the Resistance; she even managed to survive clashes with the Gestapo. Ella never claimed to have done any of the things that cousin Ernestine had done, but anyone from the always-in-a-hurry British or American press wanting to check about a prominent Baroness van Heemstra in the Netherlands who had worked for the Resistance; well, there she was, easily documented.

When Audrey arrived in New York City later in September 1951, Ella didn't accompany her. In fact, the baroness failed to gain entry into the United States because of the paperwork attached to her name and the murky legal status of this woman who not only had once described herself as a fascist but also had earned a rating of "unreliable" by Dutch police after the war. So Audrey ventured into the concrete jungle on her own and placed herself in the hands of two veteran press agents attached to Richard Miller's production of *Gigi*.

Richard Maney had been handling flak for Broadway shows since the Roaring Twenties. The other publicist on the case, Frank Goodman, was the son of Austrian immigrants who had cut his teeth in Orson Welles' Mercury Theater.

Maney found Hepburn "so lovely and refreshing, so coltish and eager, that she enchanted critics." Even better from his perspective, "She had an exciting background and an exotic origin. Daughter of an Irish father and a Dutch mother, throughout World War II she had lived in Arnhem, Holland, under the Nazis. Often she went hungry. Her male relatives were dragged off to labor camps. When she danced, it was to raise funds for the Dutch Underground. All this made copy."

Maney and Goodman knew just how to spin Audrey's war stories to maximum benefit. Because Ella had already helped her daughter clean up the record, and because Audrey had spent her life as a private, introverted person, it came natural to her to keep the record straight. Publicity surrounding *Gigi* would serve as precedent that followed Audrey to *Roman Holiday* and then *Ondine* on Broadway and on through her career in the 1950s and '60s. False trails about where and when she performed during the war would be laid here for all Hepburn biographers to contend with, especially in the spate of books that appeared after the actress's death in 1993.

But Audrey quickly became adept at throwing writers off the scent as well. When she sat down with famed columnist Hedda Hopper for an interview in Los Angeles on 11 September 1953, one of Hedda's first questions was, "All right, now tell me all about yourself."

Audrey smiled her charming smile and replied, "There's so little to tell." Her eyes fixed on a framed *TIME* magazine cover of Hedda on the far wall and Audrey exclaimed, "Isn't that wonderful. Look at that!" The notoriously vain Hopper, a former actress, took the bait hook, line, and sinker. The survivor had once again survived and avoided any pointed questions about the past. She steered the remaining interview with deftness, using gentle charm, a process she would repeat in the months and years to come. Before long she earned the power to turn down interviews, or grant them only to trusted writers. Her instincts regarding the press were as unerring as those that allowed her to choreograph and to act.

Another survivor in the family, Ella, Baroness van Heemstra, finally entered the United States with great fanfare in December 1953 after Audrey had wrapped production of *Sabrina* for Paramount Studios. Daughter was there to welcome mother with a bouquet of signature Dutch tulips and a warm for-cameras-only embrace. Why did it take so long for Ella to make it across the border? And who was it that finally broke the logjam? Circumstantial evidence points to Paramount Pictures, which had a long-standing friendly relationship with FBI head J. Edgar Hoover.

Once Ella gained entry into the United States, she came and went freely, so no status of "unreliable" had followed her from Europe. Her arrival signaled the end of freedom for Audrey, who, during the time away from her mother, had made and broken an engagement to young English businessman James Hanson, fallen in love with her hell-raising co-star William Holden during production of *Sabrina*, and then quickly settled down with American actor Mel Ferrer, a man eleven years her senior and the new father figure in her life. Ferrer had worked his way up the ladder to almost-A status, with his most recent success the role as villainous Marquis de Maynes in MGM's swashbuckling spectacle, *Scaramouche*. His career would stall after that. He kept working through the 1950s with big roles in small pictures and supporting roles in big ones, while also earning descriptors around town that included "ambitious" and "fussy" and "high-strung." And where Audrey was concerned, he earned the name "Svengali," because he became her de facto manager and took over her career.

Because Audrey was beautiful, charming, and mysterious (in short, she had it all), the most-asked question in Hollywood became, "What does *she* see in *him*?" The answer for anyone who knew the lonely Dutch girl who had survived World War II was simple: She craved affection, and Mel made Audrey the center of his universe. And that's what mattered to her. For the next dozen years, the prime of Audrey Hepburn's career as a leading lady, Ferrer would battle Ella for leverage over the affections of the woman caught in the middle.

And what a career it was. Audrey Hepburn became a screen legend even though the actress starred in only nineteen feature motion pictures for Hollywood studios. She followed up her Academy Award win as Best Actress for *Roman Holiday* with four more Best Actress Oscar nominations, for *Sabrina* in 1954, *The Nun's Story* in 1959, *Breakfast at Tiffany's* in 1961, and *Wait Until Dark* in 1967. Her instincts as an actress remained sharp until the end, despite the ongoing terror she faced at any performance that didn't involve dance. She always considered herself a dancer at heart, and specifically because she wasn't an actress, the desire to accept film roles had gone away by the mid-1960s. The son she finally had with Mel Ferrer in 1960 after four miscarriages, Sean Ferrer, had become the most important thing to her. Above all she wanted to give Sean the sort of stable life she had never been able to experience after the abandonment of her father.

Her marriage to Mel fell apart and they separated in 1967. A year later they were divorced at about the time she met Italian psychiatrist Andrea Dotti, who was fussy Mel Ferrer's antithesis. Audrey found the nine-years-younger Dotti not only handsome and charming, but "such an enthusiastic, cheerful person." Dotti represented a fresh start, and they married in January 1969. Soon thereafter she became pregnant—just in time to learn of her new husband's roving eye. Son Luca was born in February 1970, an event that sealed Audrey's retirement from the screen. "I am totally crazy about my sons," she enthused. She said she had done nothing but work, and work hard, from the time she had begun dancing under Marova in Arnhem at age twelve straight through the completion of filming for *Wait Until Dark* at the Warner Bros. studios in Burbank. After twenty-seven years, she wanted only to raise the children she had dreamed of having all her life. As she stated flatly, "I have absolutely no desire to work."

She just wanted to live quietly in Italy as Mrs. Andrea Dotti. "I'm a Roman housewife, just as I want to be," she told the press. She expressed gratitude that she was able to be what she wanted in a modern world that bore no resemblance to the Nazi-occupied Velp of 1944, a time of privation, and "that my child can eat three meals a day and be free and with no danger of somebody banging on the door." She said she had finally learned to accept that "I'm not going to be taken away, or my family taken away, as were millions of others who once lived around us."

Years passed and her sons grew. Audrey was lured back to starring film work in 1975 when an offer came to play Maid Marian to Sean Connery's Robin Hood in *Robin and Marian*. She delighted in the opportunity to portray a woman in her forties, sort of a more worldly Sister Luke of *The Nun's Story*, which she had made sixteen years earlier. But the experience of making *Robin and Marian* in Spain wounded her soul. Director Richard Lester shot at a frantic pace with multiple cameras rolling at the same time, often in natural light—none of this suited Audrey's need for the kind of traditional blocking, lighting, and makeup used by the great directors who had groomed her. Nor did it allow for a meticulous study of the script, another of her trademarks and a factor in her success. On the set in Spain she pined for the star treatment of her Hollywood days that so mirrored the politeness of a van Heemstra's titled European background. There was none of that visible at these grimy locations. *Robin and Marian* would be the filmmaking experience that made Audrey Hepburn realize her career as a leading lady had ended.

That was okay in the big picture, because she had never aspired to become an actress anyway. When asked or, rather, accused by Dutch interviewer Ivo Niehe of desiring early on to become a screen star, Audrey countered, "No, oh no, I wanted to be a dancer. I still do. (laughs) It *still* is my dream. And I must say when I go to the ballet, I'm so emotional and moved by beautiful ballet."

Not that movie producers stopped calling with film offers. With banner headlines about the Hepburn return to the screen resulting in big business for *Robin and Marian* in spring 1976, producer Joseph E. Levine asked Audrey to portray Kate ter Horst of Oosterbeek in his upcoming epic film about the battles for Arnhem and Oosterbeek, *A Bridge Too Far*. If anyone in the world could bring authenticity to the role of ter Horst, reasoned Levine, it was this Dutch girl. It would only call for a few weeks' work, and in the Netherlands at that.

The offer forced Audrey to visit Cornelius Ryan's work on which the movie was based. "When I read that book, I was destroyed," she said. "The same as when I first read Anne Frank's diary." Audrey had spent her parenting life preaching against war to sons Sean and Luca, to the extent that she refused to sit and watch any war movies they chose. She wasn't about to make a war movie now, especially not *this* war movie that would force her to relive the destruction of elegant old Arnhem and the mauling of her beloved Airborne.

Three years after turning down Joseph E. Levine, Audrey and Dr. Andrea Dotti separated. "I was no angel," Dotti admitted. "Italian husbands have never been famous for being faithful."

"I hung on in both marriages very hard, as long as I could," said Audrey, "for the children's sake, and out of respect for marriage. You always hope that if you love somebody enough, everything will be all right, but it isn't always true." As she did with Mel Ferrer and his son, Sean, Audrey nurtured the relationship between Andrea and son Luca. She knew the importance of a father; she refused to say a negative word about either man.

Then she met actor Robert Wolders, seven years her junior. He had been born in Rotterdam and spent the war near Arnhem. After modest success in films and television in the 1960s, he met and fell in love with actress Merle Oberon, a close friend of Audrey. Oberon and Wolders married in 1975 and Oberon died of a massive stroke four years later, at about the time Audrey's marriage fell apart. Both Audrey and Robert were melancholy when they met; in time they became inseparable.

Wolders was old-school European, quiet and dignified, and earned respect from the opinionated Ella, Baroness van Heemstra. Said Audrey of her mother, "She opposed both my marriages, maybe knowing neither man was going to be totally good to me. But I must say, she adored Robbie; she sensed he was really good to me."

Finally, Audrey had found peace in a relationship. The couple didn't marry; instead they retired to a rambling mansion in the guise of a farmhouse two-and-a-half centuries old in the remote village of Tolochenaz, Switzerland, where Audrey could enjoy her sons and her "Robbie," along with omnipresent dogs, an orchard, and a lush garden that became world famous.

For the first time since the Beukenhof in Velp, she allowed herself to put down roots. She described her home, which was called La Paisible: "It's a long house with eight bedrooms, lots of shutters, plants growing up things, simple, homey, cottagey. The walls are white, couches yellow and pink. I love bright colors."

Ella had spent part of the 1960s in San Francisco, where she volunteered to help Vietnam War veterans get benefits. Finally, she ended up living at the house in Switzerland and managing its staff. Said Audrey's son Luca with enthusiasm, "Ella was fantastic as a person. I grew up with her and I loved her. For a boy growing up, she was more fun than anything else. My mother was extremely sweet. She would never talk about gory things—ghosts, blood, scary things. She would say, 'You have to love, be sweet, and respect one another.' At Christmas my mother would give me a tenth red sweater, but Ella would bring me Dracula and Frankenstein [model] assembly kits from the States. She knew exactly what a boy like me wanted. She told me horrific ghost stories, murder stories.... Ella was terrifying! When she would tell a creepy story, you would shake all night and love it and ask her to tell it again the next day."

Meisje moved to Switzerland as well—as her health began to fail, Audrey arranged for her aunt to have the finest nursing care in a facility near La Paisible, where Meisje lived her last three years.

To Audrey's credit as a loyal daughter and stubborn Dutchwoman, no stories of a Nazi past ever came to the attention of the press from Audrey as Joseph and Ella lived out their lives. When Audrey learned that her father was living in Dublin, she screwed up her courage and visited him there in 1959; he returned the favor and spent time with Audrey a decade later in Switzerland; she would rush to his bedside right before he died in Dublin in October 1980.

Hepburn biographer Barry Paris quoted the baroness's friend Leonard Gershe, screenwriter of the 1957 Hepburn-Fred Astaire film *Funny Face*, on the relationship of mother and daughter: "She [Ella] had great humor and so did Audrey, but unfortunately they didn't have it together—they didn't share laughs. I adored her mother, but Audrey did not like her very much." Journalists who spent time with Audrey over the years also saw glimpses of deep-seated contempt harbored by the star toward her mother after what can only be described as a lifetime of Ella's domination. More than one reporter noticed icy control on Audrey's face as the subject of her mother came up. Leonard Gershe even said that Audrey had mentioned her mother's fascist past to him, and it was clear that she resented Ella for it.

Audrey's son Luca said of his mother and grandmother, "There was this big tension between the two—this big love and this big tension. Now I've come to understand that the underlying reason for all that was rooted in the political past of my grandmother. My mother had a very clear black-and-white, good-and-bad notion about the whole Nazi era."

Elder son Sean said his mother resented "both her parents for their political and social views, which is also why she let all of the family's titles of nobility die and be buried with my grandmother." But none of this resentment would be allowed for public consumption because of the van Heemstra–Dutch mastery of self.

In 1976 biographer David Pryce-Jones released *Unity Mitford: A Quest* and identified Ella in a photograph taken at the Braunes Haus in Munich, the same image Ella kept proudly on display in a frame in Arnhem. But, explained Ella once again, she had been way back then under the influence of an evil husband. In 1984 the biography *Audrey Hepburn* by Ian Woodward also mentioned the 1935 German connection, but since both Ella and Audrey were still living, the author carefully followed the line of logic that had been established eight years earlier: Ruston was the villain, and

Ella merely a pawn. Ella died in Switzerland soon after on 26 August 1984. To the end she received round-the-clock care from her daughter. When Meisje became gravely ill shortly thereafter, Audrey visited her often in the nursing facility. According to Wolders, Meisje—who had never remarried—departed the world in 1986 in Audrey's arms.

Audrey's half-brother Alex had died in 1979, but Alex's wife, Miepje, would outlive Audrey by thirteen years and pass on in 2006. Ian Quarles van Ufford, Audrey's other half-brother, died in 2010.

The most beloved man in Velp, Audrey's benefactor in the dark days, Dr. Hendrik Visser 't Hooft, remained a man of action and letters into the 1970s. While on a trip to Switzerland, with plans to go mountain climbing, the man who had deviled the SS and SD in Gelderland suffered a massive stroke and died soon thereafter at age seventy-one. Audrey kept her old Dutch life separate from that of mother and retired movie star, so it's unknown if she received word of Visser 't Hooft's passing.

For all that she would become, Academy Award-winning actress, Givenchy fashion plate, and international jet setter so at home on the Riviera or in Rome or Paris, the war years remained all too close. The sound of jackboots on the cobblestone streets of Arnhem never left her ears. The faces of Jews in cattle cars, adults and children, haunted her. Vivid sunsets in the western sky sometimes became the blood-red curtain of a burning Arnhem. Memories of bombs falling in Velp awoke her at night. The slaughter of Otto and Schimmelpenninck were a gunshot away.

"When my mother wanted to teach me a lesson about life," said Luca Dotti, "she never used stories about her career. She always told stories about the war. The war was very, very important to her. It made her who she was."

Audrey spent her last four years of life on the road as an ambassador for UNICEF, trying with her five-foot-seven frame that barely cracked a hundred pounds to will a planet of vengeful adults away from starting wars, because those wars create powerless victims in the children. She knew all about it.

Audrey came back from Ethiopia, Venezuela, and Ecuador in 1988; from Guatemala, Honduras, El Salvador, Mexico, the Sudan, and Thailand in 1989; from Vietnam in 1990 and Somalia in 1992 with her heart broken after every journey through barren, contested lands where children were starving. Or dying. Or already dead. She bled for them on the inside until she couldn't live with the pain anymore.

In an interview with Audrey's friend, Anna Cataldi, Barry Paris documented a telling moment from October 1992 in Nairobi. Cataldi visited Hepburn to say good-bye after they had been in Somalia at the same time, Audrey for UNICEF and Cataldi on a magazine assignment. "When I hugged her, I was scared," Paris quoted Cataldi as saying. "I had a shiver. She [Audrey] said, 'War didn't kill me, and this won't either.' But I had the feeling that sooner or later, war kills you. She was so skinny. I felt something was really wrong." Cataldi said that Audrey mentioned she was having nightmares about the dead children of Somalia, and couldn't sleep, and was crying all the time. "She had seen a lot of terrible things with UNICEF, but she broke in Somalia," was Cataldi's conclusion.

Luca said that unlike every other mission, where she had found beauty in the children, "When she came back from the Somalia trip, she was devastated. Totally devastated. Hopeless."

And her health was failing fast. "She wasn't feeling well," said Sean. "At first she felt tired. Then we all thought for quite a while that she had caught a bug in Somalia, maybe some intestinal flu or some complicated disease."

The work on behalf of UNICEF that had been inspired—no, demanded—by the years in Arnhem and Velp attacked her insides as ferociously as the malnutrition and binges and diets plagued a girl who, after all she had endured, could never again master the simple task of eating. As sure as if a Nazi bullet had finally tracked her down, World War II claimed this woman who had cheated death in the Netherlands time and again. The date was 20 January 1993. At the age of just sixty-three, when she should have been vital and happy, enjoying the love of her life, her "Robbie" in their Swiss hideaway and delighting in sons Sean and Luca—both now adults—the war caught up and took Audrey Hepburn in a matter of weeks. The cause of death: abdominal cancer.

Chapter Notes

1. Rapture

Many sources provided context for the heady times of the 1935 Reichsparteitag in Nuremberg. First and most important were the two short pieces that Ella wrote for the British fascists, which captured her point of view as a European looking at Hitler's accomplishments. At this time, Ella's thinking mirrored that of Diana Mitford, who as Diana Mosley wrote *A Life of Contrasts: The Autobiography of Diana Mosley*, a book that clearly described the Munich and Nuremberg of 1935 and especially provided a perspective on Hitler that contrasts the hindsight of today. Leni Riefenstahl's *Triumph of the Will* set the scene and the mood for events of September 1935 because it had been shot just a year earlier at the same locations. *The Nuremberg Rallies* by Alan Wykes provided logistics on the week of activities. Ella blithely stumbled into a crossroads in history, met Hitler, and then watched the world come apart in the intervening ten-year period. And as events unfolded, her daughter came of age.

2. The Blood of Frisia

Various family trees and Dutch histories were consulted to develop the history of the van Heemstra family. The Gelders Archief in Arnhem provided birth and marriage registrations for most of the van Heemstras who lived in Gelderland. Background on A.J.A.A., Baron van Heemstra, and his cousin, Schelte, Baron van Heemstra, was courtesy of Huygens ING and various clippings from the *Arnhemsche Courant*. Ella's description of her father appeared in an unpublished autobiographical novel that she wrote. Barry Paris's landmark *Audrey Hepburn* was the starting point on Ella's marriages and the globe-trotting of her youth. Several sources provided depth on Sir Oswald Mosley and the BUF movement, primarily Nicholas Mosley's *Rules of the Game* and *Beyond the Pale*, plus Robert Skidelsky's biography *Oswald Mosley* and Anne de Courcy's *Diana Mosley*. The published letters of the Mitford sisters were extremely valuable, as was Diana Mitford Mosley's memoir, *A Life of Contrasts*. And of course, Ella van Heemstra's two published pieces on behalf of the British fascists speak for themselves. Background on the Reichsparteitag came from *The Nuremberg Rallies* by Alan Wykes and from Leni Riefenstahl's *Triumph of the Will*.

Sean Ferrer provided his mother's memories of going gliding with her father in *Audrey Hepburn, An Elegant Spirit*. Various documents in the Gelders Archief prove Baron van Heemstra's ownership of Villa Roestenburg on the Pietersbergseweg in Oosterbeek in the 1930s, and site visits there with my guide, historian Robert Voskuil, provided rich detail about the "playground" of Ella's children during this period. Audrey Hepburn's reminiscences about the departure of her father are recounted here from various interviews, primarily for *US* magazine, 17 October 1988, and *Parade*, 5 March 1989. It was in the later interviews that Audrey felt more comfortable psychoanalyzing herself about the traumas of childhood. Luca Dotti provided perspective on his mother's relationship with Joseph Ruston in my June 2018 interview with him.

3. Exile

Ella's writings detail her involvement in the Nuremberg Rallies and visit to Munich. Unity Mitford's 19 September 1935 letter mentions "Heemstra" by name and places her at the Osteria Bavaria, the restaurant Hitler visited daily. Every letter sent by Unity was on Nazi stationery with a swastika, and each ended, "Heil Hitler!" Meanwhile, back in England, six-year-old Audrey lived in a suddenly less colorful world, as described in a 2 May 1996 newspaper article from County Kent as well as the March/April 2015 issue of *Bygone Kent* magazine. Audrey spoke about her school and life in Elham in a November 1953 interview for *Modern Screen*. The Gelders Archief provided details about the van Heemstras in Oosterbeek and the *Arnhemsche Courant* noted the passing of the Baroness.

Documents in the Gelders Archief settled once and for all the idea that the elegant old Castle Zijpendaal of Sonsbeek, Arnhem, "belonged" to Ella's father, or as Hepburn biographer Robyn Karney put it, that Zijpendaal was "one of the comfortable family estates just outside the city." The reality was, well, reality: The baron was a pensioner and merely rented rooms at Zijpendaal for three years. He wasn't forced out by Nazis; Nazis didn't confiscate his property or bank account.

Research work done by the Airborne Museum of Oosterbeek in preparation for the 2017 "Ella & Audrey" exhibit determined that the date of Audrey's passage from Gatwick to Schiphol on an orange DC-3 was 14 December 1939. There is some anecdotal evidence suggesting that the flight occurred earlier in the autumn because at least one person remembers seeing Audrey in Arnhem in October, but nothing concrete can be determined. Audrey recounted the experience of the airplane ride for Dominick Dunne in *Vanity Fair*'s May 1991 issue.

4. Edda

While in the Netherlands, I asked several people of the war generation what it meant to be Dutch, and what made them special. Their answers provided some of these descriptions; other parts resulted from reading Dutch war diaries and from visits to various homes and churches. Audrey spoke testily about the lack of van Heemstra wealth in the *Philadelphia Inquirer*'s 13 May 1990 issue and about her need for love in Richard Brown's 1991 article for the *My Fair Lady* restoration program. Descriptions of the apartment building on Jansbinnensingel in Arnhem Centraal come from my site visits and from Miepje Quarles van Ufford's description in the 23 December 1993 issue of *De Gelderlander* in an article entitled "The Foggy War Years of Audrey Hepburn" by Hélène van Beck. Some authors have described this address, Jansbinnensingel 8A, as a house, but it was and still is a storefront with apartments above it. Robert Wolders' description of Ella was found in the Barry Paris papers at the University of Pittsburgh. Wolders sat for a lengthy interview about Audrey conducted after her death. Audrey's descriptions of the Holland of her mother were taken from Ivo Niehe's 1988 interview with Audrey for AVROTROS television in the Netherlands, an extended version of which was broadcast on 6 August 2018.

The concept of "Edda van Heemstra" was puzzling to me—the popular mythology is that Edda was an invention to keep the occupying Germans from knowing that Audrey was English. But Audrey was enrolled as Edda in grade school five months before the Germans marched in. On the other hand, documents in the Nationaal Archief confirm that the baroness was very much pro-German before and after the 10 May 1940 occupation, so Ella herself must have wanted to downplay the fact that her daughter was English because her Nazi friends would look upon it with disfavor—Germany and England were then at war. Audrey was quoted about her early Dutch school experiences in Ian Woodward's biography, *Audrey Hepburn*. A very interesting Dutch source was the 3 October 1953 issue of *Het Vrije Volk* in which her teachers and classmates were interviewed at the time of Audrey's appearance in *Roman Holiday*, just a dozen years after Audrey/Edda attended the Tamboersbosje school.

Biographers haven't understood the importance to Audrey Hepburn's life of the 29 December 1939 war benefit at the Schouwburg. It was here that she first experienced a ballet performance in Arnhem—and a performance by her eventual teacher, Winja Marova, at that. The evening's activities were covered extensively in the *Arnhemsche Courant*, and supporting documents in the Gelders Archief placed Audrey in the Queen's Gold Circle seats. My April 2018 tour of the theater and its two balconies gave authenticity to the narrative. Documents related to the Sadler's Wells Dutch tour were found in the Paris papers, including Annabel Farjeon's diary. Margo Fonteyn's memory of standing on the bridge appeared in *Autobiography: Margo Fonteyn*, and Audrey's reminiscence about the ballet evening were found in the May 1991 *Vanity Fair* interview. I couldn't help but foreshadow the battle of Arnhem because of how tied to the "Bridge Too Far" the van Heemstras were. All three of the structures beside the bridge ramp had been inhabited by van Heemstras or van Limburg Stirums and all would be destroyed in the thick of the fighting on 18 and 19 September 1944.

5. The Unthinkable

My site visits to Arnhem Centraal are the backbone of this and all the other Arnhem chapters. Audrey was eloquent in describing the day of German occupation. She discussed it in *Vanity Fair* with Dominick Dunne and was quoted in Ian Woodward's *Audrey Hepburn* as well as in the 6 August 1994 issue of the *Sydney Morning Herald*.

Time and distance have sapped the drama of the time, and I thought it important to present to the reader the tension and unreality of German troops in Arnhem after they had so carefully avoided setting foot in the Netherlands in the Great War. Detail about 10 May in Arnhem and elsewhere in the Netherlands came courtesy of Robert Kershaw's *A Street in Arnhem* and several eyewitness reminiscences, including Sid Baron's *The Way It Was* and Cornelia Fuykschot's *Hunger in Holland*.

6. Dancer

Loe de Jong's masterwork, *Het Koninkrijk der Nederlanden in de Tweede Wereldoorlog*, provided the backbone of the Dutch perspective on the war and a day-by-day account of the deepening German occupation. *The Lion Rampant*, the account of the Nazis in Holland written by de Jong and Joseph W.F. Stoppelman and published during the war, was also invaluable. Audrey spoke of "hearts and minds" in her *Donahue* TV appearance in 1990. Information about Ella and the Diaconessenhuis was found in CABR dossier number 108579 on Ella van Heemstra in the Nationaal Archief at The Hague. The quote from Marova about Audrey appeared in the 1953 *Het Vrije Volk* article, and Audrey's about Marova appeared in Paris's *Audrey Hepburn*.

Another myth to be dispelled about Audrey Hepburn concerned the supposed use of the name Edda throughout the war. In truth, she was billed as Audrey Hepburn-Ruston in every dance program, in the newspaper, and in other advertising about the Dansschool and its performances from 1941 on. Ella had no problem promoting her daughter using a very English-sounding name.

Site visits to Zijpendaal helped me paint a picture of this peaceful setting, and my interview with Joop Onnekink set the scene for the baron's rooms inside. Audrey's descriptions of her childhood reading habits appeared in Woodward. Mevrouw Zegwaart's papers related to Zijpendaal are housed in the Gelders Archief and provided colorful detail about the back and forth between her and the baron.

Two of the most important people of Audrey's youth have all but disappeared from history—her aunt and uncle, Meisje and Otto. As Audrey grew into adolescence and had neither a father nor an affectionate mother, her uncle and aunt filled these roles.

She would mention Otto often as an adult but never speak in emotional terms about him in life. I believe she had to shut out the loving memories because they were too painful, given what happened in August 1942.

7. Pencil Scratches

It seemed to me that showing Audrey at various points of her life would help readers to understand just how much a product of the war she was. She became who the war made her. This chapter is based on information about her personality gleaned from all the research. It also contains information from Lindsay Anderson's production diary that became the book *Making a Film: The Story of 'Secret People'* and from viewings of this interesting, important, and overlooked picture in the early career of film star Audrey Hepburn.

8. Unacceptable

Information about Otto Ernst Gelder, Count van Limburg Stirum, was found in the Gelders Archief, and articles on his cases appeared in various issues of the *Provinciale Drentsche en Asser Courant*. A description of the seemingly silly case of the man accused of singing a song—the case that was Otto's undoing—was found in "Rechters in oorlogstijd: de confrontatie van de Nederlandse rechterlijke macht met nationaal-socialisme en besetting," compiled by the Boom Juridische Uitgevers of The Hague and published in 2007 by the Radboud Universiteit Nijmegen.

Information about Draaisma's involvement with the NSB was found in dossier CABR 108802 in the Nationaal Archief at The Hague. The Monné description of Ella came courtesy of the *De Gelderlander* article. Audrey's professional debut at the Wehrmachtheim was covered extensively in the *Courant*, and the memories of Marova were found in *Het Vrije Volk*. Because of the extreme postwar backlash against anything Nazi, Audrey was careful never to mention that she first danced for an audience of German soldiers.

It was a fact that could do nothing but harm her career. She carried no guilt about this; she was a dancer and she danced, but would the world understand that?

The Mozart celebration organized by Ella proved conclusively that she was pro-German and working with the Arnhem NSB at this point in the war. Articles in the *Courant* detailed the preparations for this event and then its execution, and lavish praise was heaped upon the baroness for her wonderful work to honor the German hero, Mozart. The Gelders Archief provided background on the various van Heemstras and their roles. Loe de Jong's work led to understanding of the reason for Otto's autumn 1941 dismissal from the Arnhem court as ordered by J.J. Schrieke.

9. Born for the Spotlight

Audrey discussed her mother in the November 1953 issue of *Modern Screen* magazine. The quotes from Ella van Heemstra and Alfred Heineken III were found in Paris. Evidence that Audrey attended the H.B.S. Meisjes School in Arnhem was provided in the family history of one of her classmates, Koosje Heineman. Ella's letter to Chiel de Boer is in the collection of Theater Instituut Nederland in Amsterdam. Audrey's quote about wanting to dance solo roles was found in Alexander Walker's *Audrey: The Real Story*. Annabel Farjeon's diary was found in the Paris papers, and Margot Fonteyn's quote about the rigors of dance was taken from her *Autobiography*. I followed the route Audrey walked from Jansbinnensingel 8A to the Muziekschool in Arnhem during site visits.

Rosemarie Kamphuisen of Velp connected me with information provided by her friend Koosje Heineman, whose family historical record settled the matter of whether Audrey had attended secondary school in Arnhem.

Steven Jansen's *dagboek*, or diary, is one of the most important sources to the *Dutch Girl* narrative. Jansen was a resident of Oranjestraat in Velp and kept a running account of daily life in the village through the war years, which was published in 1945 as *Velp en de Oorlog 1940–1945*. Details about the winter and the institution of the *Kultuurkamer* were found in *The Lion Rampant* by de Jong and Stoppelman. Seyss-Inquart's quote was found in his Nuremberg testimony. Details about Draaisma were taken from CABR 108802, dossier E12945 PR. A. Arnhem 7462 in the Nationaal Archief at The Hague. Information about the baron's decision to leave Zijpendaal and about his new home, Villa Beukenhof, was found at the Gelders Archief; this includes the fact that he didn't own this villa but rather rented it from the Reformed Church after it had been bequeathed by a private party. Descriptions of the house found in this book are based on photos and blueprints also filed at the Gelders Archief, and descriptions of Rozendaalselaan in Velp are the result of several site visits. Details of the arrest of Otto, Count van Limburg Stirum, were found in his diary, which is filed at the NIOD, the Dutch War Archive in Amsterdam.

10. Death Candidate

The story of Otto, Count van Limburg Stirum, is important to the van Heemstras and also to Dutch history. This wasn't some poor anonymous soul a grainy newsreel showed being shot by the Nazis; this was a member of Audrey's immediate family with whom she had lived in Arnhem. He was also among the first five civilians to be executed in all of the Netherlands since the occupation began. Otto's story is fascinating and heartbreaking, and Audrey mentioned his death so often, always positioning it as the most shocking thing that she experienced in the war. For these reasons I felt the need to explore Otto's situation. Luckily my Dutch researcher, Maddie van Leenders, found his diary at NIOD and painstakingly translated it from archaic, handwritten Dutch to English. This became my primary source, with excellent support from the diary of Robert Peereboom, which was published in 1945 as *Gijzelaars in Gestel*. I made site visits to the former Kleine Seminary Beekvliet in

Sint-Michielsgestel. The magnificent front portion of the complex remains, while the many wings added on behind have been demolished. Maddie and I were able to explore the building inside and out, and we also visited the place of execution near Tilburg, which gave authenticity to the descriptions of Otto's last twenty-four hours. My good fortune continued on the Tilburg visit as Maddie connected me with the owner of the land containing the execution site, now a national monument. There, I was able to touch replicas of the five poles planted in the ground, and pay my respects at the graves of the count and Baron Schimmelpenninck. An interview with the landowner contradicted some of the information found in an article titled "Vijf zwarte palen herinneren aan oorlogsdrama" (Five black poles remind of war drama) by Pierre van Beek, which appeared in *Het Nieuwsblad van het Zuiden* on 12 August 1975. This was the first documentation of the executions that I found, and I worked backward from there to fill in (and correct) the story from its beginning with Otto's arrest and continuing past the horrible morning of 15 August 1942.

11. Paranoid

This chapter was another gamble because once again the focus is not Audrey. But the conclusion of the previous chapter was so shocking and made so little sense to any rational mind that telling the back story of what had gone on outside Otto's knowledge was essential to giving perspective to the episode. Facts were found in de Jong's World War II narrative, including the historical perspective on the *Driemanschap* and Rutger Jan Schimmelpenninck. It begs the question: If Queen Wilhelmina had not been visiting the United States at this time and if she had not addressed Congress, would Count van Limburg Stirum and Baron Schimmelpenninck have been chosen for execution?

During the Nuremberg trials, Seyss-Inquart said on Monday, 10 June 1946: "I can take full and absolute responsibility for what happened in the hostage camp in St. Michielsgestel. It was not a hostage camp in the actual sense of the word: I took Dutchmen into custody only when they had shown themselves to be active in Resistance movements. The camp at St. Michielsgestel was not a prison. I visited it. The inmates of the camp played golf. They were given leave, in the case of urgent family affairs or business matters. Not a single one of them was ever shot. I think the majority of the present Dutch Ministers were at St. Michielsgestel. It was a sort of protective custody to temporarily hinder them from continuing their anti-German activities." (Nuremberg Trial Proceedings Vol. 15, 151st day, Monday, 10 June 1946.)

But after reading about Otto's experiences, we all know better. Seyss-Inquart was a rat and not forthcoming on the topic of the executions of "the five." It was entirely fitting that the man responsible for the deaths of Otto and thousands of others would be hanged in Nuremberg on 16 October 1946 at the age of 54.

The owner of the property that includes the execution site, a man of about 80, was once the employer of Marinus van Heerebeek, and he heard the story of the morning of execution from van Heerebeek personally. Nowhere has this account been told accurately until now—how van Heerebeek saw Green Police, heard the volley in the woods, and later put two and two together based on the shocking news that Dutch civilians had been executed.

Some of Meisje's papers, including the letters quoted, were found in the Gelders Archief.

12. The Secret

Audrey's quote about Otto appeared in "Somalia: The Silent Children." She made the statement about pain and loss to Shara Fryer of KTRK-TV in Houston on 21 March 1990 in connection with the Anne Frank tour. The reasoning for Ella's move with Audrey from Arnhem to Velp was built on circumstantial evidence. The issue of *Oranjekrant* listing Baroness van Heemstra as "Gestapo" is filed at the Nationaal Archief in The Hague. Research in the Netherlands revealed the importance of the van Pallandts of Castle Rozendaal to the van Heemstras. They were families allied by marriage for a century and by titled status for much longer. Ella's quote about the titled class appeared in her untitled auto-biographical novel. Audrey's quote about growing up with older people was found in Woodward. The Jansen diary became more important once Ella and Audrey moved to Velp since he was writing about conditions in the village from a perspective very near the Villa Beukenhof. Information about Velp itself and about the Deelen Air Base is the result of visiting both. I spent a great deal of time walking the streets of Velp, a village that hasn't changed much since the war except for destruction caused *during* the war. The *Courant* covered the February 1943 Dansschool performances at the Schouwburg. An interview with Dick Mantel in his home on Rozendaalselaan in Velp—he lived across the street from the Beu-kenhof—provided wonderful detail about life in the village, and so close to the van Heemstras, during the occupation.

Audrey's negative comments revealing a low self-opinion of her looks show up like a rash through many interviews over many decades. The quote used here was found in a syndicated piece from September 1953 coinciding with the release of *Roman Holiday*, and the quote about her shoulders was contained in the raw transcript of her interview with Hedda Hopper of 11 September 1953, which is in the Hopper papers at the Academy of Motion Picture Arts and Sciences Margaret Herrick Library.

Several newspapers carried the announcement of the marriage of Alex Quarles van Ufford to Maria Margarethe Monné in June 1943. Information about the German roundup of workers was found in Jansen, and the story about the baron's visits to the Man-tel home was provided by Dick Mantel. Audrey talked about the capture of Ian often; this quote appeared in the December 1953 issue of *Screenland* magazine. As for her fierce resistance to fielding questions that were too personal, in addition to the October 1955 issue of *Cosmopolitan*, quotes were found in the June 1954 issue of *McCall's*, the August 1962 issue of *Good Housekeeping*, and Glenn Plaskin's syndicated May 1991 newspaper feature, "She Hardly Goes Lightly Through Life." Clearly, she put up a wall at the beginning of her public life to keep reporters from asking questions about certain aspects of life, including or especially the war.

13. Soul Sister

Thanks to Audrey's 1990 collaboration with composer and conductor Michael Tilson Thomas to bring "From the Diary of Anne Frank" to American audiences in four cities, Audrey spoke a great deal about the spiritual connection she felt toward the "other Dutch girl." The quote about first reading the *Het Achterhuis* manuscript appeared in Walker. The quote about Uncle Otto appeared in an extensive interview and writeup by Lesley Garner for the 26 May 1991 *Sunday Telegraph*. The quote about Audrey as soul sister and being happy to read her words appeared in a syndicated newspaper article that circulated in late March 1990, including in the *Journal Times* of Racine, Wisconsin. An interview with the *Miami Herald* covered Audrey's day with Otto and Elfriede Frank.

Audrey was always talking about her fear of public speaking, including on this tour when she mentioned it in New York City to Bridget Foley of the Fairchild News Service. Michael Tilson Thomas's quote about Audrey's way of reading the words of Anne Frank was the first and most widely printed comment in press accompanying the tour from city to city. Finally, my visit to the Anne Frank House and Museum in Amsterdam helped greatly in the writing of this chapter.

14. Just Dutchmen

Background on the Jewish situation in the Netherlands was courtesy of the report commissioned in 1950 by the Rijksinstituut voor Oorlogs-documentatie (the Netherlands State Institute for War Documentation). This report, which was estimated for completion in 1952, took fifteen years to come to fruition because of the complexity involved in documenting the Holocaust as it occurred in the Netherlands. Dr. Loe de Jong was the director of this organization and the primary advocate for this report, which was written by Dr. Jacob Presser. I am indebted to both men for their superb work.

Audrey spoke often and eloquently about what she witnessed regarding the Jews in Arnhem from 1941–43. Some of her quotes used here were found in Walker and Woodward. She also spoke about the matter in *Vogue* in 1971 and on her 1990 *Donahue* appearance.

The onderduiker situation in Velp—those who had gone into hiding for one reason or another—was covered by Gety Hengeveld-de Jong and the Stichting Velp voor Oranje (Velp for Oranje Foundation) in *Verborgen in Velp*. This terrific volume, published in 2013, documented dozens of accounts of Velpenaren risking their lives to hide Jews who had been marked for death by the Nazis.

15. Warmest Praise

Audrey's quote about the regimentation of dance was found in the typed transcript of her 1953 interview with Hedda Hopper. Facts about the establishment of Seyss-Inquart and his government in Velp in 1943 were revealed in interviews on the ground in Velp. Steven Jansen described the confiscation of homes in his diary. Detail about Fliegerhorst Deelen resulted from my site visits to the base museum and Diogenes command bunker accompanied by historian Johan Vermeulen, with additional information found in *Duits Deelen* by Ineke Beltman. The bombing of Castle Rozendaal was covered in the *Omroep Gelderland* article "Bommen op Kasteel Rozendaal," which was published on the seventy-fourth anniversary of the incident. A letter from David Heringa to author Barry Paris describing Ella's Christian Science activities was found in the Paris papers at the University of Pittsburgh. Audrey spoke about the increasing difficulties of dancing during the war and about the *Kultuurkamer*, in the October 1956 issue of *Dance* magazine. The 8 January performance of the dansavond and its many encores were covered in the *Arnhemsche Courant*. My understanding of the Eighth Air Force bombing missions of Big Week resulted from my core research conducted for the book *Mission: Jimmy Stewart and the Fight for Europe*.

Another of the untold stories in this book concerns the Resistance in Velp as led by its physicians based in the Ziekenhuis. Information on this topic was collected during a series of interviews with Velpenaren, including Clan and Annemarth Visser 't Hooft, daughters of huisarts Dr. Hendrik Visser 't Hooft; Ben van Griethuysen, son of radiologist Dr. Bernhard van Griethuysen; and Rosemarie Kamphuisen—her family members were patients of Dr. Visser 't Hooft. A great deal of supporting information was found in *Verborgen in Velp* and in the 1992 commemorative volume, *100 Jaar Ziekenhuis Velp* by J.P. Kooger.

To show how an entire project can turn on a dime, it was an off-handed comment by Clan about her father, who said often with pride that Audrey had worked as a volunteer for him, that became a key to *everything* about the Dutch girl in the latter half of the war. Suddenly, so many of the events she had described, her participation in events that seemed far-fetched to some, had a context because she was in direct contact day-to-day with the L.O. Resistance leader in the entire area—and a very charismatic leader at that, a man of action who could inspire action in others.

The quote by Marova about Audrey's physical condition was found in Paris. The quote wherein Audrey stated that the town carpenter put up a barre for her appeared in *Dance* magazine, October 1956. However, this statement has been misinterpreted. The "village carpenter" didn't put a barre in Villa Beukenhof. He installed it in one of the rooms of the N.H.V. at Stationsstraat 5 in Velp. This was a Reformed Church utility building that served as a local meeting place and it was here that Audrey conducted dance lessons for village children. The quote about her former students staying in touch also appeared in *Dance* magazine.

16. Black Evenings

Audrey spoke about the food shortages many times, including in *The Guardian* of London on 29 March 1988. The Velpsche Ziekenhuis staff was discussed in V*erborgen in Velp*. Village resident Rosemarie Kamphuisen described Drs. Visser 't Hooft and van der Willigen in conversations with me in Velp and via email. The various Dutch Resistance groups at work in the Netherlands were described by CIA historian Stewart W. Bentley, Jr. in his book *Orange Blood, Silver Wings*. The example of Visser 't Hooft's run-ins with the Nazi police and tending of Seyss-Inquart were provided in interviews with Clan Visser 't Hooft.

Early in her career, Audrey spoke often of dancing in the zwarte avonden. She mentioned it as early as 13 January 1952 in an interview published in the *Daily Oklahoman*, and again in a *Modern Screen* November 1953 interview. As for the Rotterdamsche Bank being turned into a notorious SD torture facility, Jansen mentioned it on multiple occasions, and Audrey touched on it in a 1991 televised interview on CNN's *Larry King Live*. The experiences of various clergy in Velp were covered both by Jansen and by Hengeveld-de Jong.

Audrey's comment to Sidney Fields was, "In between running around with food for the pilots and anti-Nazi literature we gave what were called 'Black Performances,' dancing in private houses to raise money for the Underground." True to her mother's lifelong teaching that one must never call attention to oneself, and Audrey's belief that she should never use the war for publicity purposes, she never revealed more about how she helped pilots during the most critical period of the Eighth Air Force bombing campaign of the Reich in 1944.

Her adventure with the English-speaking soldier in the forest was told first by Anita Loos through a description that Loos herself called "melodramatic" in a 1954 article in *The American Weekly*. In this original version, the soldier was an "English paratrooper" and Audrey led him to a house where he could wash up before turning himself in to the Nazis. "Before they parted," wrote Loos, "the young man gave Audrey his only possession of value, a silver locket with the Lord's Prayer engraved on it."

The story as written by Loos makes no sense on many levels. English paratroopers weren't landing near Velp one at a time. During Operation Market Garden 10,000 landed many kilometers west of Velp, and on that occasion, for weeks afterward it was far too dangerous for a girl to be leaving home to go anywhere, let alone the forest. Nor were soldiers "turning themselves in" to the Nazis after a refreshing bath and shave. They were desperate to avoid capture. On the other hand, American and British airmen were shot down and seen floating to earth on parachutes every day, and this one was likely a downed fighter-pilot because they were the only British fliers in the air during the day, escorting American bombers across the Netherlands.

Annemarth Visser 't Hooft told me of the German fortified camp, known to the Dutch as "het moffendorp," and of the fact that civilians were forbidden to be anywhere near it.

17. Het Vaderland

Audrey's quote about having a good cry appeared in the *Philadelphia Inquirer* in an article entitled "Breakfast at UNICEF" on 13 May 1990. The attacks on Deelen were described in Beltman's *Duits Deelen* and Jansen mentioned the curious events—without having any context for them. The mass, unorganized retreat up through Arnhem from the Belgian border has been described by many authors, including Cornelius Ryan in *A Bridge Too Far*, and Robert Kershaw in *A Street in Arnhem*. Jansen described the German hordes descending on Velp's hotels, shops, and restaurants. Audrey's description of herself as "awfully young" appeared in the 5 August 1985 *Washington Post*. Dutch researcher Maddie van Leenders spotted Ella's classified ad in *Het Vaderland*, and the rationale for Ella placing it was based on a contextual analysis of the situation, and on Luca Dotti's descriptions of his grandmother's sensibilities.

18. If, If, If

Then there were the battered German commanding officers, Model and Bittrich. There were others, too, but I felt I had to boil the story down to its elements. The Germans needed someplace to collect themselves and lick their wounds after brutal fighting around Normandy and then across France. Arnhem, Audrey's city, became doomed when Model moved into the Tafelberg in Oosterbeek and ordered his troops to regroup practically in the laps of the van Heemstras. Their decision opened up Pandora's Box for everyone in Gelderland. How many deaths resulted? How much privation? The ripples would go on and on for decades and, I maintain, result ultimately in the tragic early death of Audrey Hepburn.

19. The Hun on the Run

I saw no way around pausing to ground the reader in Market Garden, one of the most romanticized battles of World War II, and an event that changed millions of lives, including that of Audrey Hepburn. No fan of the great actress and international personality would stop to think that the course of Audrey's life was directly connected to the fact that the Soviet army would get to Berlin before the British and Americans. This is history at its most compelling and worth a few pages to set up the Allied plan to capture the eastern part of the Netherlands.

20. The Netherlands in Five Days

Since the purpose of this tour was war relief, and the Dutch girl was back home and visiting Oosterbeek and Arnhem, I saw an opportunity to "flash forward" to look at Audrey just nine years after she had experienced the liberation. At this point she had already won an Oscar for *Roman Holiday* and a Tony for the Broadway run of *Ondine*. *Sabrina* was still doing smash worldwide business months after its U.S. release.

Dutch press coverage of the five-day tour of the Netherlands by Mel and Audrey Ferrer was extensive. Articles in the 6 November 1954 *Democratisch-Socialistisch Dagblad* and *Het Vrije Volk* were especially illuminating. The country's no-nonsense reporters clearly loved their favorite daughter, but not her brusque-to-the-point-of-rudeness husband. Ferrer's behavior rated headlines in the Dutch press, and they pulled no punches in describing his treatment of everyone from a cheese-toting little girl to his own wife. Through it all, Audrey is described as remaining above the fray.

21. Ultimatum

Audrey spoke of "the war diet" on the Anne Frank tour. Maddie van Leenders positioned the logic of Ella's move to The Hague—she was seeking a safe harbor for herself and Audrey and these were the reasons why The Hague was the right place to settle after leaving Velp. *Dolle Dinsdag* is one of the most famous days in Dutch history and has been written about extensively. All the diaries mention it, and so do all the histories. The air attack on Wolfheze and the sudden appearance of SS Panzer vehicles and troops in Velp seemed to be random incidents as mentioned by Jansen and others, but they signaled much grander events. These were opening movements in what would become the Operation

Market Garden saga, and so they have been covered by Ryan, Kershaw, and Martin Middlebrook in his opus, *Arnhem 1944*, among a legion of other authors.

22. The Devil's Picnic

Audrey's quote about the opening of the battle was taken from Woodward. Greta Stephany's account of the first bombing runs appeared in *The Dutch in Wartime Series Volume 7: Caught in the Crossfire*. Many Market Garden histories chronicle the opening bombardment; I used Kershaw and Middlebrook. For the perspective of the Velpenaren, I consulted local diaries and also interviewed survivors. Kate ter Horst's diary was published as *Cloud over Arnhem: Oosterbeek—September 1944*. Kate's daughter, Sophie, who was a survivor of the battle, handed a copy in English to me in the ter Horst garden, where fifty-nine Tommies had been buried. Receiving Sophie ter Horst's embrace in that place, a moment arranged by battle historian Robert Voskuil, was something I will never forget.

Various Market Garden histories detail the impressive response of Model to the landings he observed to the west. He did not react as portrayed in the screen version of *A Bridge Too Far*, because as director Richard Attenborough said more than once, "I'm not making history—I'm making a movie!"

The actions at the Hotel Naeff were relayed in the oral histories of interview subjects in Velp. As for the movements of the van Heemstras on this day, I was guided by the common experiences of the various reporters in Velp, including Jansen (on Oranjestraat) and van Hensbergen (on Rozendaalselaan). These two and others I interviewed responded to the sirens and the nearness of aircraft engines; otherwise, they were out of doors trying to see what was going on. Very early on, the people of Velp knew they were living a moment in history.

Over the course of three investigations in two-and-a-half

years, I covered the entire area of the battles for Arnhem and Oosterbeek, from the British landing zones on Ginkel Heath eastward through Oosterbeek, Arnhem, and Velp. All these visits were key to my ability to write about the events of 17 September.

23. Cakewalk

Historian Robert Voskuil, who led me on tours of the entire battle area, found Piet Hoefsloot's mini-story of the battle in the archives of the Society of Friends of the Airborne Museum. Accounts of Frost's men were found in Middlebrook and Kershaw, and I used Frost's descriptions from his memoir, *A Drop Too Many*. Wilhelmina Schouten's account also came from Middlebrook. An understanding of the city of Arnhem and the terrain from St. Elisabeth's to the Arnhem Road Bridge resulted from multiple site visits to the area.

The pre-dawn moment when a woman flung open her window and frightened the Tommies was courtesy of teenager Anje van Maanen's incredible diary that was published in 2015.

Perspectives of the Velpenaren, including Audrey's, were provided through diaries and in many interviews with people who were children then, Audrey's age or younger, and who vividly recalled their proximity to the battle. They suddenly found themselves in the middle of frightful commotion, a deafening cacophony, and a growing force of German troops and captured Tommies. Among those interviewed were Clan and Annemarth Visser 't Hooft, Herman van Remmen, Ben van Griethuysen, Rosemarie Kamphuisen, and Dick Mantel. All remained in Velp through the entirety of the battle.

24. Aflame

One of the most vivid September 1944 memories of those living in Velp was the blood-red western horizon on the first nights of the battle as Arnhem burned. The account of the last days of Cornelia, Countess van Limburg Stirum, was found in *Biographische woordenboek Gelderland: bekende en onbekende mannen en vrouwen* by P.W. van Wissing.

Site visits to Oosterbeek and research at the Gelders Archief provided background for descriptions of the village as a scene of battle.

Many accounts talk about the refugees streaming out of Arnhem, and Audrey would speak of the heartbreak of it often, as in a syndicated article that appeared in the 13 November 1953 *Joplin Globe*, a biographical feature in the April 1954 issue of *Modern Screen*, and a feature promoting *Funny Face* in the October 1956 issue of *Dance*. The SS view of the Tommies was taken from *Das Reich* by Max Hastings, and confirmed by Frost in *A Drop Too Many*. Reports of tanks on Rozendaalselaan were confirmed by Dick Mantel, who spent the battle there. Jansen and van Hensbergen both wrote of the situation in Velp, with refugees streaming in from the west and fresh German troops from the east. Above all, interviews with the Velpenaren who experienced the battle allowed me to tell this story.

25. Champagne for One

Audrey's statement about living conditions after the battle was taken from an interview after the Somalia trip in autumn 1992 that was to run in *International Newsweek*. Loe de Jong chronicled the railway strike in his Dutch war history. Audrey's quotes about the refugees appeared in *Dance*. Ter Horst's quote came from *Cloud Over Arnhem*, and the German officer's quote from Middelbrook. Jansen's diary entries proved invaluable to set the scene in Velp, as did interviews with the eyewitnesses.

Deane-Drummond's story first appeared in his memoir, *Return Ticket*. In the original 1967 edition from Collins in London, he referred only to "a local baroness" who "sent round a bottle of champagne." But a second edition capitalized on his proximity to the van Heemstras in Velp, and, suddenly, he was describing meeting young Audrey and the baroness during his time on the run. He referred to them being "next door" when in fact Rozendaalselaan 32 and Schaapsdrift Overbeek 16 were a fraction of a mile apart. Velp historian Gety Hengeveld-de Jong took me on a tour of the homes and buildings where Deane-Drummond hid, and based on geography alone, it's quite unlikely that the phantom major met up with Ella or Audrey in person. I put some faith in his original account that a baroness, probably Ella, sent him a bottle of champagne "for the road." But that's about it. His quote toward the end of the chapter was taken from *Return Ticket*.

The surprising revelation that the van Heemstras sheltered a Tommy at the Beukenhof was provided by Luca Dotti in a June 2018 interview. Because Audrey worked for Dr. Visser 't Hooft, the story works in all ways. As Luca said, "My mother wasn't one to make up stories." And since the van Heemstras were not shot, it's clear the British fugitive made it out with the help of the Dutch Resistance. Her quote about Les Gueux was found in Harris.

26. The Princess

Every writer needs an angle, but Eleanor Harris writing in the August 1959 issue of *Good Housekeeping*, ostensibly on the release of the picture, *The Nun's Story*, went to the extreme to find some "dirt" on Audrey Hepburn. It's not often that a star is taken to task for not having faults, but that was Hepburn's sin on this occasion. The quote by Hepburn about her mother was taken from Edward Klein's 5 March 1989 feature in the *Parade* newspaper supplement.

27. Hunters

The opening quote was from a syndicated 13 November 1953 personality profile that appeared in the *Joplin Globe*. Information about the 2nd TAF appeared in Davig Wragg's *Fighter Operations in Europe & North Africa 1939–1945*. Audrey spoke of the incident with the Spitfire in Ivo Niehe's 1988 interview for AVROTROS. The situation in Velp was described in interviews and in the diaries of Jansen and van Hensbergen. Ben van Griethuysen told me of the rocket attack that killed his mother in a June 2017 interview; Annemarth Visser 't Hooft provided her perspective in an April 2018 article, and van Hensbergen and Jansen both described the attack. The Allied pilot's view by Sir Kenneth Adam was courtesy of *The Lost Evidence: Breakout from Normandy* from Flashback Television and The History Channel in 2006.

28. The Magic Stamp

The quote about complaining appeared in the *Joplin Globe*. Jansen reported on the 5 October rocket attacks, on the food situation, and on the refugees from Gennep and its impact on the already-critical shortage of food; van Hensbergen remarked on the steps he took to try to find food for his family in October. Loe de Jong covered the Gennep attack in his World War II series.

Jansen devoted many diary entries to the rumors about Velp's pending evacuation. Gety Hengeveld-de Jong discussed that situation with me and Clan Visser 't Hooft mentioned that her father kept a handcart loaded with supplies for the moment the evacuation order came. *Verborgen in Velp* discussed the one version of how Velp was spared; Dick Mantel provided the story of the prized Dolfuss stamp and seemed confident of its truth. Because of Mantel's reliability as an eyewitness, the story seems valid, although Hengeveld-de Jong's rationale about the necessity of keeping Velp a thriving town is compelling. Audrey's vivid description of life at this time was found in the insightful *Joplin Globe* piece. Ben van Griethuysen spoke about his time with Audrey in the June 2017 interview.

The fact that Audrey worked as the volunteer aide of Dr. Visser 't Hooft is critical to understanding why she was asked to carry messages or deliver the Resistance newspaper. She mentioned her stint as "papergirl" in the *New York Post*, 22 April 1991. Clan and Annemarth Visser 't Hooft discussed their father the Resistance leader and his activities in our April 2018 interview.

Velp resident and aviation historian Johan Vermeulen accompanied me on a tour of the sprawling air base, the Diogenes command bunker, and Museum Vliegbasis Deelen in June 2017. The worsening food situation in November 1944 was covered in van der Zee's *The Hunger Winter*.

29. Streaking Evil

Audrey's quote about the last potatoes was taken from an undated article that described a UNICEF press conference in the Dutch city of Maastricht. The story of the Green Police raid on the Ziekenhuis was covered in both *Verborgen in Velp* and in *100 Jaar Ziekenhuis Velp*. The story of *Sinterklaas* and this particular Sint-Nicolaas Eve was found in van Hensbergen and Jansen, with the Audrey angle provided by Clan Visser 't Hooft. Ella's discussion of Sinterklaas was found in her unpublished manuscript. Audrey's quote about children was taken from Richard Brown's article in the *My Fair Lady* restoration program. Maddie van Leenders provided perspective on the adult traditions of Sint-Nicolaas. Her quote about the use of humor in dark times was taken from the Ivo Niehe AVROTROS 1988 interview.

I can only wish that someone had mentioned the term V1 to Audrey to get her reaction, because the V1s became a life-or-death matter in Velp beginning in mid-December 1944 and held the attention of everyone every day. The diaries return to the topic daily and even seventy-plus years later, mention of V1 triggered vivid memories among my interview subjects.

The account of the civilians in the cellar was found in Louis Hagen's *Arnhem Lift: A German Jew in the Glider Pilot Regiment*. Jansen provided details of the ever-more-severe rationing and van der Zee an overview of the food situation in December.

30. Peace on Earth. Yeah, Right.

Audrey's quote about dwindling food supplies appeared in *The Guardian*, 29 March 1988. Dick Mantel provided details about the baron's nighttime visits to listen to Radio Oranje. The shelling from Nijmegen was described by Jansen. Audrey's description about family members entertaining each other appeared in the Joplin Globe. Van Hensbergen's cynical quote about peace on earth was found in his diary. John Hackett's *I Was a Stranger* is perhaps the best account of a member of the British Airborne living amongst the Dutch, and from his vantage point in Ede, Hackett had a clear view of the V1s over Velp. Audrey's statement about the last few months of the war was taken from the autumn 1992 UNICEF interview after the Somalia trip. The quote by Cornelia Fuykschot was taken from her book, *Hunger in Holland: Life During the Nazi Occupation*. Art Bos described life in Amsterdam in *The Hunger Winter*, Book 8 in *The Dutch in Wartime: Survivors Remember* series.

31. A Tree

This chapter was drawn from a thirteen-page statement Audrey gave Christopher Dickey after visiting Somalia. The document is titled "Somalia: The Silent Children" by Audrey Hepburn; I found it in the Barry Paris papers at the University of Pittsburgh. I scrutinized the Somalia trip because of its effect on Audrey. She told her friend Anna Cataldi, "War didn't kill me, and this won't either," but, said Cataldi, "I had this feeling that sooner or later, war kills you. She was so skinny. I felt something was really wrong."

A June 2018 interview with Luca Dotti provided additional insight on the trepidations of Luca and Sean about the trip and its devastating impact on Audrey.

32. The Race

Audrey's quote about the food situation was found in the 1 May

1953 issue of the *Paris News* [Texas]. Henri van der Zee's *The Hunger Winter* provided information about conditions in the Netherlands in February and March 1945. Her quote about eating tulip bulbs appeared in the 20 January 1992 issue of the *Chicago Tribune*, and her quote about stretch marks from edema appeared in the 26 May 1991 issue of the *Sunday Telegraph*.

In her acclaimed book *Hunger: An Unnatural History*, Sharman Apt Russell provided an overview of the Minnesota Experiment, begun in 1944 with volunteers at the University of Minnesota to understand the effects of semi-starvation on humans so that once the war ended, the Allies would know how best to treat survivors in the Netherlands and elsewhere. Conditions for the volunteers simulated what the Dutch were experiencing, with unsettling results. After reading about the Minnesota Experiment, I could piece together what Audrey and others in Velp endured. Up to now, only Audrey's descriptions have been available, and she shied away from any graphic details about those dark months of the Hunger Winter. Audrey's Somalia document included her statement about bartering belongings for food. Details about the breaking of the famine were found in van der Zee.

Many times Audrey told the story about Meisje urging them all to stay in bed the next day because there was no food. I took the quote from *Parade*.

The ambush of Rauter's car was detailed in van der Zee and also described by Loe de Jong. I visited the remote spot of the ambush and then the executions of Dutch civilians—all of which took place near the Woeste Hoeve Inn. Jansen reported on the German reprisals that went on across Velp. Audrey described the executions in her 1988 interview with Ivo Niehe, the near kidnapping in the June 1954 issue of *McCall's* magazine, and the shelling in her 5 June 1991 appearance on CNN's *Larry King Live*. The shootdown of the V1 that came to earth on Oranjestraat was detailed in Jansen and discussed in my interview with Herman van Remmen, who lost four siblings in the explosion. Despite the fact that the explosion occurred in the middle of the night and therefore after curfew, just about every citizen in the village rushed to the scene because everyone knew everyone in Velp. I couldn't imagine that the van Heemstras would be the exception. Jansen detailed the new and more generous rations after the welcome arrival of a food shipment.

33. Gates of Hell

My starting point for this project was early research about the last year of the war and Velp's role in it. Many of her past biographies boil this part of Audrey's life down to, "Audrey lived under German occupation for five years." Then the next sentence might begin, "After the war..." But the stunning thing is, this girl with the big brown eyes not only lived under German rule, but she saw the final days of World War II. She lived it. I wanted to bring the reader inside her world and make the connection between the shy fifteen year old and the entertainer/humanitarian who is still beloved more than a quarter century after her passing.

Audrey's quote about anemia appeared in the 1 May 1953 issue of the *Paris News*, and Clan Visser 't Hooft identified Dr. Adriaan van der Willigen as the Velpsche physician who had become expert in issues related to edema because he had treated Clan and her sister Annemarth for the same condition. The detailed reports in Steven Jansen's diary described the action of the fighters over Velp and general destruction as days passed. Van Hensbergen in his diary gave specifics about the situation on the van Heemstras' street, Rozendaalselaan, and Dick Mantel provided his own descriptions based on his vantage point within yards of the Beukenhof. Audrey's quote about parts of her house being shot away was taken from the Ivo Niehe interview.

Her quote about having nothing to talk about because nothing had happened during the day appeared in the *Joplin Globe*, 13 November 1953. It's a telling quote because a great deal was indeed happening all around her, just not in the cellar of Villa Beukenhof.

The picture I painted on 14 April as Audrey and the baron ventured outside is drawn from what was known to be going on that day. I can't say for certain that Audrey stood on the street and looked left and right, but it's not unreasonable to expect that she did, and if she did, this is precisely what she would have seen—based also on my many visits to the spot. Neighbors were dying in a radius around the Beukenhof; Audrey might have been just another casualty of war if the wind had changed the course of just one rocket or grenade.

Diarists and interview subjects described the last days of the occupation and the final battle for Velp. Audrey spoke about the village being liberated house to house on *Larry King Live*, and she wasn't exaggerating. German troops had been ordered to fight to the death, and that's exactly what they did. Many had nothing to lose because they had nowhere else to go; their homeland had been destroyed and, in many cases, their families along with it.

I intentionally omitted a story that appeared in the 14 September 2010 *New York Times* obituary of writer Michael "Micky" Burn. The story claims the following: Micky Burn was part of the 269-man commando unit that took part in the destruction of the German-held port of St. Nazaire, France, which was the only dry dock on the French coast that could service German battleships. In what was known as Operation Chariot, a British battleship loaded with explosives rammed the dry dock, and the commandos spilled out and destroyed the remainder of the facility, making the daring mission a success even though most of the raiders were killed or captured—Micky Burn among them. Burn was sent to the German prison facility at Colditz Castle in Germany. Soon after the 28 March 1942 battle, Baroness van Heemstra attended the German cinema in Arnhem and saw a newsreel about the incident. There on the screen for a brief moment she saw her old friend

Micky Burn flashing Churchill's V for victory sign. She tracked Burn down through his wife and Ella sent her old friend one or more Red Cross packages at Colditz.

Three years later, Burn "returned the favor after his release," read the *Times* obituary and many others that appeared in major newspapers, "sending food and cigarettes to the baroness in the Netherlands, where her daughter, Audrey Hepburn-Ruston, was suffering from an infection and other ailments brought on by malnutrition. By selling the cigarettes on the black market, she was able to buy the penicillin that kept her daughter alive." Great story! However, the 1945 portion of the time line has problems. Burn was liberated from Colditz by American forces on 15 April 1945. Ella and Audrey were liberated a day later on 16 April, at which time food arrived in Velp courtesy of the UNRRA, and cigarettes courtesy of the Canadian Polar Bears, killing the "black market" for both. Audrey's health had already begun to improve after the March food shipments, and she always had a supply of penicillin at hand courtesy of Dr. Visser 't Hooft. Photos taken just after liberation show a healthy-looking Audrey posing with a bouquet of flowers, so while the Burn story may contain portions of truth, it didn't happen as presented in the obituary.

34. First Cigarette

Audrey spoke about the morning of liberation on *Larry King Live*. Her description of creeping up the stairs, interacting with the soldiers, and seeing the tanks roll in appeared in a syndicated feature for *Gigi* that appeared in the 13 January 1952 *Daily Oklahoman*. The description of the onderduikers was drawn from *Verborgen in Velp*. Steven Jansen's diary contributed to capturing the euphoria, as did my several viewings of film footage shot on Liberation Day by Dr. Bernhard van Griethuysen, who roamed Hoofdstraat from his home in the east of the village all the way west to Rozendaalselaan. Dr. Visser 't Hooft is clearly visible in some of the shots, but none of the van Heemstras could be identified among the hundreds of Velpenaren visible in this rare footage, which is housed in the Gelders Archief—although it's likely both Ella and Audrey are there in the crowd.

Descriptions of retribution against collaborators are drawn from the van Griethuysen footage, as he gained access to police headquarters to capture scenes of female sympathizers undergoing head shaving. He also aimed his camera at the gauntlet through which Nazi sympathizers ran as their loyalist neighbors jeered. Information about Ella's interrogation by Captain James was pulled from the Ella van Heemstra dossier in the Nationaal Archief at The Hague.

The bulldozing of downed trees, minesweeping, and military traffic officer are all visible in the Griethuysen film footage. Interviews with Velpenaren provided details about Liberation Day, and Audrey's quote about watching the Allied military traffic "night and day" was found in *TIME* magazine's cover story of 7 September 1953. Her statement about not staying sick for long appeared in the *Daily Oklahoman*.

35. Sorting

Audrey's quote about people learning little from war was first documented by Hollywood historian James Robert Parrish in his book *The Glamour Girls*. Considering the climate of mistrust and accusation that ruled in the Netherlands after the war, it's telling indeed what Audrey said of her neighbors. Whispers about Ella's early war activities began at once and resulted in an investigation that wouldn't conclude until early 1949. The Ella van Heemstra dossier in the Nationaal Archief presents the case against her.

Audrey spoke of the UNRRA food crates in "Somalia: The Silent Children." Jaap Besseling told Gety Hengeveld-de Jong the story of Meisje, the Renault, and the book presented Jaap's father.

Information about Sonia Gaskell was found in *Herinneringen aan Sonia Gaskell* by Rudi van Dantzig. Barry Paris stated that Ella took a job at the Royal Military Invalids Home at the border between Arnhem and Velp, and that Audrey volunteered there as well. The facility is now Museum Bronbeek, interpreting Dutch colonial history in the East Indies, and also still serves as a retirement home for "old soldiers" of the Royal Netherlands Indonesian Army.

David Heringa's letter to Barry Paris documented Ella's attempts to land Audrey a role in *Theirs Is the Glory*—and dispels recent notions that she appeared in the film.

The grim reclamation of bodies at the execution site of Otto and his companions was covered in "Vijf zwarte palen herinneren aan oorlogsdrama" ("Five black poles remind of war drama") by Pierre van Beek, which appeared in the 12 August 1975 issue of *Het Nieuwsblad van het Zuiden*. The owner of the property, who was told the story of what really happened by Marinus van Heerebeek himself, corrected the 1975 newspaper narrative during my interview with him. He did not wish to have his name appear in print but said that he well remembered visits to the grave site by the Countess van Limburg Stirum and other members of the family.

36. Crossroads

Audrey discussed moving to Amsterdam with Larry King. Details about Ella's work were found in Paris. Audrey's quote about Sonia Gaskell appeared in the Dutch article, "Audrey Hepburn—Angel of Love," and Annemarth Visser 't Hooft described Gaskell in an email to me. Details about Audrey's April 1946 return engagement at the NHV in Velp were uncovered in interviews and articles in the *Velpsche Courant*, and her appearance at the Hortus was mentioned in Paris.

The oddity *Nederlands in Zeven Lessen* is available for viewing on YouTube. One wonders what might have been going through Audrey's mind—a mere eight years earlier she had flown into

Schiphol Airport to begin life as a Dutch girl. She had survived the war and grown up, and here she was, back at Schiphol.

Information about the investigation into Ella van Heemstra was found in CABR dossier van Ella van Heemstra, Nationaal Archief Den Hag Centraal Archief Bijzondere Reichspleging; CABR 108579 PF Arnhem, dossier BV15982—Ella van Heemstra en 'De Schandpaal, personen die werken voor en in opdracht der Gestapo', *de Oranjekrant* 4 (1942).

Audrey spoke of Gaskell and the audition for Rambert in the Lesley Garner interview for the *Sunday Telegraph*, 26 May 1991. Her quote about needing money was found in the January 1965 *Modern Screen*; the quote about Rambert appeared in the 15 November 1952 issue of the *Saturday Review*; her assessment of how she stacked up against other dancers who hadn't been stifled by war appeared in the October 1956 issue of *Dance* magazine, which also contained information about Audrey's time under both Gaskell and Rambert.

The physical and emotional tendencies of people who had survived situations of famine were examined in *Hunger: An Unnatural History*, and Audrey spoke of overcompensating in the June 1959 issue of *Cosmopolitan* and of the jam jar in the *Birmingham News*, 22 February 1987. She spoke of the need to earn money on the stage in the October 1955 issue of *Cosmopolitan*.

37. Completely Nuts

Audrey's quote about resilience appeared in *US* magazine 17 October 1988, and the quote about temptation in *Cosmopolitan*, October 1955. She spoke of landing the job in *High Button Shoes* in the January 1965 issue of *Modern Screen*. Her statement about how she repeated her one line over and over was quoted in Paris from a 10 January 1954 radio interview with Tex McCurdy.

Information about Ella in this time frame was taken from the confidential dossier at the Nationaal Archief; Luca Dotti provided documents proving that Ella had petitioned to change her name to Ella Hepburn in May 1951. Audrey spoke about her work schedule being "completely nuts" to Hedda Hopper in the 11 September 1953 interview, in which she also mentioned making a screen test for *Quo Vadis*. The quote about stumbling into movies appeared in the January 1965 issue of *Modern Screen*.

Audrey became, if anything, even more self-effacing and introspective as she sat for a revealing interview for *Parade* just short of her sixtieth birthday. The resulting article was titled, "You Can't Love Without the Fear of Losing."

38. Peace

Audrey spoke of becoming a movie star despite the Nazis in the January 1965 issue of *Modern Screen*.

Sharman Apt Russell detailed the Minnesota Experiment in *Hunger: An Unnatural History*. Audrey talked about overcompensating with food in the October 1955 issue of *Cosmopolitan* and again in the June 1959 issue of *Cosmopolitan*. She spoke of the privacy issue in the October 1955 *Cosmopolitan* piece. Her quote about personal questions appeared in the July 1969 issue of *McCall's*, and her statement about being green and naive in the 26 May 1991 *Sunday Telegraph*.

Part of the *Roman Holiday* interview shot after her screen test is available for viewing on YouTube. For his book *Audrey Hepburn* Barry Paris interviewed director Thorold Dickinson about that on-camera interview. It was clear from her responses to Dickinson's questions in London in September 1951 that long before arriving in New York City, Audrey had sorted out what she was willing to talk about and what must remain private.

The fact that Ella had difficulty leaving England for the United States was discerned from material in the police dossier at The Hague. Given Ella's protectiveness and need for control over her daughter, only legal entanglements would have kept her in England when Audrey was about to hit stardom in New York City.

Richard Maney discussed Audrey Hepburn in his 1957 memoir, *Fanfare: The Confessions of a Press Agent*. Audrey's clever diversion of Hedda Hopper, who was about to discuss Audrey's early life, appeared in the transcript of their 11 September 1953 interview.

The relationship between J. Edgar Hoover and Paramount Pictures dated to 1938 when Paramount bought story rights to Hoover's first book, an anthology of true-life crime stories entitled *Persons in Hiding*. Paramount released four feature films based on chapters of the book, *Persons in Hiding* and *Undercover Doctor* in 1939 and *Parole Fixer* and *Queen of the Mob* in 1940. Thereafter, the egomaniacal Hoover would have a soft spot for Paramount boss Adolf Zukor and the studio that helped to cement Hoover's name in American government and popular culture. In effect, Paramount validated bureau chief Hoover. Just fifteen years later, Paramount—possibly Zukor himself—may have been motivated by the extreme success, and potential vulnerability, of his new star Hepburn to call FBI headquarters. Somehow he must have learned of the legal entanglements and shady European past of the starlet's mother, Baroness van Heemstra. What happened next is unknown, but the fact is that files should exist today in the FBI archives on Audrey Hepburn and Ella, Baroness van Heemstra, and neither file can be found despite the fact that experts were looking.

Audrey's life with new husband Andrea Dotti was covered in the July 1969 issue of *McCall's*. She spoke of her love of ballet to Ivo Niehe in 1988. She was quoted speaking about the offer by Joseph E. Levine to appear in the epic film version of *A Bridge Too Far* in the book *The Audrey Hepburn Treasures*. She spoke of hanging on in her marriage to Dotti in the 17 October 1988 issue of *US*. She described her Swiss mansion in the *Richmond News Leader*, 24 May 1991. Luca Dotti described his grandmother to me in a June 2018 interview.

Barry Paris presented quotes by Leonard Gershe and Anna Cataldi in his Hepburn biography, and Sean was quoted concerning his mother's resentment for both Ella and Joseph for their fascist beliefs in *Audrey Hepburn, An Elegant Spirit*. Luca told me in a May 2018 phone conversation about his mother's always using the war to teach lessons about life and described the impact of the Somalia trip in a June 2018 interview. Sean's description of his mother's final illness was found in the Niehe AVROTROS interview.

A 27 October 2009 abstract in the *Journal of the National Cancer Institute* looked at the issue of increased cancer rates for Jews who had survived World War II on the European continent versus Jews who had spent the war away from the area of conflict. Factors examined were "physical and psychological stress, such as famine and mental stress." The report, entitled "Holocaust Survivors At Higher Risk For All Cancers," confirmed the results of previous studies of non-Jewish wartime populations and noted, "Likely exposure, compared with non-exposure, was associated with statistically significantly increased risk for overall cancer risk (all cancers combined) for all birth cohorts, and for both sexes. The strongest associations were with breast and colorectal cancer. Earlier exposure, i.e., at a younger age, seemed to be particularly associated with increased risk of all-site cancer."

The disease that claimed Audrey's life, *Pseudomyxoma peritonei*, or PMP, saw a polyp grow on her appendix, resulting in what the U.S. Library of Medicine at the National Institutes of Health refers to as a "'blow out' and subsequent slow leak of mucus-containing epithelial cells from the adenoma. In most cases appendicular perforation is an occult event. The epithelial cells within the peritoneal cavity continue to proliferate producing large quantities of mucus." It had been progressing silently for a while, certainly through the exhausting Somalia trip that had been "too much."

By the time the disease was diagnosed, it had spread throughout her abdomen. The odds of contracting PMP are two in a million and the survival rates over five years are pretty good for low-grade cases; iffy for high-grade cases. It also bears mentioning that Audrey's grandfather the baron had lived to eighty-six, her mother to eighty-four, and her father to ninety-one. But Audrey had experienced Nazi rule for five stress-filled years, most of them as a sensitive adolescent, and the last under almost continuous fire. The increasing hardships year by year in the Netherlands, coupled with the lasting effects of the Hunger Winter and her own biology, all but guaranteed that she would not, and could not, win her final battle of the war.

Acknowledgments

Dutch Girl was a magical project that couldn't have been completed without the help of a number of people. Thank you, Tim Streefkerk at the Airborne Museum in Oosterbeek for accepting my cold call on an April afternoon and for taking my project seriously from the start. Tim put me in touch with Dutch historical researcher Maddie van Leenders, who had just worked on the museum's "Ella and Audrey" exhibit. Maddie became my eyes and ears in the Netherlands, conducting research at the Nationaal Archief in The Hague and the Gelders Archief in Arnhem. Maddie unearthed the diary of Otto, Count van Limburg Stirum, and made her way through all 180 pages. She also did many other translations of rare documents for me. Maddie then led me through what she had found at both facilities and also organized a day trip—accompanied by Matthijs van de Laar—to the seminary at Sint-Michielsgestel and the execution site in Goirle. Thank you, Maddie, for being a tireless and meticulous detective in the name of Audrey and history.

Tim also introduced me to Joop Onnekink, who as a boy had gone to Zijpendaal with his father to trade collectible postage stamps with Baron van Heemstra. And Tim put me in touch with Robert Voskuil, whose parents lived through the battle of Oosterbeek. Robert was born in the village soon after the war and grew

358

up on what remained for years a relic-strewn battlefield. I spent fascinating days with Robert roaming from Ginkel Heath to Velp, learning about the conflict from both British and German perspectives. Robert showed me remaining scars of battle near the Arnhem Road Bridge and slit trenches near Wolfheze and shared personal stories about his friends John Frost, Roy Urquhart, and many others of the 1st Airborne Division. Perhaps most amazing of all, Robert arranged a meeting with Sophie ter Horst, and we sat in the garden of her home where seventy-three years earlier her mother, Kate, had tended hundreds of British wounded. I was shown the spot where fifty-nine Tommies were buried in temporary graves, and then Sophie handed me a copy of her mother's book, *Cloud over Arnhem*, and gave me a warm Dutch embrace. Thank you, Sophie, for your graciousness; thank you, Robert, for making all these experiences possible.

Velpsche historian and author Gety Hengeveld-de Jong helped me get familiar with Velp through personal tours and introduced me to several Velpenaren who became key contributors to the book, namely Rosemarie Kamphuisen, Annemarth Visser 't Hooft, Ben van Griethuysen, Herman van Remmen, Ben de Winter, and Dick Mantel, who shared memories and documentation of World War II. Annemarth introduced me to her sister, Clan Visser 't Hooft, who was a year younger than Audrey and so shared a teenager's perspective of the war in Velp. Gety also put me in touch with Johan Vermeulen, who lived with his family in Arnhem Centraal until his house was burned to the ground during the battle. Johan led me on guided tours of Arnhem and Velp, with stops at the site of the Tamboersbosje school, Diaconessenhuis, Fliegerhorst Deelen, Woeste Hoeve execution site, and many others. Soon my Dutch friends were family, and I was spendiing afternoons in the garden of the Boekhandel Jansen and de Feijter in Velp asking a thousand questions and listening to fascinating stories about Audrey and the war. Thank you, Gety, for arranging all of this and for serving as

Acknowledgments

an interpreter on some important occasions.

After building the narrative through three trips to the Netherlands, I contacted Audrey's son Luca Dotti, the family historian, about my project. Luca greeted my communication with enthusiasm and matched up my efforts to his own research to sort out his mother's wartime history. He provided memories of "Mum" and her lessons about the war as well as access to Ella's unpublished novel and the family archive. Thank you, Luca, for all your wonderful contributions to this book, and for being moved to write the foreword. This was a special honor.

Stateside, my longtime friend and WWII expert, Dr. Walter Powell, provided a steady flow of resources about Market Garden and Holland along with encouragement to keep digging. Ann Trevor combed the federal archives for information about Ella, Audrey, the Nazi connection, the Dutch Resistance, and everything else she could think of. In the end Ann, a career-long D.C. researcher, became convinced that the FBI file on Ella van Heemstra had been removed from the federal record. Marina Gray provided a wealth of research on the van Heemstras, on Otto and his four companions, and on the Nazi regime in the Netherlands. Barry Paris, author of the definitive 1994 Simon & Schuster bio, *Audrey Hepburn*, advised me on the "lay of the land" in terms of Audrey and her world. He was gracious on the phone, and I especially want to thank him for donating his research to the University of Pittsburgh, where I spent many hours reviewing a wealth of original source material. Barry's work became a foundation for my own. Thank you also to William Daw and other staff at the University of Pittsburgh Library System, Archives & Special Collections, Curtis Theatre Collection, Barry Paris Papers.

My special thanks go to the peer reviewers who devoted time and expertise to a thorough assessment of the manuscript and its presentation of Audrey Hepburn, Dutch, and World War II history. They are Luca Dotti, Walter Powell, Robert Voskuil, Gety

Hengeveld-de Jong, Clan Visser 't Hooft, Annemarth Visser 't Hooft, Marina Gray, and Maddie van Leenders.

In addition to the family photos Luca Dotti provided from the Ella van Heemstra and Audrey Hepburn collections, photos of Velp were provided by mevr. C.L. Bosma-van het Karr, mevr. W.G. Matser-Wassink, and Brouerius van Nidek; photos showing Dr. Visser 't Hooft were provided by Annemarth and Clan Visser 't Hooft; the photo of Audrey at the Bouma birthday party was courtesy of Melinda Limbertie, Annelies Bouma, and Steven van Rossem; other photos were secured with the help of Jamie Owen and Jennifer Jeffrey at AKG, Martin Smit at Aviodrome, Anthony Livius at the Gelders Archief, and Ellen Dosse and Laurencia Ekkers at Spaarnestad.

In addition, I would like to thank the following: James V. D'Arc; Leendert de Jong at Filmhuis Den Haag; Jill Fornof; Patrick Jansen; Clem Leone; Michael Mazzone; John McElwee; Mike Pappas; Sandy Smith; Stacey Behlmer, Kristine Krueger, Rachel Bernstein, and other staff at the Academy of Motion Picture Arts & Sciences Margaret Herrick Library; Anneke de Feijter and Walter Jansen at Boekhandel Jansen and de Feijter, Velp; Zahra Ghanem and other staff at the Stadstheater Arnhem; Anthony Livius and other staff at the Gelders Archief; Gety Hengeveld-de Jong and Stichting Velp voor Oranje; the Society of Friends of the Airborne Museum; Johan Vermeulen and everyone at the Fliegerhorst Deelen Museum; Annie Whitehead of Harvesting Light Photography; and at Good-Knight Books, editor Mary Rothhaar, designer Sharon Berk, photo restorer and graphics specialist Valerie Sloan, map and family tree designer Amelia Williams, and publicist Sarah Miniaci.

Selected Bibliography

Airborne Museum. *Moederliefde: Ella and Audrey.* Program for the exhibit, 2017.

Anderson, Lindsey. *Making a Film: The Story of 'Secret People.'* London: George Allen and Unwin Ltd., 1952.

Baron, Sid. *The Way It Was: Growing Up in Wartime Holland.* Bellingham: Exxel Publishing Company, 2007.

Beltman, Ineke. *Duits Deelen: Van vliegbasis tot jeugdzorg.* Zutphen: Uitgeversmaatschappij Walburg Pers, 2007.

Bentley, Stewart W. Jr. *Orange Blood, Silver Wings: The Untold Story of the Dutch Resistance During Market-Garden.* Bloomington: AuthorHouse, 2007.

Bijvoet, Tom, ed. *The Dutch in Wartime Survivors Remember, Book 1. Invasion.* Niagara Falls: Mokeham Publishing Inc., 2011.

Bijvoet, Tom, ed. *The Dutch in Wartime Survivors Remember, Book 2. Under Nazi Rule.* Niagara Falls: Mokeham Publishing Inc., 2011.

Bijvoet, Tom and Anne van Arragon Hutten, eds. *The Dutch in Wartime Survivors Remember, Book 8. The Hunger Winter.* Niagara Falls: Mokeham Publishing Inc., 2013.

Davelaar, Evert G. *Al seen feniks uit zijn as: De Arnhemse tram in het Netherlands Openluchtmuseum.* Een uitgave van Nederlands Openluchtmuseum.

De Courcy, Anne. *Diana Mosley: Mitford Beauty, British Fascist, Hitler's Angel.* New York: William Morrow, 2003.

de Jong, Louis and Joseph W.F. Stoppelman. *The Lion Rampant: The Story of Holland's Resistance to the Nazis.* New York: Querido, 1943.

Deane-Drummond, Anthony. *Return Ticket*. London: Collins, 1967.

Dotti, Luca with Luigi Spinola. *Audrey at Home: Memories of My Mother's Kitchen*. New York: Harper Design, 2015.

Erwin, Ellen and Jessica Z. Diamond. *The Audrey Hepburn Treasures*. New York: Atria Books, 2006.

Ferrer, Sean Hepburn. *Audrey Hepburn, an Elegant Spirit*. New York: Atria Books, 2003.

Fonteyn, Margot. *Autobiography*. New York: Alfred A. Knopf, 1976.

Frank, Anne. *Het Achterhuis/The Diary of a Young Girl*. New York: Doubleday, 1952.

Frequin, Louis, Henri A.A.R. Knap, and W.H. Kruiderink. *Arnhem Kruisweg*. Amsterdam: Uitgeverij Promotor, 1946.

Frost, (Major-General) John. *A Drop Too Many*. London: Cassell Ltd., 1980.

Fuykschot, Cornelia. *Hunger in Holland: Life During the Nazi Occupation*. Amherst: Prometheus Books, 1995.

Hackett, (General Sir) John. *I Was a Stranger*. Aylesbury: Hunt Barnard Printing Ltd., 1977.

Harris, Ben and Sebastian Raatz, pubs. *Anne Frank: A Light in History's Darkest Hour*. New York: Centennial Media, 2018.

Harris, Warren G. *Audrey Hepburn: a Biography*. New York: Simon & Schuster, 1994.

Hastings, Max. *Das Reich*. Minneapolis: Zenith Press, 2013.

Hengeveld-de Jong, Gety. *Verborgen in Velp: Nooit vertelde verhalen over moed, verzet en onderduikers*. Stichting Velp voor Oranje. Zutphen: Koninklijke Wöhrmann, 2013.

Hofstede, David. *Audrey Hepburn: A Bio-Bibliography*. Westport, CT: Greenwood Press, 1994.

Hutten, Anne van Arragon, ed. *The Dutch in Wartime Survivors Remember, Book 4. Resisting Nazi Occupation*. Niagara Falls: Mokeham Publishing Inc., 2012.

Hutten, Anne van Arragon, ed. *The Dutch in Wartime Survivors Remember, Book 7. Caught in the Crossfire*. Niagara Falls: Mokeham Publishing Inc., 2013.

Jansen, Steven. *Dagboek: Velp en de oorlog 1940-1945*. Zutphen: Wöhrmann Print Service/ Koninklijke Wöhrmann B.V., 2006.

Selected Bibliography

Karney, Robyn. *Audrey Hepburn: A Charmed Life.* New York: Arcade Publishing, 2012.

Keogh, Pamela Clark. *Audreystyle.* New York: HarperCollins, 1999.

Kershaw, Robert. *A Street in Arnhem: The Agony of Occupation and Liberation.* Philadelphia: Casemate Publishers, 2014.

Kooger, J.P. *100 Jaar Ziekenhuis Velp.* Den Haag: CIP-Gegevens Koninklijke Bibliotheek. 1992.

Levy, Daniel S. *Anne Frank: Her Life and Her Legacy.* New York: Time Inc. Books, 2017.

Lovell, Mary S. *The Sisters: The Saga of the Mitford Family.* New York: W.W. Norton & Company, 2001.

Maney, Richard. *Fanfare: The Confessions of a Press Agent.* New York: Harper & Brothers Publishers, 1957.

Middlebrook, Martin. *Arnhem 1944: The Airborne Battle.* Boulder: Westview Press, 1994.

Mosley, Charlotte, ed. *The Mitfords: Letters Between Six Sisters.* New York: Harper Perennial, 2007.

Mosley, Diana. *A Life of Contrasts: The Autobiography of Diana Mosley.* London: Gibson Square Books Ltd., 2003.

Mosley, Nicholas. *Beyond the Pale: Sir Oswald Mosley 1933-1980.* London: Secker & Warburg, 1983.

Onnekink, Joop. *Seven days in the Witches' Cauldron: A child's memories of the Battle of Arnhem.* Published by www.tekstbureauderaaf.nl.

Paris, Barry. *Audrey Hepburn.* New York: G.P. Putnam's Sons, 1996.

Parish, James Robert and Don E. Stanke. *The Glamour Girls.* New Rochelle: Arlington House Publishers, 1975.

Peereboom, Robert. *Gijzelaar in Gestel.* Zwolle: Uitgeverij de Erven J.J. Tijl N.V., 1945.

Presser, J. *Ashes in the Wind: The Destruction of Dutch Jewry.* Detroit: Wayne State University Press, 1988.

Pryce-Jones, David. *Unity Mitford: A Quest.* London: Weidenfeld and Nicolson, 1976.

Russell, Sharman Apt. *Hunger: An Unnatural History.* New York: Basic Books, 2005.

Skidelsky, Robert. *Oswald Mosley.* London: The Macmillan Press Ltd., 1975.

Stichting Velp voor Oranje. *Herinneringen aan de Bevrijding van Velp.* Zutphen: Koninklijke Wöhrmann, 2006.

Sullivan, Robert, ed. *Audrey: 25 Years Later.* New York: LIFE BOOKS, 2018.

ter Horst-Arriëns, Kate A. *Cloud over Arnhem: Oosterbeek-September 1944.* Uitgeverij Kontrast, 2009.

Urquhart, Major-General R.E. *Arnhem.* London: Cassell & Company Ltd., 1958.

van der Zee, Henri A. *The Hunger Winter: Occupied Holland 1944-1945.* London: J. Norman & Hobhouse, 1982.

van Heemstra, M.J. (Baroness). *Friesland as it is.* Amsterdam: Lankamp & Brinkman, 1952.

van Maanen, Anje. *Tafelberg Field Hospital Diary Oosterbeek 17-25 September 1944.* Uitgeverij Kontrast, 2015.

Walker, Alexander. *Audrey: Her Real Story.* New York: St. Martin's Griffin, 1994.

Woodward, Ian. *Audrey Hepburn.* New York: St. Martin's Press, 1984.

Wragg, David. *Fighter Operations in Europe & North Africa 1939-1945.* Barnsley: Pen & Sword Books Ltd., 2012.

Wykes, Alan. *The Nuremberg Rallies.* New York: Ballantine Books. Inc., 1970.

Zaloga, Steven J. *V-1 Flying Bomb 1942-52: Hitler's infamous 'doodlebug.'* Oxford: Ausprey Publishing Ltd., 2005.

Index

Index

The Hollywood in World War II Trilogy

Dutch Girl: Audrey Hepburn and World War II completes Robert Matzen's "Hollywood in World War II" trilogy, published by GoodKnight Books. The three volumes span the United States and Europe and document human stories set during the darkest times in history.

Fireball: Carole Lombard and the Mystery of Flight 3 (2013) chronicles the unexpected death of America's "screwball queen." When her plane goes down near Las Vegas six weeks after America's entry into the war, a desperate search begins. *Fireball* covers Lombard's tumultuous life, the looming threat of global conflict, the others on Flight 3, and the effect of the plane crash on the nation, Hollywood, and her husband, Clark Gable. Matzen's research included two government investigations into the plane crash as well as TWA's secret files and the reminiscences of many who knew Lombard and Gable.

Mission: Jimmy Stewart and the Fight for Europe (2016) brings to light the previously unknown combat career of America's "boy next door." After the war and for the remainder of his life, Stewart refused to discuss his combat experiences, causing biographers to shy away from that period. Matzen located the combat mission reports for the 20 missions flown by Stewart, found written accounts of life in Stewart's bomb group of the Eighth Air Force, and spoke with many who took to the air with him. The book begins and ends with production of *It's a Wonderful Life*, a picture Stewart made while suffering the effects of what we now know as PTSD.

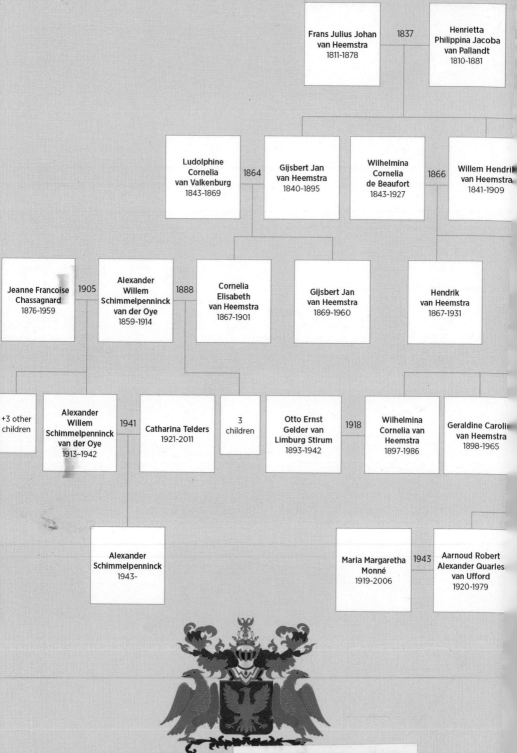

van Heemstra